W.

D1498138

WN

Conversations with Tim O'Brien

Literary Conversations Series
Peggy Whitman Prenshaw
General Editor

Library & Media Ctr.
Carroll Community College
1601 Washington Rd.
Westminster, MD 21157

Conversations
with Tim O'Brien

Edited by Patrick A. Smith

University Press of Mississippi   *Jackson*

Books by Tim O'Brien

If I Die in a Combat Zone. New York: Delacorte, 1973.
Northern Lights. New York: Delacorte, 1975.
Going After Cacciato. New York: Delacorte, 1978.
The Nuclear Age. New York: Knopf, 1985.
The Things They Carried. Boston: Houghton Mifflin, 1990.
In the Lake of the Woods. Boston: Houghton Mifflin, 1994.
Tomcat in Love. New York: Broadway Books, 1998.
July, July. Boston: Houghton Mifflin, 2002.

www.upress.state.ms.us

The University Press of Mississippi is a member
of the Association of American University Presses.

Copyright © 2012 by University Press of Mississippi
All rights reserved
Manufactured in the United States of America

First printing 2012

∞

Library of Congress Cataloging-in-Publication Data
Conversations with Tim O'Brien / edited by Patrick A. Smith.
    p. cm. — (Literary conversations series)
  Includes index.
  ISBN 978-1-61703-678-1 (cloth : alk. paper) — ISBN 978-1-61703-679-8 (ebook)
  1. O'Brien, Tim, 1946– —Interviews. 2. Authors, American—20th century—Interviews.
  PS3565.B75Z465 2012
  813'.54—dc23
                        2012014161
British Library Cataloging-in-Publication Data available

Contents

Introduction vii

Chronology xxi

Interview with Tim O'Brien 3
  Larry McCaffery / 1979

Tim O'Brien: "Maybe So" 22
  Eric James Schroeder / 1984

An Interview with Tim O'Brien 41
  Martin Naparsteck / 1989

Staying True to Vietnam: Writer Tim O'Brien Aims for the War's Nerve
Center 52
  Gail Caldwell / 1990

An Interview with Tim O'Brien 58
  Steven Kaplan / 1991

Artful Dodge Interviews Tim O'Brien 68
  Daniel Bourne and Debra Shostak / 1991

Responsibly Inventing History: An Interview with Tim O'Brien 88
  Brian C. McNerney / 1994

Tim O'Brien Interview 100
  Tobey C. Herzog / 1995

About Tim O'Brien: A Profile 115
  Don Lee / 1995

The Heart under Stress: Interview with Author Tim O'Brien   120
  James Lindbloom / 1998

Journeying from Life to Literature: An Interview with American Novelist
Tim O'Brien   125
  Lynn Wharton / 1999

Tim O'Brien: An Interview   143
  Anthony Tambakis / 1999

Tim O'Brien: Author of *July, July* Talks with Robert Birnbaum   160
  Robert Birnbaum / 2002

"Every question leads to the next": An Interview with Tim O'Brien   173
  Jonathan D'Amore / 2007

An Interview with Tim O'Brien   180
  Steven Pressfield / 2010

On War, Heroes, and the Power of Literature: A Conversation with Tim
O'Brien   184
  Patrick A. Smith / 2011

Key Resources   197

Index   203

Introduction

"I came to writing because of the war. When I returned from Vietnam, I had something to say: I had witnessed things, smelled things, imagined things which struck me as startling and terrifying and intriguing in all sorts of ways," Tim O'Brien tells Larry McCaffery. "Although Vietnam was the impetus and spark for *becoming* a writer, I do not consider myself a war writer."[1] After publishing a well-received memoir, *If I Die in a Combat Zone, Box Me Up and Ship Me Home* (1973), while still in his twenties and winning almost universal critical acclaim—and a National Book Award—for his novel *Going After Cacciato* (1978), O'Brien spoke with McCaffery in April 1979. That lengthy conversation is an apt starting point for a collection of sixteen pieces that explore O'Brien's work and many common themes, with subtle differences: the experience of Vietnam and its influence on O'Brien's writing, as well as the extent to which he considers himself a "Vietnam writer"; his youth in Minnesota and the expectations of a Midwestern upbringing; the shifting boundaries of truth and fiction, memory and imagination; love as a motivating force; gender issues; and the process and craft of writing. O'Brien meets each of those topics and a host of others with a directness and evident passion that resonates with both readers and prospective writers.

Many of the interviews in this collection—organized chronologically and spanning more thirty years, from the McCaffery piece to a conversation that I had with O'Brien in October 2011—are drawn from literary journals for their breadth and depth, which allows O'Brien the freedom to respond to questions without worrying after sound bites. Briefer profiles and interviews (Gail Caldwell, Don Lee, and Steven Pressfield) provide snapshot images of the author at a specific point in time and contain useful biographical information (as do most of the introductions to the interviews). In the longer pieces, O'Brien can be ebullient, reflective, angry, even morose, though his passion for the writing process and the ineffable wonder that comes from crafting sentences never wavers. As a writer, O'Brien writes and rewrites, drafts and revises, ruminates—even fulminates—on the essentials of story and the nuts and bolts of the words on the page. He does much the same in his spoken responses, turning thoughts back on themselves and exploring avenues of inquiry in ways that are often profound and rarely less than enlightening. The author clarifies (although hardly demystifies) his relationship to the stories that come to him: "Works of art are not explicable, in my opinion, any more than a human life is explicable. Human lives are, like books, mysteries, combinations of circumstance and what's said and what's done. To explain away the flesh and blood of art is a kind of murder."[2] Indeed, any collection of this scope, representative of the myriad ideas and contexts—historical, social, and cultural—that O'Brien addresses in his writing and based largely on his Vietnam experience, has its limitations, an issue remedied, in part, with the inclusion of a bibliography of key interviews, articles, and books.

A reader cannot understand O'Brien's work without first knowing something about Vietnam. In the introduction to the 1979 interview, McCaffery, a contemporary of O'Brien's, recalls 1968 with something less than dewy-eyed nostalgia. "Vietnam was on everyone's mind that long, hot summer, especially if you were, as I was, twenty-two years old, engaged to be married, about to enter graduate school, and the recipient of a draft notice. I spent a lot of time that summer thinking about what I would do if I were given a gun and told to shoot someone," McCaffery writes. "Luckily I failed my induction physical—my asthma had finally done me some good—so I didn't have to make these sorts of painful decisions."[3] O'Brien, of course, underwent much the same process of soul-searching as McCaffery, though the upshot of receiving his own draft notice that summer was profoundly different. O'Brien spent a year in country, earning a Purple Heart when he took shrapnel from a grenade and a Bronze Star after rescuing a fellow soldier during a firefight (both of which events he downplays in a later interview with Tobey Herzog). He returned, as so many others had, changed by the experience. Unlike the others, O'Brien will be recognized as one of the most cogent and compelling literary voices of his generation.

Between *If I Die* and *Cacciato*, O'Brien published his first novel, *Northern Lights* (1975), a thinly disguised pastiche of Ernest Hemingway that the author later disavowed. Although that book draws obliquely on Vietnam— one of the story's competing brothers returns from war, like Hemingway's Jake Barnes, with a life-altering injury—*Northern Lights* seems to be more rehearsal for the later fiction than fully formed literary vision, a bridge between the too-real experiences of Vietnam detailed in the memoir and the more expansive (and, in some ways, even darker) shadow world of O'Brien's imagination. With *Cacciato* (a book treated thoroughly here by McCaffery, Eric Schroeder, Steven Kaplan, and others), a story about a soldier's vivid escape fantasy as he stands guard on an observation post in Vietnam, the die had been cast.

When O'Brien won the National Book Award for *Cacciato* in 1979, besting John Irving's *The World According to Garp* and John Cheever's *Stories*, he validated the fiction of Vietnam—a doubled-edged sword for a writer who has dealt, in a dozen different ways over the years, with the question of the extent to which Vietnam has influenced his writing. In explaining the inevitable connection between his time in country and the characters inhabiting his stories, O'Brien tells Don Lee in 1995, twenty-five years after returning from the war, "'All writers revisit terrain. Shakespeare did it with kings, and Conrad did with the ocean, and Faulkner did with the South. It's an emotional and geographical terrain that's given to us by life. Vietnam is there the way childhood is for me.'"[4] In a later interview with Anthony Tambakis, the author offers a more pointed response: "It's like calling Toni Morrison a black writer, or Melville a whale writer, or Shakespeare a king writer. Or saying John Updike is a writer for the suburbs, which he isn't in the slightest. . . . I don't write about bombs and bullets, after all. I write about the human heart. That's my subject matter more than anything else."[5] Later still, softening his stance on the issue, O'Brien tells Robert Birnbaum, "I'm flattered to be known as a Vietnam writer. I can't and I don't want to write the same books over and over. And haven't."[6]

To confine O'Brien to a single place or a particular style is to willfully ignore the intricacy of the work. *Cacciato* and the later short-story cycle *The Things They Carried* (1990) showcase O'Brien's writing, a high-wire act synthesizing descriptive prose and dreamlike, surreal flights of fancy, images arising from the author's fragmented recollection of Vietnam and the schizophrenic chaos of the battlefield, simultaneously raucous and impossibly isolated. Similar observations removed from the battlefield underpin the Cold War paranoia of *The Nuclear Age* (1985), John Wade's tormented conscience in *In the Lake of the Woods* (1994), the comic malfeasance of Thomas Chippering in *Tomcat in Love* (1998), and the ensemble novel, *July, July* (2002).

Even if O'Brien routinely uses Vietnam to ground his stories in a recognizable context, though, the characters who survive and thrive in his fiction do so through a burgeoning awareness of the wider world and a forced self-evolution that, in the end, rarely has as much to do with place as it does with the characters' moral grounding. "All of my characters are shaken out of a state of stasis—a kind of innocence, a kind of belief in the world that's grounded in a thoughtless traditionalism, and by thoughtless I mean that it is accepted or taken for granted—by some kind of outside, global event," O'Brien tells Steven Kaplan. "In all of the books except maybe *Northern Lights* some outside event intrudes on that innocence. The characters, like Rip Van Winkle, are shaken awake and forced to confront their own na-ïveté, their own jejune acceptance of an order."[7] Within the subject of war, O'Brien explores the world from the perspective of both the beleaguered, dispassionate observer—particularly when the emotion evoked by an action exceeds a character's ability to articulate it, as in the serio-ironic death of Ted Lavender in "The Things They Carried"—and the protagonist tuned to life's elaborate harmonies. Points of view shift as well, from the introspec-tion of the intimate, first-person narrator employing a modified stream-of-consciousness (*If I Die, Tomcat in Love*) to an objective third-person narra-tor recording events in graphic, though distanced—and distancing—detail (*Northern Lights, The Nuclear Age, In the Lake of the Woods, July, July*).

A forthcoming O'Brien expresses a sentiment that appears throughout these conversations: namely, that he chose to participate in Vietnam not because he believed in the war, but because he feared that his unwillingness to join the effort might be perceived by those at home as an act of coward-ice, a refusal to fight for American values, a young man's turning his back on the traditions of a society that had always valued, at least publicly, the principled stand. O'Brien, barely a month out of college, having graduated *summa cum laude* and Phi Beta Kappa from Macalester College in St. Paul, Minnesota, with a degree in political science and his sights set on a gradu-ate degree, fought the desire to dodge the war with every fiber of his being. Upon receiving the letter, O'Brien's initial response was to run for Canada or Sweden. Instead, he chose the same route as many young Midwestern men of the time, fulfilling his obligation by fighting in Vietnam. In truth, what choice did he have? His parents had both served in World War II, his father in the Pacific theater and his mother as a WAVE, a division of the Navy that consisted entirely of women. "I was bred with the haste and dispatch and careless muscle-flexing of a nation giving bridle to its own good fortune and success," O'Brien writes of the roots of his aversion to war and to the Mid-west generally. "I was fed by the spoils of 1945 victory."[8]

Indecision and a young man's fit of conscience were, finally, no match for "the town, my family, my teachers, a whole history of the prairie. Like magnets, these things pulled in one direction or the other, almost physical forces weighting the problem so that, in the end, it was less reason and more gravity that was the final influence."[9] O'Brien reiterates a contentious relationship with his native Midwest as late as October 2011, tying the perceived close-mindedness of the region to the inefficacy of literature to affect change: "I'm resigned to the knowledge that I'm not going to change the Midwest, and the Midwest is not going to change me. . . . I feel the same powerlessness, I might add, in regard to mankind's appetite for war. I look back on my years as a writer—all those books, all those scenes and sentences and paragraphs, all that struggling over bits of language—but what real fruit did it bear? The world is as full of self-righteous bellicosity as when I began."[10]

Those contradictory impulses, one to run, the other to fight even when "Certain blood was being shed for uncertain reasons,"[11] inform the author's later writing style and predict the fiction's dominant themes. O'Brien's attention to complex matters—jaundiced notions of honor and family, the power of place, the sacred and the profane—requires complex examination, a task that the author takes as his *raison d'être*. The rigor with which he examines those issues comes through in the interviews collected here.

Before an invitation to war, however, there was a relatively uneventful, if at times challenging, childhood in the nation's heartland. Young Tim grew up fascinated by magic and storytelling (related here in Lee, Brian McNerney, and Lynn Wharton), and he often equates the two when discussing the craft of writing. O'Brien's mother, who had become an elementary-school teacher after serving in World War II, encouraged reading and contributed to her son's obsessive attention to language. His father, an alcoholic insurance salesman, was by turns attentive, aloof, and cruel as O'Brien recalls in an especially candid moment in a 1995 interview with Tobey Herzog: "It was a difficult relationship, like everything, complicated. On one hand [my father] was a model—his intelligence, his wit, his grace in public, an extremely stylish guy. A charming man. . . . We had a lot of problems, too. I was picked on a lot as a kid. For reasons that I still don't understand, I was teased relentlessly, at least it seemed to me, from the time I was nine years old until I left for college. I felt that I was never good enough for him, could never please him no matter what I had accomplished."[12] That capricious treatment seems to have ensured O'Brien's understanding, on some level, the contradictions and vicissitudes of adulthood, a lesson that stood him in good stead in the rice paddies and jungles of Vietnam and, upon his return to the States, when he enrolled in Harvard's Ph.D. program in political science; a later stint as a reporter at the *Washington Post* allowed O'Brien to hone the reportage and straightforward observation that give his stories a clarity of purpose unmatched by his contemporaries.

Perhaps, too, because of the cognitive dissonance that characterized both his formative years in Minnesota and his tour in Vietnam, O'Brien comes across in interviews as inscrutable and complex. Under the right circumstances, however, usually after rapport has been established with the interviewer, he opens up in an expression of the Keatsian "Negative Capability" that allows the author to struggle with competing ideas on the way to discovering some version of the "truth." "There's a frustration that comes from uncertainty and ambiguity, but there's also a beguiling fascination that comes with it," he tells Karen Rosica in an attempt at bridging the gap between experience and writing. "It's maybe why I'm captivated by gambling— the uncertainty of it. . . . I, as a writer and as a human being, make do with what I can [in terms of] ambiguity and uncertainty and try to plod onward writing these novels."[13]

The decade of the 1990s was a watershed for O'Brien (he had published *The Nuclear Age* in 1985 to mixed reviews), and interviews and profiles proliferated in the wake of his masterwork, *The Things They Carried.* Although Martin Naparsteck's 1989 conversation with O'Brien was the first to discuss *The Things They Carried* (the book had yet to be published when Naparsteck conducted the interview in April 1989, and O'Brien was making final edits to the manuscript when the two met in the author's home outside Boston), Gail Caldwell's *Boston Globe* profile of March 1990, reprinted here, brought O'Brien and his book to the attention of a broad audience, describing the author's pleasant demeanor, even in the throes of a national book tour, and his important relationship with Houghton Mifflin publisher Seymour Lawrence, a partnership that ended only with Lawrence's death in early 1994. Those interviews, all cognizant of the immediate impact of *The Things They Carried* on American letters, tend to focus on the book's organization, unique for the lengths to which it takes its search for "truth." Of "How to Tell a True War Story," which is anything but, O'Brien tells Naparsteck, "In a way it's part essay and part fiction, but in a way it's neither. I think that when you're reading the thing you have a total effect. To me, it has a singleness or unity to it. . . . Literature should be looked at not for its literal truths but for its emotional qualities. What matters in literature, I think, are pretty simple things—whether it moves me or not, whether it feels true. The actual literal truth should be superfluous."[14]

Four years later, after the publication of the well-received *In the Lake of the Woods*, a fragmented, quasi-documentary novel rooted in mystery, several pieces chronicle O'Brien's continued exploration of the nature and origin of truth. Taken in the aggregate, the decade's interviews show a writer at the top of his form, confident in his grasp of craft, consistent in decrying war, and agile in examining both specific and general aspects of literature and current events.

Despite the striking success of *The Things They Carried* and the critical and commercial achievement of *In the Lake of the Woods*, O'Brien's career took a dark turn in 1994 when he contemplated giving up writing entirely. That self-imposed exile lasted several months—an eternity, one can imagine, for a writer accustomed to spending seven days a week at the keyboard. Still, before year's end, he had published a poignant essay titled "The Vietnam in Me." O'Brien spent two weeks revisiting the ground that so profoundly changed him more than twenty years before; at the same time, a long-term personal relationship comes to its inevitable, sorrowful end. The essay appeared on the cover of the *New York Times Magazine* on October 2, 1994. "Later in the night, as on many other nights, we talk about the war. I try to explain—ineptly, no doubt—that Vietnam was more than terror. For me, at least, Vietnam was partly love," O'Brien writes, struggling to come to terms with the experience and the delamination of his personal life. "With each step, each light-year of a second, a foot soldier is always almost dead, or so it feels, and in such circumstance you can't *help* but love."[15]

The tone of that passage echoes the morass of shock and loss detailed in *In the Lake of the Woods*, a novel predicated on the participation of the book's protagonist, John Wade, in the war's infamous My Lai massacre. Led by Lieutenant William Calley, an unassuming draftee from Columbus, Georgia, the four-hour attack—the worst documented war crime in United States history—on March 16, 1968, claimed the lives of some five hundred Vietnamese, many of them women and children. In the essay recalling his return to the country, the unfiltered recollections offer a rare glimpse into the deepest recesses of O'Brien's mind, stripped clean of everything save the essential humanity of his ideas and the importance of words in his life. The piece also calls into question the author's shifting notions of identity and the extent to which we can (or cannot) know our enemies or our lovers (an issue he takes up here with Kaplan, Daniel Bourne and Debra Shostak, McNerney, and others).

O'Brien expresses unease at how little time passes—one generation— before events that once held audiences rapt in righteous indignation have been utterly forgotten. "More than 25 years later, the villainy of that Sunday morning in 1968 has been pushed off to the margins of memory," he writes. "In the colleges and high schools I sometimes visit, the mention of My Lai brings on null stares, a sort of puzzlement, disbelief mixed with utter ignorance."[16] In addition to the obvious unthinkable savagery of the act, O'Brien and his fellow soldiers, unaware that the atrocities had even occurred when they arrived in the area in 1969, were put at risk. "These acts caused among the populace that we were trying to save, not just anger, but incredible sorrow and grief that was palpable as we walked around this place," O'Brien recalls. "And the response to all the savagery on the part of the enemy was to litter the place with land mines and blow the shit out of us."[17] The influence of My Lai is felt most strongly in *Lake of the Woods* in transcribed passages from court martial proceedings, a kind of documentary frame upon which the nebulous plot hinges. The massacre is the basis for John Wade's humiliation in a national political campaign and, it seems, the catalyst for his wife's disappearance and Wade's own suicidal plunge into the Minnesota wilderness. Despite his obvious disgust with what transpired, O'Brien offers commentary from both sides of the issue, refusing to come to any conclusion regarding Mrs. Wade's disappearance.

O'Brien has spoken openly about the difficulty of being on the ground in the My Lai area when anti-American sentiment in Vietnam had reached a crescendo, and he discusses how the war undermined the American myth on which he and his generation were raised:

> So along comes Vietnam, which disrupted all of these myths and stereotypes— "disrupted" is the wrong word, but erased all these myths—and substituted a kind of hard, tough reality: America is not always good. It's hard to distinguish the white hats and the black hats. You can't always tell them apart. Sometimes they commingle. Sometimes a man can do something beautiful and sublime one moment and something horrendous the next. Witness My Lai. So, in a sense, all of my writing about Vietnam has been a kind of delayed response to the simplistic images and icons that were presented to me as a young man through pop art.[18]

O'Brien's continued disillusionment with war in the later novels includes an increasingly stronger articulation of his disdain for Americans who accept the inevitability of war and trust the infallibility of American ideology, the very attitudes that allow us to fight in a place like Vietnam. "Evil has no place, it seems, in our national mythology. We erase it. We use ellipses," O'Brien writes, in a stance echoed throughout these conversations. "We salute ourselves and take pride in America the White Knight, America the

Lone Ranger, America's sleek laser-guided weaponry beating up on Saddam and his legion of devils."[19]

Since 1999, O'Brien has taught creative writing in the MFA program at Texas State University in San Marcos. His reputation is as an attentive, demanding mentor; in that sense, his teaching reflects the work ethic of a tireless writer, an inveterate tweaker whose success mirrors the hard-earned grace of the baseball stars he grew up idolizing.[20] Commenting on his critical reception and his status as a cult figure in the closed world of fiction workshops and MFA programs, O'Brien reminds Robert Birnbaum, "I'm the guy who sits in his underwear in front of the computer all day. People forget that. That's how I spend my days for four years in a row."[21] One of the most revealing descriptions of the writing process and the profound effect that writing can have on a reader comes in a 2007 conversation with Jonathan D'Amore. "It's part of the skill of the writer, to have the details of the story activate the soul of the reader to feel pain and to feel joy and to feel terror, to wince and to wonder, to feel awe at the unfolding of the extents within the story," O'Brien says. "It also has to do with the sound of the prose, with the music beneath of the story. . . . There's a little-boyish feel to it. I don't want anything getting in the way of the dream of the dream."[22]

Although O'Brien first expressed his Vietnam experience through memoir as a way of exploring and even mitigating the psychological impact of the war, the writers who influence O'Brien's later work—he cites Jorge Luis Borges, Joseph Conrad, Toni Morrison, Ernest Hemingway, William Faulkner, Gabriel García Márquez, John Dos Passos, and others in the interviews collected here—represent an eclectic mix of styles, genres, and backgrounds. Undoubtedly those writers helped O'Brien to mold his writing, which includes memoir (*If I Die*), realist fiction (*Northern Lights, The Nuclear Age, July, July*), magical realism (*Going After Cacciato*), comedy (*Tomcat in Love*), and experimental fiction (*The Things They Carried, In the Lake of the Woods*). Still, O'Brien contends, "the huge 'influence,' finally, is the life that surrounds me—people, places, events."[23]

Certainly, O'Brien's fiction was influenced by his contemporaries, many of whom experienced the war first hand: memoirists Philip Caputo, Michael Herr, and Ron Kovic, poet Bruce Weigl, dramatist David Rabe, and novelists Stephen Wright and John Del Vecchio, among others. Much of that work feeds off the zeitgeist of the early- and mid-1960s and the introduction of the New Journalism, a style popularized by Tom Wolfe in *The Electric Kool-Aid Acid Test*, Norman Mailer in *The Armies of the Night*, and

Hunter S. Thompson in *Hell's Angels*. Eric Schroeder compares O'Brien's early work to that of Thompson and Wolfe, asserting that "while O'Brien's authorial stance is not as megalomanic as Thompson's, the narrative nonetheless depends on the author's first person viewpoint for its formal cohesion; furthermore, his content, his participation in the Vietnam War . . . is presented as a shared experience and, more importantly, as a *believable* one."[24] O'Brien's work, with its push and pull of competing ideologies and attitudes, creates moving, lasting art. "Books are a little bit like our dreams and memories," O'Brien tells Scott Sawyer of the resonance of stories. "They continue to live in our heads long after they've passed away. Like dead puppies from our childhood, or a set of friends from Vietnam, they operate on the ghost principle."[25] It is from the ashes of his experiences and through the pain of memory that O'Brien creates his most powerful literature.

Remarried now and raising a family outside Austin, Texas, O'Brien talks openly about the joys and challenges of fatherhood, the wonder of it all. Having published his last novel, *July, July*, a decade ago, he continues to write, this time with an eye toward his two sons' futures. "I'm not sure what it is *exactly*, though I know inexactly—a mix of fiction and nonfiction, like many of my books—with a focus on my being an older father," he says. "Partly that, and partly a kind of memoir, the stories I tell my kids about my own life as a writer and a soldier and a father. It's partly fiction, too, little tales I tell to my kids at bedtime."[26]

For O'Brien, writing, imagination, reaching after truth, a sense that writing can make a difference—those are the necessary components of storytelling. But writing goes deeper than that. "We think of the imagination as kind of a flighty thing when, in fact, it's an essential component of our daily lives," O'Brien tells Schroeder, reinforcing the notion that reality devoid of imagination can never make art or accurately describe the human condition. "The central theme of [*Cacciato*] has to do with how we use our imaginations to deal with situations around us, not just to cope with them psychologically but, more importantly, to deal with them philosophically and morally."[27]

In Tim O'Brien's fiction, it makes perfect sense, then, that a contradiction forms the beating heart of the stories awaiting readers: "Truth doesn't reside on the surface of events. Truth resides in those deeper moments of punctuation, when things explode," he posits.

"You tell lies to get at the truth."[28]

I've looked forward for several years, since finishing a critical exploration of the author's work for *Tim O'Brien: A Critical Companion* in 2005, to editing a Literary Conversations volume on O'Brien. First, many thanks go to Walter Biggins at the University Press of Mississippi, who encouraged the project from the outset and was patient and prompt in answering all questions I sent his way. Managing editor Anne Stascavage gave the manuscript the kind of close attention any writer is fortunate to have.

It was also a pleasure to get to know, at least through correspondence, the scholars and writers whose work I've read and admired over the years, including Robert Birnbaum, Daniel Bourne, Jonathan D'Amore, Tobey Herzog, Larry McCaffery, Steven Pressfield, and Eric Schroeder. I'm gratified that they all agreed so readily to sign on to this project. Also, a special thanks to contributor Lynn Wharton, whom I tracked down in Shropshire, England. This volume is better for her intimate knowledge of O'Brien's work, her own insightful interview with the author, and her sage replies to my queries. Also, I always appreciate the help of the libraries and librarians dedicated to keeping the written word alive—in this case, the Bainbridge College Library and Jeff Dowdy, the Florida State University Libraries, and the Library of Congress.

Thanks, too, go to the people instrumental in gaining permission to reprint the interviews collected here, including Jill Barnes, Wayne Chapman, Andrea Drygas, Annie Foral, Matthew Hotham, Michael Khavari, Anne McKenna, Michael Nye, Megan Sexton, and Alasdair Spark. Marilyn Litt, who maintains the web's most comprehensive site on O'Brien and his work, was kind to make possible my connection with the author.

These projects are never brought to fruition without the help and generosity of friends and family, and I want to thank Dan Bowser, Guy de la Valdène (Push: Send!), Bob DeMott, Wes Potter, Martha Smith, Matthew Smith, and Jessica Teisch for their encouragement and editorial comments. And Patricia Boyett, whose cheerful support and sympathetic ear were an inspiration throughout the process.

I'm especially grateful for the participation of Tim O'Brien and his willingness to be interviewed for the book's closing piece. In the course of our conversation we discovered common ground, the children who have graced our lives.

This book is dedicated to my brilliant sons, Eric and Matthew, with love and hope.

PAS

Notes

1. McCaffery, 131.

2. Herzog, 78.

3. McCaffery, 129.

4. Lee, 201.

5. Tambakis, 98.

6. Birnbaum, http://www.identitytheory.com/people/birnbaum72.html.

7. Kaplan, 99.

8. *If I Die*, 11.

9. *If I Die*, 18.

10. Smith.

11. *The Things They Carried*, 40

12. At the time of the interview, Herzog was preparing to write a Twayne volume on O'Brien and dug deep into the author's biography. Later in the conversation, O'Brien clarifies the relationship with his father: "I hope you downplay some of this information as much as you can. I don't mind you using this stuff, but I don't want to make it appear as if this guy is all foul. He had many, many virtues and to this day still does. And I want to make sure that those virtues balance the negative aspects of my Dad's problem. Among his virtues is his intelligence; he's also well-read. He was extremely supportive of me in things like Little League and managing the team. Played ball with me all the time. Taught me to golf. Took me golfing with him all the time. Took me on trips with him when he would go out and sell insurance. A lot of times when he was sober he was a terrific father. And I want to make it real clear that his influence on me was probably dominantly affirmative as opposed to dominantly negative, but coming across in our conversation, because we are spending so much time on it, is the dominantly negative. It was the opposite. It was a dominantly positive influence" (81).

13. Karen Rosica. "Interview with Tim O'Brien—From Life to Fiction." 15 May 2004. http://www.lighthousewriters.com/newlett/timobrie.htm.

14. Naparsteck, 9.

15. "The Vietnam in Me," 51

16. "The Vietnam in Me," 52

17. Herzog, 87.

18. Twister Marquiss. "Westward Ho! (Chi Minh): Tim O'Brien and the Wounding of the American Cowboy Mythos." *Southwestern American Literature* 29.2 (2004): 11.

19. "The Vietnam in Me," 52

20. After having thrown away thousands of pages of prose that most writers would gladly have taken as their own (*The Nuclear Age*, published in 1985, was apparently the worst instance of this), O'Brien still adheres to a regimen that he likens to that of one of his great influences,

Joseph Conrad, who claimed that the "sitting-down" is the most important aspect of the act of writing.

21. Birnbaum, http://www.identitytheory.com/people/birnbaum72.html.

22. D'Amore, 37.

23. Karen Rosica. "Interview with Tim O'Brien—From Life to Fiction." 15 May 2004. Web. http://www.lighthousewriters.com/newlett/timobrie.htm.

24. Schroeder, Eric James. "The Past and the Possible: Tim O'Brien's Dialectic of Meaning and Imagination." In *Search and Clear: Critical Response to Selected Literature and Films of the Vietnam War*. Ed. W. J. Searle. Bowling Green, OH: Bowling Green State U Popular P, 1988. 117.

25. Scott Sawyer, "In the Name of Love: An Interview with Tim O'Brien." *Mars Hill Review* 4 (Winter–Spring 1996): 117-26.

26. Smith.

27. Schroeder, *Vietnam, We've All Been There*, 129.

28. Schroeder, *Vietnam, We've All Been There*, 132.

Chronology

1946   William Timothy O'Brien, Jr., born 1 October to William Timo-
        thy, an insurance salesman and World War II veteran, and Ava E.
        Schultz O'Brien, an elementary-school teacher and former WAVE,
        in Austin, Minnesota. A sister and a brother would follow.

1956   Moves with family to Worthington, Minnesota, "The Turkey Capi-
        tal of the World." O'Brien would describe—and question—his Mid-
        western upbringing in some detail in his Vietnam memoir, *If I Die
        in a Combat Zone*. Around this time O'Brien, an avid reader and
        amateur magician, writes his first fiction, a short story titled "Tim-
        my of the Little League."

1964   Enrolls in Macalester College in St. Paul, Minnesota, in the fall of
        the year. O'Brien would become an honors student and student-
        body president. Macalester inspired the setting for O'Brien's later
        novel, *July, July*.

1967   Travels abroad in Europe, including Prague, Czechoslovakia, and
        begins a novel. Campaigns for Senator Eugene McCarthy, who runs
        for president as an anti–Vietnam War candidate.

1968   Graduates Phi Beta Kappa from Macalester College. While working
        at a local golf course, O'Brien receives a draft notice. After briefly
        considering ignoring the notice, he reports to the Army in August.

1969   Begins tour of duty in Vietnam's Quang Ngai province after the
        infamous My Lai massacre in the same area the previous March
        claimed some five hundred Vietnamese lives. While there, he pub-
        lishes vignettes based on his experience in the *Minneapolis Star*
        and the *Worthington Daily Globe*. O'Brien receives a Purple Heart
        for a shrapnel wound sustained from an exploding grenade and
        Bronze Star for rescuing a fellow soldier.

1970   In March, returns from Vietnam holding the rank of sergeant. In
        September, O'Brien begins a Ph.D. program in government at Har-
        vard and starts work on a memoir, *If I Die in a Combat Zone, Box
        Me Up and Ship Me Home*. O'Brien would leave the university six

years later without finishing his dissertation, although he would continue to live in and near Cambridge, Massachusetts, for much of the next three decades. *Playboy* publishes a short piece about landmines called "Step Lightly," which would appear later in *If I Die*.

1971   Brought on as a summer intern at the *Washington Post*, a position he would hold the following summer as well.

1973   Based on internship experience, hired as national affairs reporter for the *Post* and covers national and international stories. Early that year, after establishing a relationship with legendary editor Seymour Lawrence, publishes *If I Die*, about which Annie Gottlieb writes in the *New York Times*, "It is a beautiful, painful book, arousing pity and fear for the daily realities of a modern disaster." O'Brien marries Ann Weller, an editorial assistant at Little, Brown.

1975   *Northern Lights* published. O'Brien himself would later take the book to task for its "gratuitous repetition," the work of a beginning novelist, and consider revising the book at various points during the next three decades.

1976   Wins first of four O. Henry Memorial awards for "Night March," a piece excerpted from the forthcoming novel *Going After Cacciato*.

1978   *Going After Cacciato* published to immediate and widespread critical acclaim. "Speaking of Courage," another story excerpted from the novel, wins a second O. Henry Award for O'Brien. The novel won the National Book Award, beating out the favorite, John Irving's *The World According to Garp*.

1982   Garners a third O. Henry award for "Ghost Soldiers," a story originally published in *Esquire*.

1985   *The Nuclear Age* published.

1989   "The Things They Carried," the eponymous piece in the forthcoming short-story cycle, wins a National Magazine Award in Fiction.

1990   *The Things They Carried* published to widespread acclaim. The novel would be shortlisted for the Pulitzer Prize and the National Book Critics Circle Award and win both the Melcher Award and France's Prix du Meilleur Livre Étranger.

1994   *In the Lake of the Woods* published. The novel won the James Fenimore Cooper Prize. O'Brien speaks publicly about his decision to give up writing. He returns to Vietnam for the first time since the war and in October writes "The Vietnam in Me," a lengthy essay ruminating on his experiences in country and a failed long-term relationship, for the *New York Times*. "Last night suicide was on my mind," O'Brien writes. "Not whether, but how." Within nine months, he would write the opening passages of a comic novel, *Tomcat in Love.*

1998   *Tomcat in Love* published.

1999   Accepts a teaching position in the MFA program at Texas State University in San Marcos. "The Things They Carried" selected for inclusion in *The Best American Short Stories of the Twentieth Century*, edited by John Updike.

2002   *July, July* published.

2003   Fourth O. Henry award for "What Went Wrong," a story originally published in *Esquire.*

2010   Reads and lectures in support of the twentieth anniversary of the publication of *The Things They Carried*, which was chosen from more than thirty selections by the National Endowment for the Arts to be featured in the "Big Read."

2011   Lives with his family outside Austin, Texas, where O'Brien continues to teach at Texas State University and to work on a book "meant to be a record for [my two sons] Timmy and Tad of their own youth, the things they said or did or experienced. Most of what we experience as children is almost instantly erased, gone forever, and I'm hoping the book might preserve for my sons a few glimpses of their own swiftly passing childhoods. I look at the book as a little gift I can leave behind for Timmy and Tad."

Conversations with Tim O'Brien

Interview with Tim O'Brien

Larry McCaffery/1979

From *Chicago Review* 33.2 (1982): 129–49. A version of this interview also appeared in *Anything Can Happen: Interviews with Contemporary American Novelists* (Urbana: University of Illinois Press, 1983), 262–78. Reprinted with permission of Larry McCaffery.

Everyone over twenty-five remembers the spring and summer of 1968, a period so jammed with tumult, confusion, high emotions, violence, and death that today it's hard to believe so much could have happened in only a few short months. But as with John Kennedy's assassination, everyone today can still recall exactly what they were doing during the big moments of that year: McCarthy's victory in New Hampshire; Johnson's announcement that he wouldn't seek a second term; King's assassination; Kennedy's assassination; the scenes on the streets of Chicago at the Democratic Convention.

And Vietnam.

Vietnam was on everyone's mind that long, hot summer, especially if you were, as I was, twenty-two years old, engaged to be married, about to enter graduate school, and the recipient of a draft notice. I spent a lot of time that summer thinking about what I would do if I were given a gun and told to start shooting at someone. Could I really do that? Or could I really say "fuck it" to friends, school, family, and take off for Canada or Sweden, or go underground the way some of my friends already had? Luckily I failed my induction physical—my asthma had finally done me some good—so I didn't have to make these sorts of painful decisions. But like most other Americans whose sensibilities were formed during that confusing period of our history, I have done a lot of thinking about Vietnam during the past ten or twelve years: I've wondered what it was like to be there (or to run away from it), and about my own tacit complicity in the horrors and confusions that war produced. And like many other Americans, I've sought help in understanding what our experiences in Vietnam meant to our nation and to the poor sons-of-bitches who fought, were wounded (in all senses of the word), and died there. I've listened to newscasters, talked with Vets (most of us have shared the conversation which ends: "You can't understand where I'm coming from, man, you don't know what I *saw* over there, what I *did* over there."), gone to the movies. And I've read novels. The best of the lot, the book which seemed to me to speak most eloquently and viscerally about the experience of the war and how the war effected the imaginations of the men who fought there, is Tim O'Brien's *Going After Cacciato*. On April Fool's Day 1979 I spent the afternoon talking with O'Brien in his Cambridge, Massachusetts, apartment about *Cacciato*, about Vietnam, about his other writing. What follows is an interview based on that conversation.

In 1968 Tim O'Brien was also recently graduated from college, also twenty-two years old, also the recipient of a draft notice. Unlike me, however, O'Brien passed his physical and was sent to Ft. Lewis, Washington, for basic training. While there, he almost decided to desert the Army, abandon family and friends, and slip across the nearby Canadian border to start a new life. Eventually O'Brien didn't desert—he was subsequently sent to Vietnam, where he served as an infantryman—but the imaginative possibilities of deserting became the seeds of *Cacciato*, a novel which, as he suggests in our interview, starts with the premise of "What if I *had* deserted?"

It was when O'Brien's *Going After Cacciato* won the prestigious National Book Award in 1978 (it won out over the highly favored *The World According to Garp*) that the literary world began to pay serious attention to a writer who had published two previous works: *If I Die in a Combat Zone* (1973), a collection of nonfictional anecdotes about his experiences in Vietnam, and *Northern Lights*, a novel set in the Minnesota wilderness of O'Brien's youth which deals with the issues of how courage and bravery develop. Although these earlier novels were well received when they appeared, they certainly didn't prepare readers for the astonishing performance of *Cacciato*. Because of the subject matter and because of O'Brien's clear, crisp sentence rhythms, comparisons with Hemingway were inevitable; but a more useful analogy is probably with García Márquez's *One Hundred Years of Solitude*, for like Márquez, O'Brien blends an eye for realistic detail with a sense of the fabulous to produce a work of magical realism. Indeed, like a number of other important works of the late 1970s—works like Toni Morrison's *Song of Solomon*, Robert Coover's *The Public Burning*, and John Barth's *Letters*— *Cacciato* suggests that writers have successfully assimilated the formally experimental approaches of the late 1960s and that they are now ready to re-engage the world through these new approaches.

Larry McCaffery: Two of your three books to date have dealt directly with Vietnam, and your third—I'm thinking of *Northern Lights*—might be considered a marginal case. At this stage in your career do you consider yourself to be primarily a "Vietnam writer"?

Tim O'Brien: No, I don't. It's true, of course, that I came to writing because of the war. When I returned from Vietnam, I had something to say: I had witnessed things, smelled things, imagined things which struck me as startling and terrifying and intriguing in all sorts of ways. At that point I didn't care much about technique or language or structure or any of that craft stuff. All I had was a body of acquired experience that impelled me to write. But since the publication of *Cacciato* in 1978, I've been working in entirely different ways. My new book, which will be called *The Nuclear Age*, deals with a new set of issues and concerns. So, no, I'm not a Vietnam writer. Although Vietnam was the impetus and spark for *becoming* a writer, I do not consider myself a war writer.

LM: Had you received any writing training at all before you went to Vietnam?

TO: Term papers. I wrote a make-shift novel when I spent the summer of 1967 in Czechoslovakia. A college novel, a crappy little thing, an exercise.

LM: Could you clarify the chronology of your writing career up through *Going After Cacciato?* I understand that in between writing projects you were also a graduate student and a newspaper reporter . . .

TO: I was drafted in 1968, went to Vietnam in 1969, and came home in '70. I arrived at Harvard to pursue a doctorate in government in September of 1970. During my first year in graduate school I began writing *If I Die in a Combat Zone*. I finished that book sometime in 1972. In 1973–74, I took a year off from Harvard to work as a reporter for the *Washington Post*—I was a general assignment reporter on the national desk; I covered a lot of Senate hearings, the first oil boycott, some veterans affairs. General politics. While a reporter, I wrote *Northern Lights* during my off hours. I wrote *Cacciato* in 1975, '76, and '77.

LM: Did your graduate studies have any relationship to the ideas that went into *Cacciato*?

TO: Sort of. I was studying American foreign policy and my dissertation explored American military interventions. Equally important, though, was my reading in political theory: Plato, Aristotle, Marsilius of Padua, Aquinas, Locke, Dante, Machiavelli, and so on.

LM: You actually wrote some of the pieces in *If I Die* while you were in Vietnam didn't you?
TO: I wrote tiny vignettes or anecdotes—little pieces of maybe four or five pages. For example, seeing a land mine kill some people, I wrote a piece called "Step Lightly" that appeared in *Playboy* and later in *If I Die*. Perhaps five or six of these things were written while I was actually in Vietnam. But even then I wasn't thinking of myself as a writer; I was writing in the sense that we all do it—in letters and postcards.

LM: Were you active in opposing the war while you were in college?
TO: I was active in the sense that activism existed then. From 1964 to 1968, while I attended Macalester College, there were no wild demonstrations against the war. Four or five local activists might wave signs saying "End the War." I wasn't among those four or five people. I was, however, a big supporter of Gene McCarthy during the 1967–68 period. I knocked on doors for him, took trips up to Wisconsin to help out during the primaries.

LM: In both *Cacciato* and *If I Die* you devote several important passages to the issue of why one goes to war even not believing that the war is just. In *If I Die*, for example, you say, "I was persuaded then and I remain persuaded now that the war was wrong, it was evil"—but you go on to say that "in the end it was less reason and more gravity" that finally influenced you to go to Vietnam. What did you mean by the last part of that quote?
TO: In both those books I tried to describe those forces which seemed, almost physically, to push me into the war. One was my background: I came from a very small town, a fairly conservative town. I was part of the prairie. My father was a sailor in World War Two, my mother was a WAVE. I sensed that the people I cared for in my life—friends, college acquaintances, professors—would have looked askance at my deserting. There was also the question of living in exile. I couldn't face that. To live in Canada or Sweden for the rest of my life was a frightening prospect. Philosophical questions also played into it. Although I did feel that the war was wrong, I also realized that I was a twenty-one-year-old kid—I didn't know everything. Our

president and his advisors were telling us the war was necessary and right. It seemed arrogant simply to give them the finger and say, "No. I won't go." The "gravity" that I was referring to in that passage was a feeling of emotional pressure—a fear of exile, of hurting my family, of losing everything I held to be valuable in my life. In the end, questions of political rightness or wrongness succumbed to the emotional pressure.

LM: One of the most vivid passages in *If I Die* is your description of your preparations for deserting the Army—preparations you later abandoned. I take it that this personal struggle was one of the germinating ideas for *Cacciato*.

TO: Yes. *Cacciato* was in essence the flip side of *If I Die*. That is, in *Cacciato* the premise I started with was, what if I *had* deserted? Would I have been happy living in exile? Would I be happy running? What would I experience? Would I be able to live with myself? Was it *right* to run? What about my obligations as a citizen? My conclusion was basically that Paul Berlin's fantasized run for Paris would have been an unhappy experience—it wasn't compatible with his background, personality, his beliefs. But while I was writing *Cacciato* I tried to keep things open-ended to allow for the possibility of a happy ending for the flight. I found I couldn't write my way into a happy ending, just as in my life I couldn't live my way into it.

LM: I noticed that in the dream sequence near the end of *Cacciato*, where Paul is asked to step boldly into his dream of escape—he bases his refusal on much the same principles as you describe in *If I Die*.

TO: There are two essential answers that Paul gives there. One has to do with this issue of emotional baggage—that constellation of emotional pressures we were just talking about. But of equal importance is his argument—and my own—that he can't mold his imagination to fit what ought to be there. He can't say, "Paul Berlin, you ought to run away—the war is wrong. Force yourself to imagine yourself running away." One can't fully control one's imagination. That's very important, not only to the book but to how we do things in our own lives. If you could imagine yourself sitting in Ft. Lewis, Washington, in 1968, trying to decide if you're going to desert or not, what would you do before you make that decision? You would attempt to *imagine* the desertion. Would I be happy? Could I get across the border? What's it going to be like sitting on the bus as I go across there? What happens if I get checked by the border guards? What would I need in the way of money and clothing? You can *imagine* yourself *imagining* all this. The decision to run or not run is based on that process. Those soldiers who actually did desert were able to imagine a happy end to it.

LM: In *Cacciato* the issue of whether or not Vietnam was a fundamentally different war for Americans is raised in a discussion between Doc and Captain Rhallon. You present both sides very persuasively, but it seemed to me that you give Doc the upper hand when he claims that the common soldier has always had the same kinds of problems and that he's never given a damn about justice or the purposes of war. Do you agree with Doc?

TO: Yes, I do. It's not a very popular belief. Many of the correspondents who came back from Vietnam base their reporting and general attitudes on the proposition that Vietnam was fundamentally different from other American wars. Vietnam, they say, was an unpopular war and was perceived as being evil by many of those fighting it. My quarrel, I suppose, is that, based on my own experience, not many of the soldiers believed that Vietnam was an evil war. Most people fighting there—the ordinary grunts like me—didn't think much about issues of good and evil. These things simply didn't cross their minds most of the time. Instead, inevitably, their attention was on the mosquitoes and bugs and horrors and pains and fears. These were the basic elements of the Vietnam War, and the same elements were present at the Battle of Hastings or Thermopylae or wherever. Captain Rhallon has a nice rejoinder to Doc's position on this. Rhallon argues that, without a clear and just purpose, soldiers will simply run. He feels that "purpose" is what keeps men fighting. I suppose in some sense Rhallon's argument may be true, although not that many soldiers in Vietnam, proportionally, ran away, deserted, or even went AWOL. For me, there's no clear-cut answer to the matter. Is the presence or absence of "purpose" or "moral imperative" the proper criterion for distinguishing one war from another? I don't know. The Nazis fought very well in defending their homeland against incredible pressures from both east and west. They were outnumbered, outgunned, outflanked, out-everythinged. Yet the German soldiers fought bravely, even though a great many of them had long since given up any sense of a great or noble purpose. Once a soldier is in battle, the rational and moral faculties tend to diminish. All we can hope for is that these faculties don't fail entirely.

LM: Why do you think that several of the most important works about Vietnam—your book, Eastlake's *The Bamboo Bed*, Michael Herr's *Dispatches*,

Apocalypse Now—have relied so heavily on surreal or fantastic effects? Is this a reaction to the type of war that was fought there?

TO: I think all good war novels have a surreal aspect. *All Quiet on the Western Front*, for example, has that wonderful scene in which the coffins are blown out of the ground. *Catch-22* deals with WWII in a great many surreal ways, *Slaughterhouse-Five*—again about WWII—has a strong surreal element to it. Even *The Naked and the Dead* in that long and really impossible march up the mountain was, if not surreal, certainly fantastic and improbable. *The Red Badge of Courage* also has a good many scenes that seem surreal. In war, the rational faculty begins to diminish, as I just said, and what takes over is surrealism, the life of the imagination. The mind of the soldier becomes part of the experience—the brain seems to flow out of your head, joining the elements around you on the battlefield. It's like stepping outside yourself. War *is* a surreal experience, therefore it seems quite natural and proper for a writer to render some of its aspects in a surreal way.

LM: But don't you feel that the Vietnamese War seemed especially chaotic and formless—in both a geographic and tactile sense—so that writers might be even more tempted to deal with it surrealistically?

TO: Every war seems formless to the men fighting it. Certainly if you read *The Red Badge of Courage* you get a strong sense that Henry Fleming doesn't know where he's at or where the lines are or where the enemy is. There's a lot of smoke and noise mixing enemy and friend together into one inseparable mass. Who's behind me, Fleming wonders? Who's in front of me? Battles as witnessed on the ground don't have that classic feel of strong, unbroken lines between friends and enemies, a strong sense of location, nor that sense of here is where I am. This wasn't quite so true for WWI, obviously, because of the trench warfare, but the chaos and general absence of order was still present in WWI fiction. It's very nice and easy to say Vietnam was special because it was formless and absurd. But certainly WWI must've seemed equally chaotic and absurd to Siegfried Sassoon or Robert Graves or Rupert Brooke or Erich Remarque. And it *was* absurd, men were slaughtered like cattle for reasons that no soldier really understood. We like to think our own way is special: especially horrible, especially insane, especially formless. But we need a more historical and compassionate perspective. We shouldn't minimize the suffering and sense of bewilderment of other people in other wars.

LM: What's your opinion about the other books that have appeared dealing with Vietnam?

TO: I liked Herr's *Dispatches*. It's very good.

LM: What about the movies?

TO: Horseshit. Simplistic and stupid. *Heroes*, *The Deer Hunter*, *Coming Home*, *Apocalypse Now*—they all came across to me as cartoons, garishly drawn rhetorical statements. Some less so than others. *The Deer Hunter* was the best.

LM: Do you have a daily writing routine?

TO: I work seven days a week, six to eight hours a day. On weekends, I may only work five to six hours. I'm slow, I need big chunks of time. It's very regularized.

LM: Do your books or stories begin in the same way for you each time, with a character, a plot, an idea, a metaphor?

TO: Most often it starts with an idea. I want to stress here that I'm a believer in substance—that is, I feel the fiction writer should have something to say. I mean this in all sorts of ways—in terms of a body of witnessed experience, the physical things that are seen and felt. But beyond that, I mean "substance" in a philosophical and thematic sense. It's not enough to say, "Here's what I saw in Vietnam" or "Here's what I experienced on my peace march." The writer needs a passionate and knowledgeable concern for the substance of what's witnessed, and that includes the spiritual and theological and political implications of raw experience. All my fiction is governed by this concern for substance—ideas with philosophical meat to them. I begin my books with a search for a dramatic vehicle for an idea. For example, *Cacciato* started with an idea: the metaphorical and literal flip side of *If I Die*—what if *I had* walked away from Vietnam? What would have happened in terms of my psychological well-being? What were the moral implications of desertion? Next, I sought a way of dramatizing this cluster of ideas and questions. *Northern Lights* began almost precisely the same way. I wanted to explore ideas of courage, hence I looked for the proper dramatic vehicle.

LM: Once you've found this dramatic vehicle, how do you proceed to develop your books? For instance, do you work straight through on a novel and then go back and revise? Or do you keep working on individual sections until you're satisfied?

TO: I have a peculiar way of approaching books: I try to make chapters into independent stories—that is, I like my chapters to have beginnings, middles, and ends. There are two reasons for this. One is very practical: I can publish chapters as stories in magazines. This has the advantage of making money, and also of testing things out, getting responses from magazine editors and readers. The other reason, which is more important, has to do with why chapters are chapters. I've always wondered why so many chapters end arbitrarily. It's much nicer to have your chapters conclude with a nice mini-resolution. There should be a sigh from the reader at the end of a chapter, the sigh signifying he's recognized a natural end and that the chapter has an internal integrity to it. Sure, the reader knows that the book will go on, but there has been a temporary resolution—not just a dramatic resolution, but also in terms of psychological development, suspense, or whatever. Again, I don't like novels that seem arbitrary. As a result, much of my time is spent trying to forge dramatic wholes, so that the first chapter of *Cacciato*, for example, is a story—the book could end there, with Cacciato up on that hill and Paul Berlin saying "Go, go."

LM: Are you happy with the way your first novel, *Northern Lights*, turned out?

TO: The book is maybe eighty pages too long. Someday, before it's reissued, I'll go over it and cut it considerably, especially in the first two-hundred pages. There's a lot of interior monologue material that's too set up, and there's a lot of unnecessary repetition. These are things that can be solved. I'm firmly convinced that style is not the most important element of good literature. Stylistic problems *can* be solved: by writing better, by recognizing your own faults and getting rid of them. What *can't* be learned, however, is passion for ideas—substance. Out of every forty books of contemporary fiction, I'm lucky to find one which gives the sense of an author who really gives a shit about a set of philosophical issues. I'm not saying that fiction should *be* philosophy, but I am saying that a fiction writer must demonstrate in his work a concern for rightness and wrongness. What I see instead is concern for style and craft and structure. I see concern for well-drawn characters, concern for plot, concern for a whole constellation of things which, however, seem peripheral to the true core of fiction: the exploration of substantive, important human values.

LM: So you wouldn't agree with someone like Grass, who feels that style is its own reward in fiction—maybe the *only* legitimate concern for the writer—or with other writers like Barth and Borges, who feel that in exploring the nature of language and fiction-making they are also exploring something fundamental in man's makeup?

TO: If these writers are interested in exploring language as a tool of human inquiry and understanding, then I'd say okay. But I would also ask: "Why aren't you doing linguistic philosophy? Why aren't you writing essays? Why use the camouflage of drama? Why do you need plot or characters? Why do you need even the semblance of a story?"

LM: Do you have a similarly negative attitude towards all the experimentalism that was so prevalent in American fiction during the early and mid '70's?

TO: Experimentalism, in various guises, has been going on since people started writing. In many ways, I think of myself as an experimentalist. I'm always experimenting with new sentences, new structures, new meanings. I'm creating what seems to me to be brand-new people, putting new words in their mouths, finding a story-telling method which accomplishes new dramatic magic. Although my experiments aren't startling—I'm not experimenting for the joy of experimenting, but rather to explore meaning and themes and dramatic discovery. For instance, *Cacciato* is structured as a teeter-totter, with the "Observation Post" chapters as the fulcrum—the present of the book. The teeter-totter swings back and forth between reality—the war experience—and fantasy—the imagined trek to Paris. Devising this structure was fun, yes, but I did it for thematic and dramatic *reasons*. I don't enjoy tinkering for the joy of tinkering, and I don't like reading books merely for their artifice. I want to see things and explore moral issues when I read, not get hit over the head with the tools of the trade.

LM: You must pay considerable attention to the sound and rhythm of your sentences—it's one of the most striking aspects of your style.

TO: Absolutely. When I start a book, I try to figure out its "moral aboutness" and then how to dramatize it. This process takes seven or eight months or even a year. But when I actually get to the typewriter, my time is spent in only one way—trying to make sentences and combinations of sentences which sound right and then work toward the creation of a dramatic dream. Rhythm is a big part of that. Dreams have rhythm. Drama has rhythm. The language mustn't be monotonous or repetitive. I like to juggle compound sentences and complex sentences and straight, declarative sentences. I watch certain words. I watch "and's," for example, to be sure too many of them don't appear. I'm very keen on catching unnecessary or showy repetitions since I used to use too many of them—in *Northern Lights*, for example. I don't like to repeat words if I can possibly avoid it, even words like "the." I don't want to say, "The train arrived at the depot." I'd rather say, "A train arrived at the depot"—something like that.

LM: Am I right in noting the influence of Hemingway in your approach to the sound and rhythm of sentences?

TO: Yes, although I don't know really how much of his style I have absorbed. I don't think *Cacciato* sounds much like Hemingway; *Northern Lights* probably has more echoes of Hemingway than any of my other books. But as to what specifically I learned from Hemingway—efficiency, drama, sentiment instead of sentimentality.

LM: In *Northern Lights*, Paul Perry is said several times to be searching for "the bottom of things," and in his last visit to the pond you say he was in "a final search for the start of things." It occurred to me that this interest is really the obverse of his father's fascination with the *end* of things, with the apocalypse.

TO: Yes, that's a good way to put it. The book revolves around the genesis of personality, the genesis of one's moral outlook. I want the reader to ask: "Why is Paul Perry so cowardly in many ways, a homebody, whereas his brother is an outgoing macho-man, a hero? What made them so different?" Consequently, I had to go back literally to the sources of personality: why do people turn out as they do? There's no simple answer, obviously, and I don't think there *can* be. But there are interesting combinations of experiences, and interpretations of experience, which can be more or less formative. For Paul and Harvey Perry, these experiences and interpretations go back to their father, and *his* father, and finally to the Kalevalan mythology. A reader rightly demands and expects a dramatic, satisfying explanation for the behavior of people. These motives and sources needn't be spelled out directly, but the raw material should be there, built into the novel's drama and context. You can let the reader shape the material, figure out what is most or least important, but nevertheless you must have this material present. Nothing infuriates me more in reading a book than unexplained behavior. There can be many, many possible explanations—not just one—but there must be at least something.

LM: Apocalyptic images abound in *Northern Lights*, and from what you've told me about your new book it will deal even more directly with the notion of the end of things. What do you find so sustaining about these particular images or metaphors?

TO: I'd say these aren't images or metaphors—they're *real*. In *Northern Lights*, when the father builds a bombshelter it's because he's afraid of dying. Dying in general, but also death by way of the Bomb. When I wrote *Northern Lights*, I didn't think critics would interpret the bombshelter as a metaphor. To me, it's a *real* bombshelter; this guy's afraid of war. There is a whole litany of things to explain *why* the father is afraid of real bombs—the whole Finnish mythology which underlies the book helps explain this, for example. Still, this fear is real. But when the book came out, a few reviewers remarked, rather snidely, that the bombshelter was a pretty crude metaphor. This upset me. It wasn't a metaphor at all—it was just a damned bombshelter. A *real* one! In the book I'm writing now—*The Nuclear* Age—there is another real bombshelter. No metaphor, no image. Real, real! The book's themes revolve around two issues: one is the whole question of how and why we become politicized and depoliticized; the second issue involves the safety of our species, of our survival. We *won't* survive if we can't stop thinking of nuclear weapons as mere metaphors. These bombs are real. Two years ago, in preparation for the new novel, I went to Kansas and looked at a Titan missile complex. Real hardware, real firepower. It didn't look very metaphorical. My new book, although it's designed to be humorous in a lot of places, treats the nuclear age in very tangible, realistic terms. That is, I want to hit people over the head with real bombs, real dangers, real perils, real possibilities. I want to ask: "Why are we so *numb* to these realities?" If you ask someone, "Is the bomb real?" they'll say, "Yeah, sure, it's real." But if you *don't* ask, it's never acknowledged; it's treated as a fairy-tale, as something that isn't quite genuine, as a dream. What motivated me to write my new book—and what motivated *Northern Lights*, too, although it wasn't recognized—was this desire to treat apocalypse as a startling fact of modern life. Not as Biblical backlash or absurd theater or *Dr. Strangelove*.

LM: Although Vietnam doesn't appear directly very much in *Northern Lights*, I felt you might be using it as a sort of muted presence, much the way that Hemingway used WWI in *The Sun Also Rises*. This connection seemed reinforced by the fact that just as Jake Barnes comes back from the war with an overtly symbolic wound, so does Harvey Perry come back blinded—a wound which seemed to be linked to what Vietnam did to many returning veterans.

TO: As far as Vietnam was concerned, no, it didn't occur to me that I was writing about it in that way. The action of the book occurs after the war, and I wanted some kind of dramatic demonstration of Harvey's macho tendencies. So I had him go to a war—you know, "There's this brave son-of-a-bitch"—and he gets wounded as a result. I *did* intend Harvey's partial blindness as a symbol of a deeper personality-blindness.

LM: The idea of escape, of running away, is obviously a central concern in *Cacciato*, but it appears in *Northern Lights* as well in regard to Harvey and Addie. In your earlier book, though, you seem to be treating escape as more of a frivolous activity than you do in *Cacciato*, where you seem more sympathetic to the idea that escape may be necessary—at least imaginatively—in an intolerable situation.
TO: Actually I think this idea is treated equally seriously in both books. Because Harvey and Addie are unsympathetic characters in some ways, I suppose the reader is justified in feeling that their attitude about escape and running away is frivolous. To me, though, it doesn't seem so much frivolous as it is a common human failing. I have it. I'm always wanting to run away: run to Tahiti, to all those places Harvey talks about. In all my works, and in what I am writing now, running away plays a big part, perhaps because running away helps open up all kinds of plot materials. In *Cacciato*, Paul Berlin is escaping a war; in *Northern Lights*, Harvey is escaping himself and his own history; in *The Nuclear Age*, my chief characters are trying to outrun their own obsessions, to escape from the Bomb.

LM: A few reviewers compared your style in *Cacciato* with the magical realism coming out of South America. Had you read García Márquez when you wrote *Cacciato?*
TO: Yes, and Borges, too, but just dabbling. To me, all realism should be magical. All reality *is* magical.

LM: *Cacciato* seems less obviously governed by realistic impulses than your previous works, mainly because so much of the book is devoted to Paul's fantasy. Was this a conscious shift on your part?
TO: I think you could argue that *Cacciato* is the most realistic thing I've written. The life of the imagination is real—it's as fucking real as anything else, especially if you happen to be a follower of Fichte, who says that *nothing* is real but what is inside our own heads. But even if we don't go that far, I know that if I'm sitting in a room by myself, daydreaming, that daydream is perfectly real. The so-called fantasy sections of *Cacciato* are no less real

than a soldier's memories of the war. The war scenes aren't happening in the present; when Bernie Lynn is killed, when Sidney Martin is fragged, these are memories which Berlin is reliving in his mind. Still, they have an internal reality—a visual and emotional and moral reality. The same principle applies to the imagination. An internal phenomenon again, real, real!

"Soldiers are dreamers"—that epigraph begins *Cacciato*. Soldiers fantasize and daydream—they live in their heads. War is horrible, and you need to escape it. Any psychologist will tell you that retreat into fantasy is a means of escape. Albert Speer, when he was in prison, used to walk around a small courtyard during his exercise period, pretending he was walking around the world. He'd count each step and say, "Today I've walked a mile and today I'm in Hong Kong." Then next day he'd say, "Today I've walked three miles and now I'm on the road to Peking." He was pretending it. Imagining it. This same sense of imprisonment and stress exists in war, only heightened by the fear of death. So you retreat into your own mind. You manufacture a new reality.

LM: Several of the characters in *Cacciato*—notably Paul and Doc—share an almost obsessive need for order in their lives. Am I right in feeling that you tie this notion of order and control closely to the controlling power of the imagination?

TO: Yes, that's one important elaboration of my interest in the imagination. A concern for the ordering of experience—whether or not it's imaginative or remembered experience—seems to be an important aspect of psychology. Even in daily life, it is often hard to recall the events of an ordinary day; it's especially hard in a situation of great stress and peril. The ability to manufacture order out of seeming chaos is important to our psychological well-being—humans are causal animals. We have an impulse to order events, seek out causes and consequences. You can imagine a murderer who's just gone out on a rampage saying, "Why did I do it?" And he'd try to sit back and remember what series of physical and psychological events produced the killing spree. Similarly, in the case of *Cacciato*, one of Paul Berlin's compelling concerns is to figure out why his platoon murdered Sidney Martin; hence all the retracing of what happened when, the fitting of events together: when did Frenchie Tucker die? what did Martin say? what about Bernie Lynn? what happened first? what caused what? how did the murder come about? The ordering provides a partial motive for Cacciato's eventual flight from the war: he had been an implicit conspirator in a murder. All this feeds into the motives which prompt Paul Berlin to consider his own flight.

LM: I found it interesting that you placed the catalogue of the men's personal histories and backgrounds—Chapter 22, "Who They Were, or Claimed to Be"—in the middle of the novel, rather than at the very beginning, as most writers might have. Why did you do it this way?

TO: If that chapter has impact, it's because of what's implied in its title—"Who They Were, or *Claimed* to Be"—the disjunction between the two. So the chapter has to do with their nicknames, the lies they tell about themselves, what they pretended to be, the kind of images they tried to project. A lot of the important character information has already been supplied by the time we get to that chapter—we know Stink is a squirrelly, quick-tempered little shit; we know Oscar is evil in a more cool, quiet sort of way; we know the Lieutenant's history from the very first chapter—that he was busted, and so on. So I came to that point in the book and decided it would be instructive to dramatize the disjunctions and discontinuities between the surface characters and the internal characters. Oscar is a good example: he claims to be from one place but all his mail comes from another place; he pretends he's from Detroit but doesn't know the names of any contemporary ballplayers. The whole business with nicknames is a way of hiding a lot of things, covering up fears, trying to become what one is not. That's common in war.

LM: Another structural aspect of the book that interested me has to do with the very opening page, which is virtually a litany of those who will die in the rest of the novel. I imagine some traditionalists would claim that this destroys some of the suspense you might have capitalized on.

TO: Books can also work as magic acts. You go into a magic theater and *know* you'll see these little chests and you know someone is going to get into one while someone else sticks swords through it. You know no one is going to really die, but you still say, "I've got to see this." You know the outcome, the story, but the mystery isn't so much in *what's* going to happen as it is in *seeing it happen.* That's one response. The names of the dead are listed in a kind of threnody in the beginning and then, one by one, they are killed off. We *see* it happen. I'm hoping that the reader is taken up with the happeningness of it. But, beyond that, the real mystery of the novel isn't given away on page one. We don't find out what happened to Cacciato—in fact, we never really find out. We also don't know what happens to Paul Berlin. A good reader will know by the second chapter that Paul is going to survive all that follows, that what we're seeing is all history. None of the important questions, then, is answered on that first page. I sure as hell didn't know what was going to happen when I wrote that first page.

LM: So you wrote that first page first?

TO: Yeah. The first chapter was the first thing I wrote. Other chapters were written later in a completely different, hodge-podgey order.

LM: Unlike most of the other Vietnam novels I've seen, *Cacciato* doesn't seem to be fundamentally an antiwar novel.

TO: I don't believe any good book could be "antiwar" in its conception. It's like writing an antifeminist book—how would one do it? One could make a caricature of a feminist and make her so shrewish and awful that every reader would hate her. But this approach would just result in a bad book. Full of stereotyping and easy straw targets. No sense of mystery. I can't think of a great piece of literature that takes an absolute, black-and-white moral stance about the rightness or wrongness of certain issues, drawing all the bad guys as really bad and all the good guys as really good. An exception might be the two Malraux books, *Man's Fate* and *Man's Hope*, but even there it's not a closed question as to who is right and who's wrong. A genuine concern for the issues and complexity and the sense of discovery is much more important. Let the reader settle things.

LM: So, a scene like the one where that absurd young pacifist girl picks up the men is partly designed to add enough complexity to your treatment of war to allow the reader to draw his own conclusion.

TO: Yes, although there's really two, simultaneous responses to that scene. One is to laugh at her. She *is* pretty grotesque. But at the same time what the men do to her is also grotesque—they steal her van and leave her stranded. I get a sinking feeling when I reread the end of that scene. What they do may be funny, but it isn't *good*. The scene has a moral edge, too.

LM: Obviously we see violence and inhumanity outside the sphere of Vietnam in *Cacciato*. The most memorable scene of this sort may be the beheading which takes place in Tehran. I assume you were using these kinds of scenes to widen the scope of the novel, to suggest that the violence we see in Vietnam is not something limited to the American involvement in Vietnam.

TO: That's right. It's hard to articulate precise reasons for placing particular material or scenes in a novel. Obviously these scenes don't just happen—the writer makes them happen—and yet the reader should have a sense of dreamlike spontaneity. In general, however, my purpose was to hint at the roots of war in peace. War *always* grows out of peace—always. As the soldiers in my novel run away from war, they encounter many of the same evils which they had hoped to leave behind—avarice, injustice, death, brutality, etc. Unhappy things occur on their own peace march, which is a way of saying that one can't just run away and expect a happy, magical ending. There are consequences in the real world to any kind of escape. There is no utopia to run to. The so-called peaceful world is full of butchery, slaughter, and tyranny.

LM: When Paul is in Paris, a tour guide tells him that, "Paris is not a place, it's a state of mind." What *was* Paris in your conception of the book?

TO: Paris was that utopia in the mind of Paul Berlin and Sarkin Aung Wang—the absence of war, the city of light and goodness. It was the peace of Paris that was a conceived antithesis to all the brutality, butchery, and uncivilized behavior of war. Of course, Paris isn't *really* that way. Paul Berlin's response is that he hopes the guide is wrong and that Paris is more than a state of mind. But the guide is right. A lot of us in Vietnam used to talk about coming back to "the World"—we called the United States "the World." The United States was also a state of mind for us—it represented the absence of violence, civility, decorum, felicity. But the States weren't really that way either.

LM: Your use of nature—or "elements," as you refer to it in *Northern Lights*— creates much of the important symbolic framework in your two novels, although in *Cacciato* the rhythms of birth and decay seem upset because of all the destruction. Is there any aesthetic or private reason why you tend to anchor your books so firmly in nature?

TO: Because *life* is anchored in these things. Another, a more practical reason is that I have a hard time writing scenes which are set indoors. I feel liberated by a sense of space when I am writing; I like the sky, not a ceiling or a wall. My best scenes, the ones which seem to me to be most vivid and alive, are those which take place outside the confines of walls. I'm not sure why this is. Most of Henry James's best scenes take place indoors. In my new book I'm trying to fight this, set more scenes indoors, but I find this very difficult because when I get people indoors I find them sitting around talking. The word "sit" is a crucial word here—it's a very passive thing, whereas when we're outdoors we're not sitting very much. It's a memorable kind of thing to sit on real grass and be stationary; we're usually walking, moving around. So I try to invent indoor scenes with movement. Good novelists understand that there should always be motion in a novel, even during dialogue. In practice, though, this is hard to accomplish, because one's concern while writing is to get the scene done—getting the dialogue out, the problem set up, the next step taken. This often becomes very static and talky.

LM: A good example of what you're talking about is the scene in *Northern Lights* where Paul must kill the muskrat—a scene which parallels the earlier one where he confronts the rat. Paul's actions and reactions in these two scenes dramatize the change that has taken place in his personality.

TO: Yes, and these scenes do this without saying, "Look—my personality has undergone a metamorphosis. I'm really a different man now." In a way I'm pleased that you saw that in those scenes, but in another way I was hoping to hide this—I wanted the reader to retain not a memory of the rat scene so much as a subconscious feeling that this guy has changed without knowing why you have been made to feel this way. The book is studded with parallel episodes like that, which I thought out very carefully. The trouble with the damn book is that there is so much crap surrounding the good stuff.

LM: You mentioned that your novel-in-progress, *The Nuclear Age*, is partly a comedy. Have you found the creation of a humorous narrative to be fundamentally more difficult, or different in any ways, than that of a straight dramatic narrative?

TO: Both forms are "dramatic," of course. For example, one of the chapters of my new novel is about my narrator as a young boy during the '50s who has converted his ping-pong table into a fallout shelter. He's afraid of bombs. He's seen all those mushroom clouds on the tube, the CONLRAD alerts on the radio, the tests of the Emergency Broadcasting Company, and he's scared to death. He goes down to the basement one day and puts bricks and rugs on top of his ping-pong table, makes it into a fallout shelter. His father and mother try to talk the kid out from under the table, but the kid can't understand their numbness and lack of fear, he can't understand why they laugh and make fun of his ping-pong shelter. Now some funny things happen in this scene, and yet it's also poignant and even sad. It's that kind of balance that I want—comedy mixed with tragedy. You can't just preach to the reader and say: "There's a gap between what the kid sees—real problems and real bombs that we should fear—and the parents' numbness." If I did that, the effect would be monotonous and predictable. However, if you can get some laughter generated in the story, then the sober, tender point in the end becomes all the more sober and all the more tender. It's like killing off a character; if you want to make it tragic, you need to elevate him properly; you need to stretch your own and the readers' emotional capacity by running the gamut of things. In my other books, the tone pretty consistently remains sober. In my new book I want to stretch this, keep the soberness, intelligence, and tenderness but broaden this out in a life-giving way—the way of laughter, comedy.

LM: You're still early on in your career, but do you think you've learned something about writing since you started writing seriously?

TO: I've learned that writing doesn't get easier with experience. The more you know, the harder it is to write. If you know that repetition can be gratuitous and self-defeating, then this makes writing harder, since you've got to find new ways to say things. If you know that you shouldn't be monotonous in the length and style of your sentences, this makes writing more difficult, it challenges your skill. The most important thing, though, is this sense I've developed that a writer's true value must be found in his substantive contribution. Thought is the critical element in writing. Hard, rigorous, disciplined thought. I've learned to pay closer attention to the dramatization of moral choices. I've learned to ponder those choices before writing a story or a scene.

LM: Are there any contemporary writers you particularly admire or feel affinities with?

TO: John Fowles. I think he's our best living writer. There aren't too many others. I did like *Garp* a lot and also what I've heard of John Irving's new book, *The Hotel New Hampshire*. I'd probably also include Graham Greene, John Updike, Walker Percy, Norman Mailer, Tom McGuane. But as I said earlier, most modern fiction seems to me to be frivolous and gimmicky and . . . well, boring.

LM: In *If I Die*, you say, "Can a foot soldier teach anybody anything important about a war, merely for having been there? I think not. He can tell stories." Do you still believe this?

TO: Absolutely. What can you teach people, just for having been in a war? By "teach," I mean provide insight, philosophy. The mere fact of having witnessed violence and death doesn't make a person a teacher. Insight and wisdom are required, and that means reading and hard thought. I didn't intend *If I Die* to stand as a profound statement, and it's not. Teaching is one thing, and telling stories is another. Instead I wanted to use stories to alert readers to the complexity and ambiguity of a set of moral issues, but without preaching a moral lesson.

Tim O'Brien: "Maybe So"

Eric James Schroeder/1984

From *Vietnam, We've All Been There: Interviews with American Writers* (Westport, CT: Praeger, 1992), 124–43. Interview first appeared in "Two Interviews: Talks with Tim O'Brien and Robert Stone." *Modern Fiction Studies* 30.1 (Spring 1984): 135–64.

Schroeder: I want to start out with your first book because I think it raises the issue of fiction versus nonfiction and how the two begin to merge in Vietnam literature. On first reading, *If I Die in a Combat Zone* strikes one as a straight autobiography. Yet the impulse was obviously there for you to fictionalize. How much did you fictionalize, or why was there the impulse to fictionalize that experience when so many other writers obviously resisted it?

O'Brien: Well, most of *If I Die* is straight autobiography. All of the events in the book really happened; in one sense it is a kind of war memoir and was never intended to be fiction. It's not fiction. But you're right that I tried to cast the scenes in fictional form. Dialogue, for example. Often I couldn't remember the exact words people said, and yet to give it a dramatic intensity and immediacy I'd make up dialogue that seemed true to the spirit of what was said.

Schroeder: That's what Gay Talese says he does in writing his New Journalistic pieces.

O'Brien: I think it's probably not very new. I think it's old. Any memoir has it, going back to anybody. Unless you're sitting with a tape recorder or taking precise notes every time something happens, obviously you have an imperfect recollection. Things like ordering chronologies, that's made up. I didn't follow the chronology of the events; I switched events around for the purpose of drama. And drawing characters and descriptions and so on. It's not even sewn, just a little vignette and another vignette and another vignette. I'm not even sure what that is, but it's a fictional technique. It doesn't really matter.

What's odd about it, though, is that a book which I published and intended to be a straight autobiography or war memoir is now called a novel by everyone, and everyone writes about it as a novel. That goes to your point, which is that for some reason (I'm not even sure what it was; it must have been largely subconscious) the book was written as a novel; that is, the form of the book is fictional.

Schroeder: When I first read the book, I assumed it was straight autobiography, and I was not aware that it might be something else until I read an annotated bibliography that described it as fiction. Then I went and examined my copy—sure enough, on the spine of the book it says "Fiction."
O'Brien: I never noticed that.

Schroeder: So I thought, "I wonder how much is fictionalized and how much is autobiographical; if the publisher is going to put the stamp on it, it's for a reason."
O'Brien: It's not on any of the other editions. That's really odd. Well, there's another reason people think it's fiction. Even my own publisher can't tell. I'm not sure it matters, to be honest. It is what it is, clearly, no matter what kind of label you put on it. It never bothered me when people began calling it a novel. I think Gloria Emerson was the first to do so. I tell them it's not a novel, but really it doesn't bother me one way or the other.

Schroeder: Do you think, then, that this perception has more to do with the book's structure than its content? As you say, its episodic method?
O'Brien: I think it's the dialogue and that sense of drawing scene. When we think of nonfiction, we think of someone telling us, "And here's what happened when they went on like this," without stopping to give us dialogue and characters and so on. If I were to tell you a story about something that happened yesterday, I wouldn't go on for four or five pages without a "scene drawing," that "he said, she said." This creates the illusion of "happeningness" which usually isn't there in nonfiction. Nonfiction is usually cast in the language of political science or history or sociology or whatever. And this is not. It's cast in an entirely different language.

Schroeder: Why did you omit your college years from *If I Die*? You're rather detailed about your early childhood and adolescence, then at the end of

Chapter 2 you begin college. At the beginning of Chapter 3 it's summer, and you've finished college and have received your induction notice.

O'Brien: This I did in the interest of selectivity. There wasn't much that happened in college that seemed to reflect on what was important. I tried to pay attention to those antecedents or seeds that bloomed in Vietnam during the course of the experience. And there was nothing in college that was there to really grow. Hence, I just didn't put anything in about it. Little references here and there—I was called "College Joe." I mention that. But there was nothing in college that seemed critical to the experience.

Schroeder: Do you think your experience was atypical in that you were a college graduate who became an infantryman and saw combat? It seems that most college graduates who went to Vietnam got out of front-line duty.

O'Brien: Most did. I never quite understood why I didn't. There were some in my platoon, probably three of us.

Schroeder: Did that in any way alienate you from the younger GIs?

O'Brien: Most didn't know I had been to college. Those who did looked at it the same way that I looked at anybody else who was sort of unusual: "You're a bartender, huh? You were a cop? I didn't know that." It was something unusual. No, there was no alienation that I can remember. I noticed that everybody seemed quite young. But I was young too. I think I was twenty-one. So I was only a couple of years older than the average soldier. I felt young there. I didn't feel that much older than anyone else, though of course I was older than many. There's no question that most of us were kids.

Schroeder: Getting back to this distinction between fiction and nonfiction, we might locate *If I Die* in a mean position between the two, or a bit more toward nonfiction than fiction. But you can clearly see it partaking of both. With *Going After Cacciato* it seems that you've gone to a much further extreme in your fictionalization; the operative word there might be a myth-making. I see this much more in tune with something of that order than with a fictional work in a realistic mode, such as the books that came out of World War II—*The Naked and the Dead*, for instance. What was your motivation for adopting this mode?

O'Brien: A whole bunch of them. It's so complicated that it's even hard to talk about. On one level I think of it as strict realism; that is, even the so-called surreal sections are very real in a way: one's imagination and daydreams are real. Things actually happen in daydreams. There's a reality you can't deny. It's not happening in the physical world, but it's certainly happening in the sense data of the brain. There's a reality to imaginative experience that's critical to the book. The life of the imagination is half of war, half of any kind of experience.

We live in our heads a lot, but especially during situations of stress and great peril. It's a means of escape in part, but it's also a means of dealing with the real world—not just escaping it, but dealing with it. And so I chose to render about half of the book in a naturalistic mode, but I also treated it as fully real. Early on in the book I try to blur the distinctions between what's real and what's imagined, so that the reader thinks that all these things are actually happening. For instance, there's this peculiar falling into a tunnel. It's written as if it were really happening. Odd things happen. What's this guy doing living in a hole? The reader has the same sensation that a person has when he slips into a daydream and then out, slipping into it and out; he doesn't treat the fantasy section as *Alice in Wonderland*–ish, as if filled with goblins and hobbits and fantasy creatures, but instead treats it very realistically, as straight declarative prose.

And there's more to it than that. One of the important themes of the book is how one's memory and imagination interpenetrate, interlock. Paul Berlin will be remembering guys dying in the tunnel, for example, and these memories will set off his imagination, and suddenly he'll start imagining that the trek to Paris has fallen into a tunnel. Hence it's the way those two things interact that seems to me important. Beyond that, one's imagination is also a way of goal setting or objective setting, of figuring out purposes. For example, before wanting to become a doctor, one would have first to imagine giving shots to people. Could you stand it? What would it feel like and look like? If you couldn't imagine being happy sticking a needle into someone, the odds are that in the real world you wouldn't become a doctor. You'd be something else. If you could imagine yourself happy as a professor, getting up in the morning and putting on a tie, having office hours, going to class, preparing lectures—if you can imagine being happy in that sort of situation, then you might go to graduate school in the real world.

Paul Berlin is engaged in the same process. We think of the imagination as kind of a flighty thing when, in fact, it's an essential component of our daily lives. Paul Berlin is using his imagination to figure out whether he would be happy running from a war or not, if he'd be happy living in exile. Would he find peace of mind and contentment, would he feel that he had betrayed his country, that his reputation has been undermined, his family? And this imagined journey is a way of asking himself the question, "Could I really do it in this other world, this world of physical reality? Could I physically do it?" It's a test of how to behave and what to do.

The imagined journey after Cacciato isn't just a way of escaping from the war in his head—it's that, too, I'm sure—but it's also a way of asking the questions, "Should I go after Cacciato, really? Should I follow him off into the jungle toward Paris? Could I live with myself doing that?" See what I'm getting at? How the imagination is a heuristic tool that we can use to help ourselves set goals. We use the outcomes of our imaginings. We do this all the time in the real world. You imagine yourself picking up the phone to call this girl. You imagine yourself dialing. What will she say? Okay, I'll say this, and she'll say that. What if she says no? What shall I do? What if you start sweating? What if she says *yes*? You really want to go out with her, and you imagine being in the car with her at the drive-in movie, and you imagine putting your arm around her, and you imagine what she will do. Somehow the outcome of that long mental process will determine whether you're going to pick the phone up and actually make the call. The central theme of the novel has to do with how we use our imaginations to deal with situations around us, not just to cope with them psychologically but, more importantly, to deal with them philosophically and morally.

Schroeder: This process of imagining is similar to what happens in *One Hundred Years of Solitude*. Were you influenced by García Márquez?
O'Brien: I haven't read him.

Schroeder: Really?
O'Brien: No. Wasn't that the *New York Times*'s "magical realism" thing? I hadn't read any of those guys. I've since read Borges, but I haven't even read much Borges. I was a political science major, so it's hard to be influenced by what you haven't read.

Schroeder: And you still haven't read *One Hundred Years*?
O'Brien: I started it once. I just hated it. My wife read it and loved it, but I got through about three pages; I just couldn't take it. I don't even know what it was about it that I didn't like. I remember the paragraphs were extraordinarily long, and I don't like wending my way through long paragraphs. I looked at another book of his, *Autumn of the Patriarch*. I tried to read that, too, but I got about halfway through that one and couldn't finish it. Borges I've really come to respect and admire. I'd feel good if that magical realism quote were directed toward Borges. But García Márquez—I'm afraid that

I still haven't finished anything he's written. Maybe I'll give *One Hundred Years of Solitude* another shot. Everybody says it's a real modern classic.

Schroeder: In an early chapter of *If I Die* you talk about the role of the soldier. You ask what it is that the soldier can teach. Will we learn from the soldier? You answer your question, "Well, the soldier can't really teach anything. The only thing he can do is tell war stories." This is what Michael Herr says in *Dispatches*. *Cacciato* seems to be doing exactly that, telling war stories, but telling them according to the older sense of the term "story," where the story had meaning for the community. Perhaps we've come to devalue the word "story."

O'Brien: It's hard for me to pin down what I mean by that because my friend Erik Hansen, to whom *Cacciato* was dedicated (he appears in *If I Die* and helped me edit it), didn't like that line in the book. He said, "It's not just storytelling; you're doing more than that," but what he doesn't understand— what I'm not communicating—is what I mean by the fullness of the word "story." How do you gather a lesson from *The Iliad* or *The Odyssey*? They're stories. They have no single moral, no single lesson. Not even a set of lessons or morals. The word you used was "myth." The story should have a *mythic* quality to it, even a short story that isn't reducible to a parable from the Bible. You can't say, "Now be kind to your neighbor and don't go to war," that sort of thing; rather, it's like the imaginative process which I was talking about earlier—where you read a story as a kind of imagined event. It *is* an imagined event—I've imagined the events of *Cacciato* just as Berlin imagines them. He doesn't draw any single moral out of the story, and I don't expect the reader to draw any single moral out of it either; but rather, by going through the process of having imagined something, one gathers a sense of the *stuff* that's being imagined, a sense of what a war is and what escape from war is. And that sense can't be pinned down to a message or a moral. It's a story, and you finish a story with a whole cluster, a constellation, of emotions and yearnings and whimsies.

There's also a tentativeness to it as there is in real life—for example, if you go through a cancer experience, you don't come out of it with the lesson, "Don't get cancer." You come out of it with a sense of exaltation that you've conquered it, a sense of knowledge of your fears—cowardices perhaps—the memory of trauma and tears and all that sort of thing. And it's not one thing; it's an experience. My point is that you can't use literature as a signpost saying, "Do this" or "Don't do that."

Schroeder: The word that keeps coming up is "imagination," and it seems that this is what really sets fiction apart from nonfiction. In fiction you have so much more freedom. Do you think that this is what makes us conceive of fiction as the greater art?

O'Brien: In a way, yes. You've done this yourself. Everybody does it. You start telling someone a true-life story and at some point you find yourself embellishing it just a bit—instead of there being four guys coming at you with crowbars, suddenly there're twelve of these fuckers, and they're six feet eight each of them (instead of six feet), because you want to hype up the story's intensity to make your story equal to what you felt personally. And so you rev up detail, heighten it, so as to create an emotion in the listener equivalent to the emotion you felt, this great fear. To say the guy was only six feet tall doesn't sound very impressive, even though it was very impressive at the time.

The sense of embellishment, letting one's imagination heighten detail, is part of what fiction writing is about. It's not lying. It's trying to produce story detail which will somehow get at a felt experience.

Schroeder: Don't you see Vietnam in particular as a subject which shouldn't need embellishment?

O'Brien: It does though. I think it does. Maybe "embellishment" isn't quite the right word. I was using an example to get at what I really mean about a sense of heightened drama. I guess drama is the important element. If you were actually to record an individual's daily experience in Vietnam, it would be boring, monotonous, because 90 percent of the time you're sitting on your butt, swatting mosquitos, putting on mosquito repellent, eating chow, walking, walking, walking. (In reality that's *not* so boring as it sounds in the telling because there's an undercurrent of impending doom always there— the next second could be broken by a mortar shell, a booby-trap could be stepped on.) Yet fiction—good writing of *any* kind—can't employ this imitative fallacy. You don't try to get at boredom by being boring in your writing. Rather you hint at these days going by, which is what the basketball scenes in *Cacciato* do—not much happens but basketball, basketball—but underneath it there's this feeling that something's about to happen.

So the novelistic trick is to hint at the boredom without *being* boring. When a writer simply apes events, when he simply holds a mirror up to the real world, it gets boring: "We sat down. Two hours later we ate chow. We played this game. We did this. And we walked." It'd be really monotonous. So you compress the monotony down. In a way, of course, it's a kind of lie, a kind of embellishing, but you're trying to get at a deeper truth. Truth doesn't reside on the surface of events. Truth resides in those deeper moments of punctuation, when things explode. So you compress the boredom down, hinting at it but always going for drama—because the essence of the experience was dramatic. You tell lies to get at the truth.

Schroeder: There are many passages in *If I Die* that presage *Cacciato*.
O'Brien: Oh, I know. Not only that, but there's a lot of events which I use in both books. You're right.

Schroeder: And the sense of embellishment does come through in *Cacciato*. The same events become a bit stranger, or maybe more significant is a better way to put it.
O'Brien: True. Yes, I did this at least three or four times. I can remember one: shooting the water buffalo. In *If I Die* the guys shoot this water buffalo, and they all watch the bullets ripping huge chunks of flesh from it. There's a similar scene in *Cacciato*. But it's not a whole bunch of guys; it's just one guy, Stink Harris, in the scene in which they meet the women. There are three or four other places where I used a real experience, a real event, and tried to turn it into something more emblematic than it was. I think those passages are probably some of the more successful in *Cacciato*.

Schroeder: The water buffalo scene is interesting because it's based on something that you actually saw.
O'Brien: Oh, yes. I did see it. It happened.

Schroeder: The difference, then, between the two passages is significant because the first is a mere retelling of something that you witnessed whereas in *Cacciato* that action becomes functional; it becomes symbolic of something larger than itself, than a simple historic event.
O'Brien: In *If I Die* the passage is cast as a lesson of sorts, the kind of message thing that doesn't work in fiction. The lesson is that we had gone through all these frustrating days and couldn't find the enemy and had lost more and more and more men. One day we were walking along this rice paddy and saw a buffalo, and for no reason the whole company started blasting the buffalo. There's a lesson there, and it's told in this "lessony" sort of way: "Here's what happens to men who get frustrated. They blow away a buffalo. Guess what else they blow away."
Cacciato, however, is not framed in that kind of "here's Tim O'Brien's

view of what happened" mode. Rather, the scene is just an event which happens on the route to Paris, and it's not framed in any kind of moral way. No one makes judgments about Stink Harris blowing away the buffalo. There's no sense of frustration in his doing it. I don't think there's any reason for his doing it. He just does it. He just blows it away. He brags about it—"Lash L. LaRue, fastest gun in the West"—that sort of thing. And it takes on a quality of its own; you remove the preaching, the moralizing, and it becomes its own event. The reader has to figure out what it means, if anything: how it fits into the whole fabric of the book. That's one of those big distinctions, one of the reasons I wrote *Cacciato*—so I could free myself from making authorial judgments and instead present a story. Let the reader make the judgments. It *does* finally take on a symbolic quality—that's the whole idea of what a symbol is, I think, that it represents something beyond that which it is.

Schroeder: Another difference illustrated in the two treatments of the water buffalo scene is a shift in point of view from the first-person in *If I Die* to this detached third-person point of view in *Cacciato*. In that sense, how closely related are the "I" in *If I Die* and Paul Berlin in *Cacciato*?
O'Brien: Not too. There are some similarities, but more differences. The Paul Berlin in the book isn't me. There are parts of him that are, but more parts that aren't. It's not a composite in any way; he's a made-up character.

Schroeder: He seems much more naïve than the "I," and yet for all of his lack of intellectualizing he is, in some way, more philosophical.
O'Brien: He's more of a dreamer than I was, I think. He spends much more of his time in dream. He takes the war and the possibility of running from war more seriously than I did. Hence his concern is more revved up than my own. He's more frightened than I was—and I was very, very frightened. He's more sensitive, I think, than I was, more aware of the nuances of his surroundings and of his fellow soldiers. And I think he noticed more. *Cacciato* is filled with more noticings, more odd detail, than I was able to render in *If I Die* because there I had to stick to exactly what I saw, and I simply didn't see as much as Paul Berlin did.

Schroeder: It seems, though, that in the long run Paul Berlin is actually outdreamed by Sarkin Aung Wan in the scene at the conference table, where something becomes more important to Paul Berlin than his dreams. This, I think, is what you try to catch in *If I Die* as well, this notion of one's sense of duty to—not only to one's country because that seems too big—but to one's immediate experience, one's family.

O'Brien: That's true. But, remember, he dreams her. He's made her up out of thin air. She's his fantasy. His alter ego, perhaps. He's at war with himself. In that Paris peace-table scene when she's talking, part of his personality is represented by her viewpoint when she says, "Go for happiness. Leave this silly war behind. You must live in Paris and be happy. You *can* live in exile. I'm more worried about death, about grotesque happenings. March into your own dream." Part of Paul Berlin is saying all that to himself at the observation post. The other part is arguing another position: "I can't run. I've got an obligation to my family, my reputation, my friends, my town, my fellow soldiers. Besides, it scares me—running away from a war is frightening." And that peace-table scene represents a schizophrenia of sorts. He's arguing with himself, and I don't judge the debate.

I try to make both sides of it as convincing as I can, roughly because that's how it was in my own experience. On the one hand, "God, I sure should walk away from this war—hey, it's a wrong war; it's evil." I felt guilty. But the other half was saying, "God, you can't do that; you've got everything else to think about: what if I am a coward, what about my family? You've gone this far; you're obliged to go the rest of the way." It's this sense of war that I'm trying to get at in that concluding scene. Internal war, personal war.

Schroeder: I'm reminded of something Michael Herr said to me: that *Dispatches* ultimately wasn't a book about war, but a book about writing a book. He went on to talk about *Cacciato*, comparing it to *Dispatches*, and said that he didn't see *Cacciato* as a book about war either.

O'Brien: I agree completely. I don't see it as a book about war either. In part it's a book about writing a book in the same way perhaps as his. Maybe mine is even more obviously that way; clearly, when I talk about imagination and memory, I'm talking about the two key ingredients that go into writing fiction. You work with your memories—those events which are critical to you—and you work with your imagination. Memory by itself is the province of nonfiction—you write what you remember, you remember what you take in notes or on a tape recorder. This is strictly memory—what really happened. The fiction writer combines memory with imaginative skills. And the outcome—the book, the novel—is part memory, part imagination—who knows what? You can't put percentages on it because it's all mixed together, but that's what it is. The very themes of the book are imagination and memory. In that sense it's about how one goes about writing fiction, the fictional process. But for me it's also about how life itself operates. I think our lives are largely, maybe totally, determined by what we remember and by what we imagine—it's a part of that goal-setting thing I talked about earlier. Whom we marry is determined partly by memory, partly by imagination. If you marry a blonde, it's perhaps because you remember this gorgeous blonde cheerleader you were hot for. But your fantasies also come into play. You imagine her as someone new. You imagine being her husband.

Memory and imagination as devices of survival apply to all of us whether we are in a war situation or not. It's a tricky question. Obviously the book is set in a war, and a large part of the subject matter has to do with war. But then you ask the question, "What is war?" It has to do with big philosophical and moral issues. Right and wrong. Being brave. How does one go about doing the proper thing? Is it right to run from the war or right to stay there? Courage and justice. Those are issues that are embedded in our daily lives. I think that as an outside reader, if I were to pick up my book and read it, my feeling would be that I wasn't really reading a war novel; I would perhaps feel that a trick had been played on me. Here's a book passing as a war novel, but it's not really that: It's not like *The Naked and the Dead*, it's not like Quentin Reynolds, it's not like Hemingway's war stuff. It's quirky. It goes somewhere else; it goes *away* from the war. It starts there and goes to Paris. A *peace* novel, in a sense.

One of the things that I worried about in writing it was that I was disobeying the conventions of war literature, the "war genre." But then I thought it's maybe just enough writing a book. It's a war novel on the surface, but it's about lots of other things too.

Schroeder: As you say, it does seem to be really a book more about peace than war, about coming to peace with oneself, making those decisions that are going to make one a man. Thus it's significant that Cacciato and Paul Berlin are running to Paris; after all, Paris was the center of the peace talks. Was that a conscious choice?

O'Brien: Yes, that was. That's largely why I chose Paris as a destination. I knew that I wanted to finish the book with a peace-table scene. In every novel there has to be a central tension if the story's going to be any good—what's going to happen to Ahab? Is he going to get the whale or not?—that kind of central, driving impetus. In *Cacciato* this has to do with how Paul Berlin's going to resolve his philosophical dilemma. Is he going to run, or is he going to stay? What's he going to decide?

There is this sense of moral decision making; the book is one long decision. And so I chose Paris not only because the peace talks were in progress there, but for all kinds of metaphorical reasons—the City of Light and Justice, the symbol of civilization, the Golden City—and also because the Peace of Paris was signed there. For all kinds of reasons it was the ideal site.

But also it makes psychological sense. For a guy like Cacciato or Berlin it would be the obvious choice of destination. I mean, where else would they go? Someone else might choose Albania or some such place if he thought there was an esoteric reason for it, though it would represent the same thing. But not those guys; they aren't the type. As you say, they aren't highly intellectual. They're naïve in a lot of ways. For a naïve person Paris is the obvious choice.

Schroeder: In the same way that Paul Berlin must come to terms with himself, must come to peace within himself, is there a larger purpose behind the book, which is to assess the American experience in Vietnam: America coming to terms with its sense of duty on the one hand and its actual purposes in Vietnam on the other?

O'Brien: I don't think so. In any case I didn't think of it that way when I was writing it. One of the things about fiction is that the writer has to be careful in assigning meaning to his own work. If we were on some kind of public forum and somebody asked that type of question, all I would say is "maybe," because you can't make decisions like that. I try to rinse away any kind of authorial moralizing, whether it's directed toward the country (as you suggested) or toward personal decision making.

Schroeder: Do you think, though, that a book like *Cacciato* does have a didactic force in bringing people back to terms with Vietnam? In recalling Vietnam to them, does it somehow make Americans aware of the experience, and in making them aware of the *issues* can it help them come to a personal peace over Vietnam?

O'Brien: Yes, that's probably true. All my work has been somewhat political in that it's been directed at big issues. It's not this sort of contemporary tendency to examine purely personal daily concerns—the minutiae of life. My concerns have to do with abstractions: What's courage and how do you get it? What's justice and how do you achieve it? How does one do right in an evil situation? There's a didactic quality to the book. It's not the answer to those questions; it's simply their posing in literature which gives them the importance that I think they deserve. Too much contemporary literature seems to me trivial and aimed at rather frivolous objectives. It's not tackling big stuff. This has become a waste of talent and technique and craft and all the rest. If one's going to spend time writing anything, it makes sense to tackle big, important stuff. Not that I even try to provide answers. My aim is just to give those issues a dramatic importance. See what I'm getting at? You don't try to answer questions. You simply pose them in human terms and make them important to readers so that they end up caring about some guy who's trying to decide what to do. "Am I going to stay in the war?" By caring about the issues maybe the reader will carry that concern over to his or her own life. I'm not trying to answer questions but to dramatize the impact of moral philosophy on human life.

Schroeder: Do you think that Americans are coming to terms with questions about Vietnam?
O'Brien: No, not with Vietnam. I think that most Americans are too comfortable. One of the reasons that I write (and one of the goals of literature in general) is to jar people into looking at important things. Much of our lives is spent thinking about clothing ourselves and our families and feeding ourselves and so on, so that we rarely try to grapple with philosophical issues. A good novel will seduce you into caring about those things—maybe only temporarily—but for the three hours it takes to read *Cacciato*, you have to pay attention to that stuff because that's what the book's about. For the average soap-opera watcher, the book isn't going to have much appeal unless the reader can somehow be seduced into the drama of the dream, of the story.

It's not really Vietnam that I was concerned about when I wrote *Cacciato*; rather, it was to have readers care about what's right and wrong and about the difficulty of doing right, the difficulty of saying no to a war. There are all these pressures on you to go to war. In my latest book, *The Nuclear Age*, I'm dealing with the difficulties of confronting the obvious: that the bombs are out there. Until very recently no one even noticed them. I look at literature (at what I do as literature, in any case) as a way of jarring people into paying attention to things—not just the war but your personal stake in the political world.

Schroeder: Vietnam nonfiction often seems much more potent than the fiction. A book like *Dispatches* has a much more powerful impact than almost all of the novels that have been written. One of Herr's constant concerns is to demonstrate the "reality" of the war's unreality. Your work is different; *Cacciato* is clearly more reflective than *If I Die*, raising as it does questions of imagination and of the nature of reality. Do you think that the failure of some of these fictional works has something to do with the realistic mode many of them are couched in? That perhaps Vietnam's "unreality" defies this particular mode?

O'Brien: No, I don't think so. I think it's just very hard to articulate. Vietnam was an experience that many people in America had felt that they had gone through because of television; they felt that they were veterans of the war. If you watch people die on television night after night, you begin to think that you are an eyewitness—maybe even in a sense a subconscious participant in that conflict. Subsequently, they are unwilling to understand that they weren't participants, that no matter how many hours you watch people dying on television, you don't have to stay up at night on guard duty, you don't worry about being killed, you don't have any personal jeopardy, and so on. I think that in that sense television made people more open to realistic nonfiction—television-like things—as a way of reliving or revalidating what they perceived as a personal experience. That's the only thing that I can think of.

For me Vietnam wasn't an unreal experience; it wasn't absurd. It was a cold-blooded, calculated war. Most of the movies about it have been done with this kind of black humorish, *Apocalypse Now* absurdity: the world's crazy; madman Martin Sheen is out to kill madman Marion Brando; Robert Duvall is a surfing nut. There's that sense of "well, we're all innocent by reason of insanity; the war was crazy, and therefore we're innocent." That doesn't go down too well.

Schroeder: Well, this seems to be a rather recent development because many of the early novels don't come across that way. Many of the novels come across in what we characterized earlier as this World War II fashion—you charge up the hill, fire your weapons, and the enemy falls down dead.

O'Brien: Yes, tick 'em off. Gustav Hasford's book is one I think of, and Jim Webb's certainly is. But when it comes to your original question, I really don't know the answer to it. I don't know why novels haven't succeeded as well as nonfiction in gaining a general widespread popularity. One possibility is that they aren't as good, that they aren't as well written. For many novels, that's true; many published novels should have been written as nonfiction because their *content* is nonfiction: the authors are not trying to imagine; they're writing purely from memory. They'll give fictitious names to characters, but you're actually seeing a home movie of what really happened to somebody. Good novels don't work on that principle. Novels will fail if you do that. Too many fail for the very reason that they should have been nonfiction; they should have been cast as war memoirs. They don't do what novels ought to do, which is to let your imagination add to memories. That's all I can think of that explains it. Personally, I don't like most of the novels nearly as well as the nonfiction.

Schroeder: Have you read *Dog Soldiers*?

O'Brien: Yes. I loved that book. I'm not sure it's about Vietnam, but of course mine isn't either.

Schroeder: I was going to say that *Dog Soldiers* seems to do the same sort of thing that both you and Michael Herr do: it's a book that uses Vietnam as a point of departure for discussing other issues and ideas.

O'Brien: It's one of my favorite books. It's a wonderful novel. I just finished *A Flag for Sunrise*—it's just a real blowout. Of the contemporary writers I admire, Stone and Herr are at the top of the list. They're it. They write literature; they do work that goes beyond the mundane. They transform their material into something that's going to last. It has resonance, vividness. It grabs your emotions and squeezes them.

Both *Dog Soldiers* and *A Flag for Sunrise* are works of a lasting writer. *Dog Soldiers* is a Vietnam book in a sense, though I don't know if Bob thinks so or not. But I suspect he does. I suspect that he looks at it as I do at *Cacciato*. It's not a war novel, exactly, but it is clearly anchored in the events and in the moral concerns and evils of that era. There is a sense of evil out there that one's trying to battle against, but always with a sense of futility. This is coupled with an impulse to try to run from it and to escape it; it's clearly there in *Dog Soldiers*, that frantic racing. After the stash, up to those mountains. What do you find when you get there? You find war. A real battle scene. The same kind of principle holds in *Cacciato*—despite that long-imagined trek to get to Paris, they end up doing barbarous things. You can't outrun it. I think that's why I admire Stone's work: he doesn't shy from evil; he really tackles it in a nice dramatic way.

Schroeder: When did you first realize or feel that you would be writing a book about Vietnam? When you first went to Vietnam, did you have *If I Die* in mind, or was it something that evolved?

O'Brien: It happened while I was there. Partly I began writing little anecdotes, four or five pages. Not stories but vignettes. But I didn't think of them as a book. I thought of them as little vignettes. I wasn't sure what they were or why I was doing it. But having got back a year later, I had accumulated a stack of them. Some of them were terrible, and some of them were pretty good. I never seriously thought it was going to be a book until it was done. At no point did I think I was writing a book. At no point did I think of even sending it to a publisher. I was in grad school, and my concerns were academic. I wanted to get through my doctoral program. I wanted to pass the orals and get the dissertation written. Writing was kind of a sidelight. At night, when I was tired of studying, I would hack out a chapter. I didn't call them chapters, just little things. Then I began putting them roughly in chronological order, but not exactly. At some point I thought, "Why not?" And then, very quickly—I mean in a month or so—I stitched it together into a book and sent it off. After sending it off, I forgot about it. And when the publisher called to say he'd accepted it, I couldn't remember sending it to him. I mean that particular guy. I knew it was someplace. I remember one of the odd things that happened was that I sent it to Knopf (this was in '72) and had a letter saying, "We like it very much, but we have a book under contract called *Dispatches*." This was about five years before Herr even finished his book.

Schroeder: And you hadn't published anything before that?
O'Brien: No books. I had published in *Playboy* a chapter of *If I Die*—or what became a chapter; also a couple of pieces that I had sent from Vietnam were published in the *Minneapolis Tribune* and in my hometown newspaper. But the *Playboy* thing was the only major piece that had been published.

Schroeder: Do you feel that *If I Die* really paved the way for *Cacciato*?
O'Brien: Yes. I'm glad I got it out of my system. Otherwise I would have ended up writing one of these books that we were just talking about, autobiography cast as fiction. The power of *If I Die* is the same sort that one gets from a book like Ron Kovic's. It's just there as a document. It's not art. I didn't know what literature was. *If I Die* is just a straightforward telling: "Here's what happened to me." But these little things that we talked about—adding dialogue, for instance—these made *Cacciato* possible. Otherwise I'd have written a *Cacciato* which wasn't *Cacciato*: it wouldn't have been nearly so good. I look at those two books, and one of them I think of as my effort at literature and one as my effort at just relating an experience that happened to me, as I would tell a friend.

Schroeder: You've made the distinction that those who write simply from memory write nonfiction, whereas those who write fiction use memory but additionally use imagination to compress and intensify experience. What if you want to write about a particular experience, though, and you have no memory, no personal experience to begin with? I'm thinking in particular of those sections of *Cacciato* set outside Vietnam.

O'Brien: In the Paris section, for example, I don't want to sound like a tourist, but I do want to describe with an informing eye, a kind of tourist's eye—what the city was like—because I figured that would be more or less what the characters in the book would have, a surface knowledge of the city. It was the only part of the book that I researched in any way at all. I figured I should know at least as much as Berlin would know—the general layout of the city—and not much more. The sections on Tehran and Afghanistan were entirely made up. That's the best way to write a novel. Again, I wasn't tied to real stuff. I made up names for things: the courthouse, for instance. A lot of language is made up. In the Mandalay section, I made up the name for the monks and so on. That's what I'm getting at. There's a sense of playfulness to it that isn't possible in nonfiction. Where you don't have to have such a sense of fidelity to fact and reality, you're not going to know all the names of things; you're going to imagine things. When I looked at it as Paul Berlin's imagination, I thought that I may as well imagine it myself, sometimes anchoring it in stuff that he might know. He might know that the SAVAK was a police agency in Tehran, and he might imagine the jail cell, and he might imagine being beheaded. But while some of that will come from what he might know of the real world—his knowledge of the SAVAK, perhaps—much of it—people being beheaded and the fly on the nose—is imagined. It's that kind of combination which couldn't happen if I had to write a book about really going to Iran; those things just wouldn't happen.

Schroeder: While surface detail is a necessary ingredient in fiction, sometimes a lack of detail can be equally effective. For instance, the character who is really the most fascinating in *Cacciato* is Cacciato himself.

O'Brien: Yes, he is, isn't he? That suggests that the less said about someone, the more compelling. It's something that every novelist should remember. Something I tend to forget. People have the feeling that the way to make character is by trying to nail down every little specific of mannerism, dress, and physical appearance—how tall? what's the exact shade of the hair?—when, in fact, some of the more memorable characters (for me, all memorable characters) are remembered for one thing. All I can remember about

Ahab is that he chased the whale, that he was obsessed by it. That's why I have Cacciato obsessed about going to Paris. Or I think of Huck Finn. Does he have red hair and freckles, or is that just on the cover of my book? I can't remember if Twain gave him red hair or not. I know in the movie Huck's hair was red. But I really can't remember if he *actually* had it. All I remember is his quest, the lighting off for the West, getting on that raft. This is something that for a novelist is so easy to forget, because you think that the way to get your readers to believe in your characters is to supply a lot of detail. But a reader doesn't remember it all; he can't process it all. The best way to get at characters is through a single idea of a character: the idea of chasing a whale, of getting on a raft. This is half "plottish"—chasing a whale—but it's also half idea, the idea of lighting out or of being obsessed by something. As a character, Cacciato is memorable because the reader can fasten on this idea of a guy who's run away from the war. The reader doesn't have to worry about a lot of physical stuff.

Schroeder: For me Cacciato is memorable precisely because he is so vague. He's more of a symbol than a person; when I think of Cacciato, I think of the scene where Paul Berlin dreams that "Cacciato's round face became the moon."
O'Brien: That's exactly how I think of him.

Schroder: That's the characteristic I remember most vividly.
O'Brien: As another example of this fiction/nonfiction split, there's a character like Cacciato in *If I Die*. In fact, Cacciato has his genesis in this fellow from my own basic training whose name was Kline. Kline was this klutzy guy with tiny beady eyes. A complete klutz. He came to reveille one morning wearing two left boots. Erik Hansen and I were always looking at each other and thinking, "Is he *really* this klutzy?" Or was it an incredible act that he was using to get out of Vietnam? Because if he's really that klutzy, he could be recycled through basic training to infinity. And it was this notion of a character who from the surface evidence was stupid that gave rise to Cacciato. Is Cacciato naïve, an innocent? Is he a cipher who acts purely on animal instinct? Or, as Berlin asks, is Cacciato smart? Has he got more going for him than everybody thinks? It's one of the mysteries of the book. I keep the reader off guard, thinking, "When am I going to meet Cacciato? When am I going to find out what his motives were? I'd like to pin this guy down." I never let this happen. Even though Berlin sees him. I stop the scene so that the reader never gets to grab the guy. If you were to grab him

and to examine him in minute detail, then you would run the risk of being mundane—Cacciato would be ordinary. His dialogue, the explication of his character, would undercut the mystery of the guy. This again is the distinction between fiction and nonfiction. In *If I Die* I treat the character in detail. I describe him, what he did, and so on, and remove the mystery: "Maybe he's really a smart kid who's acting dumb." But by describing him in such detail, I make it clear to the reader that this guy really *is* dumb. In *Cacciato*, though, I can let the mystery stand.

Schroeder: The other image of Cacciato that is so memorable occurs in the chapter "World's Greatest Lake Country." Cacciato is fishing, and everybody knows there are no fish in those craters. Yet he persists. It's as if he knows something no one else knows, or that by a sheer act of will he can *will* fish into those craters.

O'Brien: That's the feeling I'm trying to evoke. That's exactly it. It's the sense that "maybe there is something there that nobody else knows about." A sense that "well, it's not very likely, and yet maybe—" It's the sense of "maybe" that I really like about his character. And it is this sense that runs throughout the book. "Maybe so."

An Interview with Tim O'Brien

Martin Naparsteck/1989

From *Contemporary Literature* 32.1 (Spring 1991): 1–11. © 1991 by the Board of Regents of the University of Wisconsin System. Reprinted with permission of the University of Wisconsin Press.

Tim O'Brien is widely considered the best of a talented group of Vietnam veterans who have devoted much of their writing to their war experiences. Sections of his most recent book, *The Things They Carried* (Houghton Mifflin/Seymour Lawrence, 1990), have won a National Magazine Award and an O. Henry Prize and have been included in *Best American Short Stories*. It follows by twelve years his National Book Award–winning *Going After Cacciato* (Delacorte Press/Seymour Lawrence, 1978), which until recently was often called the best work of fiction to come out of the war; the critical reaction to *The Things They Carried*, however, now makes it a prime candidate for that accolade. The latest book resists easy categorization: it is part novel, part collection of stories, part essays, part journalism; it is, more significantly, all at the same time. As O'Brien indicates below, he may have created a new literary form. His other books are *If I Die in a Combat Zone* (Delacorte Press/Seymour Lawrence, 1973), a memoir of his year in Vietnam; *Northern Lights* (Delacorte Press/Seymour Lawrence, 1975), an out-of-print novel about two brothers who become lost on a cross-country skiing trip in Minnesota; and *The Nuclear Age* (Knopf, 1985), about a man who, while building a bomb shelter in 1995, recalls his life as a radical.

This interview took place at O'Brien's home in Boxford, Massachusetts, about twenty-five miles north of Boston, on April 20, 1989. O'Brien had completed writing *The Things They Carried* and was working on some final revisions.

Q. You have two Pauls in your fiction, Paul Perry in *Northern Lights* and Paul Berlin in *Going After Cacciato*. Is that just a coincidence?

A. I doubt it's a coincidence, though I can't explain it. The first Paul, the *Northern Lights* Paul—that's a terrible book. I'm embarrassed by it; it's hard to talk about it. It's the first novel I ever tried to write, and unfortunately it was published. It was done logically. Paul was chosen for Paul on the road to Damascus, the Damascus Lutheran Church [which appears in the novel], all the imagery of light throughout the book. The same thing with his middle name, Milton—you know, blindness. Whereas Paul Berlin: just sound. No reason for it.

Q. Why do you say that you're embarrassed by *Northern Lights?* It seems to me to have a lot of things that an early book has, a lot of easy Hemingway references, for example.

A. That's part of it. I was under two influences: one was Hemingway, one was Faulkner. They both penetrate that book every which way, but beyond that there are a lot of other flaws with it. Overwriting is probably the chief flaw of the book. It's maybe a hundred pages too long. Too much gratuitous repetition. I continue to use repetition in my work to this day, but not so that it's done just for its own sake. I think that if at some point I were to run out of ideas for a new work I might go back to *Northern Lights* and rewrite it. I've done that with *Cacciato* over the last year and a half or so; I've rewritten substantial portions that are appearing in the latest edition. *Northern Lights* would require at least two years of work. The story is O.K., the essential story, that wilderness stuff. The rest of it needs a lot of work, and someday I think I may do it.

Q. The ski trip is what you see as the heart of the book, then?

A. Yeah, the essential story. I like some of the other stuff, but the other stuff is out of proportion to the narrative heart of the book, I think. I know.

Q. The opening strikes me as in many ways very appealing, with Harvey coming back from Vietnam. I think a lot of stories about returning veterans oversentimentalize the return, which *Northern Lights* doesn't do; it's one of the very few stories about a veteran coming home that seems to get things right.

A. Yeah, I think those parts I do like. The story about two brothers and the father is solid, and Harvey's not sentimentalized. He's a good, hard character; I like his character. Still, it's a question of language. Language equals content. Unfortunately, there are so many echoes that are Hemingway-esque—language coming out of Harvey's mouth and descriptions and things that get in the way.

Q. Were you conscious of writing with these Hemingwayesque influences?
A. I was trying to parody Hemingway. I wrote the book not knowing it was going to be published. I was just a beginner, and I was sort of having fun with it, so I tried to spoof *The Sun Also Rises, A Farewell to Arms*, and I thought I did a pretty neat job of doing the spoofs, but unfortunately good literature should be more than just gamesmanship, and I think there is too much gamesmanship in that book.

Q. Let's move to a book you like better. Is Cacciato's decision to leave the war related to his refusal to touch the grenade? You never specifically say that.
A. It's never said directly, because Cacciato is never there to say it, but, yes, I think it's related pretty directly. The chronology of the book—of which I am fond—is all scrambled throughout the narrative. You can actually map that this event happened first, second, third, and his departure follows pretty quickly after. Refusing to touch the grenade is the first war event prior to his departure. I don't think it's necessarily the only reason for his running, but in a way it's got to be so. I try to keep him off in the horizon and try to keep his motives as removed as he is physically from the rest of the men; they can never figure out precisely what his motives were.

Q. There's something else that's never said directly: is that the grenade that kills the lieutenant?
A. Again, definitely the lieutenant's off-stage; there's no scene where they kill him. No, maybe it's a different grenade; the grenade is symbolic. I've always pictured it as being the same grenade, but it doesn't necessarily have to be.

Q. And it would be the black guy, Oscar, who throws the grenade?
A. I think that once they've all touched it, it doesn't much matter. It's like naming the executioner of Ted Bundy; who killed Bundy? It was the state, the whole judicial system. I don't know who threw the grenade; I don't think it very much matters.

Q. Except that a guy like Berlin might be able to touch the grenade, but I have a hard time seeing him being able to throw it.

A. I have a hard time seeing him do it, too, but I don't have a hard time, for example, seeing Stink do it. He's the sort of guy you'd expect to throw it. Oscar certainly would be a main candidate. But, as I say, I don't think it really matters. If I had to take a guess, it would probably be Oscar who's done it.

Q. Not answering questions like that in the book, is that deliberate?

A. Yes. It's a question of what matters, I guess, both to the writer and the reader. It doesn't matter to me who did it. It's like if you were doing a scene of the execution of Bundy and you suddenly were to concentrate on the executioner, who's really a stand-in character. The key thing is that touching.

Q. Do you ever feel that you've written so much about Vietnam that you've been typecast, like the town drunk?

A. Yeah, I do. I can't deny it's part of my material, my life, things I care about. Even if I don't write often, specifically, about Vietnam, a lot of the stuff, for example in *The Nuclear Age* and in *Northern Lights*—courage and obligation and so on—flows from that experience. Beyond that, I think all writers get typecast. I think Melville is typecast as a sea writer. And Conrad certainly is. Updike is a suburban-hyphen-domestic affairs writer. Shakespeare is a king writer. That has to happen, because an author like any other human being naturally gravitates toward a center of concerns that are particularly his or hers. Being typecast still irritates me at times, but not enough to make me say I'm not going to write about Vietnam, because I am, and I'm sure I will in the future.

Q. Your characters spend a great deal of time thinking about courage, which is a fairly common subject for Vietnam stories, but you handle it differently. One symbol that comes up a lot in other writers is John Wayne; Ron Kovic, for example, implicitly rejects that symbolism. You never mention John Wayne, and you do not write of courage as something that drew you to Vietnam. You handle courage in a more realistic way.

A. It's such a complicated subject, it's hard to know what to say. It's easy to break down courage into categories. There's moral courage versus physical courage and so on. Even that seems oversimplifying it. To break it down into categories of John Wayne and Socrates, for instance, seems to me to be really artificial. Like everything else, courage interpenetrates the whole fabric of a life. To take a strand out and say this is courage and this is something else violates a central humanness. In my own particular case, I hated the war in Vietnam and didn't want to go. I had no desire to test my capacity to charge a bunker; I had no desire to do that. Some guys did. And I never really understood it, from the moment of basic training. Why would guys want to die? Take the chance of dying? I just didn't get it. So I think my perspective on the issue probably varies a lot from that of a guy like Kovic who wanted to test himself. My concerns aren't those of other people, and the writing probably echoes that.

Q. It seems that your characters are very much concerned about courage, but they typically don't reach conclusions about it. You're not really making a statement about one type of courage being better than another.
A. The best literature is always explorative. It's searching for answers and never finding them. It's almost like Platonic dialogue. If you knew what courage is, if you had a really wonderful, philosophical explication of courage, you would do it as philosophy, as explication; you wouldn't write fiction. Fiction is a way of testing possibilities and testing hypotheses, and not defining, and so I think that more than anything the work is a way of me saying, yes, courage is clearly important in this character's life; he thinks about its importance in circumstances; the work is a way of searching for courage, finding out what it is. That's especially true in *Cacciato*, I think, where it's both a search for courage for him to walk away from that war and also a kind of search for what courage is, what the courageous thing to do is.

Q. Your first three books differ from the fourth in the treatment of courage. Courage doesn't seem to be a major theme in *The Nuclear Age*, which is more about figuring out what sanity is and is not. Do you think it was inevitable that in moving away from Vietnam you would move away from courage as a dominating topic?
A. It's the same issue. It's like the other side of the coin in that this guy in *The Nuclear Age* had the courage to do what I didn't and a lot of other people didn't, which is to risk embarrassment and censure and endure humiliation about walking away from the war. If there's a courageous character in that book, it's that William character, who despite his service in a kind of Waspism and his wimpy attitude toward the war manages to do for the most part what he thinks is right. So I think it's not a departure from the earlier work but a looking at it from another angle. To me, he's the only hero I've written.

Q. It seems to me that in your first three books you were dealing with philosophical issues, such as courage, while *The Nuclear Age* is more political. Do you feel that way?

A. Not really. I see all four books as political in that they all deal with the impact of global forces on individual lives. In my own life and in *If I Die*, this huge thing—global politics—pushed me into the war, and similarly in *The Nuclear Age*, William Cowling is pushed into hiding and pushed away from his own life by global politics. I think anything I've ever written has that as its center theme, even more than issues of courage—how individual human lives are influenced by global forces beyond the horizon.

Q. I sensed in reading *The Nuclear Age* that you were coming close to making a statement there, saying we should do something about this nuclear madness.

A. I don't think I was making a statement; I certainly wasn't trying to. I was trying to write a comedy, basically, and a book that was funny, and I think the real difference between *The Nuclear Age* and the earlier works is tone. It had a more comedic tone to it. I'm not sure people cared for that. But my intent was to be different—like Shakespeare saying, "My subject may be life and death, but I want to have a comedic perspective on it."

Q. The reviewers were not always kind to *The Nuclear Age*. Do you think a lot of them missed the comedic intent?

A. That's probably it. I was trying to write a funny book. I think it is funny. But it's up to the ages. *Cacciato* may, a hundred years from now, not be read at all, while *The Nuclear Age* could be. The best road for most writers is to turn them out at the time. *Moby-Dick*, for example, was trashed, worse than *Nuclear Age*. It was "the most hideous piece of garbage ever written," and what happens is that over time, I think, these things straighten themselves out. You can't as a writer defend your work or knock it. You have to say, "Let time take care of it." So I don't get too excited about bad reviews or good ones. I feel happy if they're good, feel sad if they're bad, but the feelings disappear pretty quickly, because ultimately I'm not writing for my contemporaries but for the ages, like every good writer should be. You're writing for history, in the hope that your book—out of the thousands that are published each year—might be the last to be read a hundred years from now and enjoyed.

Q. Was the story "Speaking of Courage" originally intended to be part of *Cacciato*?

A. Yes. It was a piece I took out. It's kind of an orphan. I've since rewritten it for *The Things They Carried*—pretty substantially rewritten it, in fact, changing everything except the lake, driving around the lake, but all the war stuff has been completely changed, and now I'm really fond of the story. I didn't care for it at all when it was originally written.

Q. Is that why it was left out of *Cacciato*?

A. Partly that and partly because it just didn't fit. It's a postwar story; *Cacciato* was a war story, and it just didn't have a proper home in that book.

Q. In rewriting it, you changed the character from Paul Berlin to Tim O'Brien.

A. The character becomes Tim, even though the Tim character is made up entirely, and then the Tim is transformed again into another guy, another character in *The Things They Carried* named Norman Bowker.

Q. Is the Tim character Tim O'Brien? In "The Lives of the Dead" there's a Timmy O'Brien.

A. Yeah, it is, in part. It's made up, but I use my own name. *The Things They Carried* is sort of half novel, half group of stories. It's part nonfiction, too: some of the stuff is commentary on the stories, talking about where a particular one came from. "Speaking of Courage," for example, came from a letter I received from a guy named Norman Bowker, a real guy, who committed suicide after I received his letter. He was talking to me in his letter about how he just couldn't adjust to coming home. It wasn't bad memories; it was that he couldn't talk to anybody about it. He didn't know what to say; he felt inarticulate. All he could do was drive around and around in his hometown in Iowa, around this lake. In the letter he asked me to write a story about it, and I did. This was after I published *If I Die*.

Q. Was this somebody you knew?

A. Yeah, in Vietnam. I sent him the story after it was published, and he said he liked it. Then I didn't hear from him for a long time. His mother finally wrote me. I wrote her and she wrote back saying he committed suicide by hanging himself in the locker room of a YMCA. So that's the terrible-happening anecdote that I include after the story in *The Things They Carried*. The commentary is partly about writing sources and partly about the writing itself.

The Things They Carried is my best book. There's no doubt in my mind about it. When I was writing *Cacciato* I had that feeling; I have that feeling now. I can tell by the strangeness of it. It's a new form, I think. I blended my own personality with the stories, and I'm writing about the stories, and yet everything is made up, including the commentary. The story about Norman Bowker is made up. There was no Norman Bowker. The point being, among others, that in fiction we not only transform reality, we sort of invent our own lives, invent our histories, our autobiographies. When Melville wrote *Moby-Dick*, he was inventing himself, for posterity.

Q. Have you ever been approached about doing movies?
A. *Cacciato* and *The Nuclear Age* have both been taken by the movies. I've seen a few scripts. I've seen three on *Cacciato*, none of which are any good. There are some good parts in them, but by and large they tend to take all the dreamlike, fantastic, surrealistic elements of the book out and tell a pretty straightforward, realistic story, which to me violates the whole aboutness of the book. The book is about the interweaving of memory on the one hand and the imagination, how one frees the other and back again, and that's gone. To me you don't have *Cacciato* anymore; you've got some new thing. I was asked to write a screenplay of the book, and I said "No," because you end up having to do what they did. You have to, the way movies are made. You have to screw up your own work, and if it's going to be screwed up, I would prefer that somebody else do it, not me.

Q. I've seen the term "magical realism" used in connection with your writing. Do you think *Cacciato* fits into that grouping?
A. I don't know. I think the term is a shorthand way of saying something that's much more complicated than that. No writer wants to be grouped in any category. Writing is being an individual; it's a creative enterprise, and a writer wants to make an individual, creative statement that's unrelated to anything that's been said before or afterward yet is simultaneously totally related not just to one thing but to everything. "Magical realism" is shorthand for imagination and memory and how they interlock, for what realism is, for what's real and not real.

Q. "How to Tell a True War Story" in *The Things They Carried* seems to me to be very directly about the interlocking of memory and what actually happened. It also strikes me that this story is as much an essay as it is a story. Did you have that sense in writing it?

A. It's a mixture, yes. It's like the rest of the book, in that it's part story, just raw story—six guys go up to the listening post in the mountains—and also a discussion about the making of the story, not a discussion by me as much as by the guys themselves. In a way it's part essay and part fiction, but in a way it's neither. I think that when you're reading the thing you have a total effect. To me, it has a singleness or unity to it. Rather than being part this and part that, it's all those things together. That story is the genesis for the idea for the whole book. When I'm talking about a happening, it seems essayish, but that stuff is invented and imagined; it isn't true in a literal sense. I don't, for example, believe that war is beautiful in any aesthetic way whatsoever. Even though the character sounds like me and says pretty point blankly that war is beautiful, the harmonies and shapes and proportions, it's not me saying that. The guy who's narrating this story has my name and a lot of my characteristics, but it isn't really me. I never felt or thought that war's pretty, even though I can see how people such as Bill Broyles have said that. My personal feeling is that it's pretty ugly. I was in danger, and my perception never let me see any beauty. All I felt was fear. What I'm saying is that even with that nonfiction-sounding element in the story, everything in the story is fiction, beginning to end. To try to classify different elements of the story as fact or fiction seems to me artificial. Literature should be looked at not for its literal truths but for its emotional qualities. What matters in literature, I think, are pretty simple things—whether it moves me or not, whether it feels true. The actual literal truth should be superfluous. For example, here's a story: four guys go on a trail, a grenade sails out, one guy jumps on it, takes the blast, and saves his buddies. Is it true? Well, yeah, it may have happened, but it doesn't feel true, because it feels stereotypical, hackneyed; it feels like Hollywood. But here's another story: four guys go on a trail, a grenade sails out, one guy jumps on it, takes the blast, and dies; before he dies, though, one of the guys says, "What the fuck you do that for?" and the dead guy says, "The story of my life, man," and starts to smile. He's dead. That didn't happen. Clearly, ever, and yet there's something about the absurdity of it and the horror of it—"What the fuck you do that for?"—which seems truer to me than something which might literally have happened. A story's truth shouldn't be measured by happening but by an entirely different standard, a standard of emotion, feeling—"Does it ring true?" as opposed to "Is it true?"

Q. The narrator of "How to Tell a True War Story" comes to a different understanding of what happens at the end of the story than he had at the beginning. At the end he climbs into the tree to pick out parts of his friend, who's died in an explosion, giving the impression that he didn't quite understand the truth at the beginning, maybe because it was too difficult to remember, too hard on him. It's the exercising of his imagination that gets him at the truth.

A. Yes, I think it is. I think exercising the imagination is the main way of finding truth, that if you take almost any experience of your own life that means something to you, that really hits you, let's say the death of your mother, over the course of time your imagination is going to do things with that experience to render it into something that you can deal with and that has meaning to it. You're going to select some details and forget others: she's lying in bed dying for five weeks; you're not going to remember every detail of that; you're going to pick out of your memory, pluck out, certain conspicuous elements, and then you're going to reorder them. The experience that you remember is going to have a power to it that the total experience didn't have. You went to fix breakfast while she was dying, the phone rang, you had to deal with it—all that random stuff that you've forgotten will be rearranged by your imagination into a new kind of experience. I think in war we tend to block out the long, hard moments of boredom, standing around, sitting around, waiting, which is a lot of what war is. It's ninety-nine percent monotony, and what the imagination does is to push that away and take what's left and reorder it into patterns that give meaning to it.

Q. In *Cacciato* you have the observation post scenes, which seem to be almost directly essays, and in one of them you talk about how to use imagination. There are a lot of dream sequences in literature, but Berlin is not really dreaming; he's wide awake, and he's controlling what he's thinking about, and what he thinks about makes up half the novel.

A. Dreams are dangerous. I don't think I've ever used a real dream. Berlin is awake the same way you and I are now, only alone, and he's staring at the beach and thinking; he's imagining in a way we all do at times. It's a kind of daydream, but it's not an *Alice in Wonderland* or Hobbity sort of thing where events happen at random that come only from the subconscious. It's a mixture of the subconscious and the directed, the same way stories are written. What Berlin is doing is what I do with a typewriter: I'm half living in a rational world and half living in a kind of trance, imagining. Berlin's process in the observation post was meant, at least in part, to echo my own process of imagining that book—not dreaming it and not just controlling it, but a trancelike, half-awake, half-alert imagining.

Q. A lot of guys from Vietnam go to the Breadloaf Writer's Conference in Vermont because they know you teach there every summer.
A. There are always some, which is good.

Q. They usually try to select you as their teacher.
A. They try to. They don't always get me. I think of myself not as a soldier anymore. That's all over. I think of myself as someone who now and then writes about the war, but my daily concerns are just the same as yours. When you're writing a book about Vietnam you don't think of yourself as a soldier; you think of yourself as a writer. The subject matter is war, and you're trying to make a sentence that's graceful, you're trying to make a character come alive, you're trying to make a scene shake with meaning and also with a dramatic feel; your attention is on writing that matters. I feel bad when I meet a vet who thinks that because we both shared this soldiering thing we can also share the other thing, writing, without work, and to me writing is really hard work. Anybody who's done it knows that just making a simple sentence is work. My chief asset as a human being, as a writer, is that I'm tenacious; I work just constantly, stubbornly, and like it. I mean I really like it—I get angry, I feel rotten, if somebody calls me in the middle of work and says, "Let's go play golf," because I like writing that much. If you want to be a writer, you've got to learn to be an eagle soaring up above and a mule who keeps climbing and climbing and climbing.

Staying True to Vietnam: Writer Tim O'Brien Aims for the War's Nerve Center

Gail Caldwell/1990

From *Boston Globe* 29 March 1990: 69, 74. Reprinted with permission.

NEW YORK—In a private dining room of midtown's literati-laden Century Club, publishing savant Seymour Lawrence is reminiscing to his guests about an old error of judgment. It was almost twenty years ago, and he had just read the manuscript of a poignant Vietnam war memoir by a young foot soldier—what would become Tim O'Brien's first book, *If I Die in a Combat Zone.* Lawrence was impressed, but, according to the memo he's quoting from tonight, he had reservations about the somber quality of O'Brien's prose. What the book needed, he wrote then, was "more prostitutes and dope peddlers"—and, let's face it, "the Platonic dialogues have to go."

O'Brien, who has just relinquished his jeans and Red Sox cap to put on a suit for this dinner in time, laughs at Lawrence's memories. "Right," he shoots back. "Throw in a couple of hookers, and we're all set."

Lawrence didn't get his way—no hookers, and the Platonic dialogues stayed—but it was nonetheless the beginning of a long relationship between author and publisher. O'Brien went on to take the National Book Award in 1979 for *Going After Cacciato,* a magical novel heralded for capturing the American experience in Vietnam in a way no straight war narrative could. He veered away from the war in his next novel, *The Nuclear Age* (1985), only to return to it in the interconnected stories of *The Things They Carried,* just published by Seymour Lawrence/Houghton Mifflin. Twenty years after he came home from a war he had almost fled—having returned as a decorated sergeant with a Purple Heart—O'Brien has written a book about Vietnam

so searing and immediate you can almost hear the choppers in the background.

So the war is still with him, though O'Brien insists that "in my normal life
I don't think about Vietnam, I don't dream about Vietnam. It's a long while
ago, like a sickness; you know you went through it on an intellectual level.
But in my waking moments, I don't feel it. And the only times I have felt it
were in writing this book. Then I did, again."

One's first impression upon meeting Tim O'Brien is that he seems like
such a regular guy—someone you'd take to a Celtics game, or expect to give
you a hand with a flat tire. Some of it is the bracing handshake and the unbroken eye contact; never mind that he's in the midst of a twenty-eight-city
book tour and is being feted at Lawrence's dinner before the night is over.
All this is a far cry from the relative serenity of his life in Boxford, Massachusetts, a town about an hour north of Boston, where he lives with his wife,
Ann, of seventeen years.

Armed with a gin-and-tonic and a pack of Carlton 100s at his Upper East
Side hotel, O'Brien—now forty-three—is by turns buoyant, inquisitive, and
disarmingly serious. Lost in thought, he drops ashes on the floor or places
his hands together to make a point; he worries aloud intermittently that he's
saying the wrong thing, or saying it badly. But it is precisely this ingenuous
sincerity—this absence of book-tour pizzazz—that makes you believe what
the man is telling you.

That same quality is inherent throughout *The Things They Carried*, a
book as hard-baked in its prose as it is unflinching in its portrayal of the war.
Its sense of intimacy is enhanced, sometimes disconcertingly so, by the appearance of the first-person narrator: a forty-three-year-old writer named
Tim O'Brien, who reminds us that "almost everything . . . in this book is
invented." The initial effect is a sense of surprise—OK O'Brien, did this happen, or not?—followed by one of heightened reality. Not that the stories are
fact, but that they are true.

The Things They Carried is dedicated to its characters. "I lived with these
guys in my head," says O'Brien. "I just wanted to acknowledge where they'd
taken me, and say goodbye to them. They were more real sometimes than
the guys I actually served with." He insists that the use of his own name—the
fleshing out of himself as a main character—was "just one more literary device, that goes along with description and dialogue and narration, to build
that sense of urgency and immediacy and belief."

The compulsion to find out how much of his book is drawn from personal experience is a kind of back-handed compliment, given how "real"

these stories seem. And if "Tim O'Brien" had any other name, the question wouldn't be quite so obvious. But this chameleonic blurring of authorial presence has a deeper meaning; it may point to an artistic catharsis O'Brien has finally realized with *The Things They Carried*.

If I Die in a Combat Zone is straightforward autobiography, the account of a year in country delivered with cool precision. *Going After Cacciato*—with its dreamy alter-ego, Paul Berlin, stationed at an observation post and fantasizing about a trek to Paris—is fluid and mystical, its intelligence the tent peg for its flights of the imagination. But *The Things They Carried* leaves third-degree burns. Between its rhythmic brilliance and its exquisite rendering of memory—the slant of sunlight in the midst of war, the look on a man's face as he steps on a mine—this is prose headed for the nerve center of what was Vietnam.

"A month into the writing of the book," says O'Brien, "I found my name appearing. I was typing, and I remember thinking, this will be fun, I'll do it for an hour, and then go back to a made-up first-person narrator of another name.

"And in that hour of writing—this is stuff I haven't talked about before, so I'm not sure what to say, exactly. But something happened in that hour, or hour and a half, where I was going down. And I wasn't 'remembering' the war; it was nothing attached to the outside world—but my stomach was doing these things." He laughs softly. "I was writing 'How To Tell a True War Story,' which is the heart of the book—about telling stories, about repetition, and that blur between memory and imagination, how it doesn't matter. And yet as I was writing, my name appeared, and this stomach thing happened, somewhere between the bowels and the heart. You pay attention to that.

"I'm not a totally intuitive writer; I know what I'm doing. But—what a joy. What a joy just to feel something like that while you're writing, to feel the return to your heart. It doesn't happen to many writers, and it hasn't happened in my life, ever, writing. So that hour was an important hour for me in my life—not just in my writing career, but in my life, as a human being. Where I felt the remembering of Vietnam—not just Vietnam, but my writing memory as well—intersecting with my life in a way that meant I was home."

O'Brien seems chagrined at what he is saying, and half-apologizes. "These aren't literary things I'm talking about, these are like—heart things. So although the rest of the book was a struggle—it took five hard years to write—it was a struggle that I was in all the way."

If O'Brien has been able to capture Vietnam in a way that seems both profound and universal, his own experience—what led him to the war—was far from typical. A Minnesota kid born in 1946, he got his draft notice in the summer of 1968, the year he graduated from Macalester College. He hated the war, had a full scholarship to graduate school at Harvard, left advanced infantry training in Tacoma to go to the library and research "AWOL and Desertion." He talked to the chaplain at the base, learned the Swedish words for "food," "drink," and "deserter." Then he got on a plane to Cam Ranh Bay.

Nowhere did this common collision between fear and courage have more of a field day than in Vietnam. It's one of the paradoxes of the war that O'Brien meets head-on in *The Things They Carried*, along with the lurid beauty of tracer fire and illumination rounds—the effects that the ambiguities of Vietnam had upon the soul:

"At the hour of dusk you sit in your foxhole and look out on a wide river turning pinkish red, and at the mountains beyond, and although in the morning you must cross the river and go into the mountains and do terrible things and maybe die, even so, you find yourself studying the fine colors on the river, you feel wonder and awe at the setting of the sun, and you are filled with a hard, aching love for how the world could be and always should be, but now is not."

O'Brien nods now at the mention of this dichotomy, at the profound power of war most people besides Patton would just as soon leave alone. He quotes another passage from the book from memory: "'. . . and the immense serenity flashes against your eyeballs—the whole world gets rearranged—and even though you're pinned down by a war you never felt more at peace.'

"This isn't to glorify war," he says. "I hate it, I was a rotten soldier, I despised the war, I thought it was the wrong thing to do. But nonetheless, only in war—only during a few moments of the war—when I felt I was next to the grave, just in those few moments had I ever—pined for tranquility. Not just intellectually, but my whole body, just pining for peace. Knowing it and wanting it simultaneously.

"The reason I'm pausing is that I'm afraid of making that experience in any way something someone should go through. It's not worth it. But you can't ignore the truth either; the truth is that I knew peace, and I wanted it. Hence I'll be writing about the war probably until I die, in some guise or another. But not what is so great about war. For the purpose of exposing ugliness to show beauty, or pain to show possibility.

"I don't look at myself as a soldier. The real content is the human heart. You have to take the material of your life—dignity and love and so on—and those are what I consider the real subjects.

". . . Fiction is made up of behaviors, crossing borders, and hopping into bed and out. It's not about wrestling in the mind. And the interesting tensions for me in fiction are those tensions where there is this world of ambiguity that's all around us. It's pretty rare in your life where it's clear what the right thing to do is."

In both *Going After Cacciato* and *The Things They Carried*, O'Brien was intrigued by what he calls "the whole theme of imagination and memory, and how they interlock in our lives." This is manifest in Paul Berlin's flight of the mind in *Cacciato*, where, stuck on the observation post, he realizes that "out of all that time, time aching itself away, his memory sputtered around those scant hours of horror." In "How to Tell a True War Story," a soldier tells a stunner of a tale about a six-man patrol on a listening-post operation in the mountains. At the end of a week, they've had their minds blown by the sounds of Vietnamese opera and cocktail chatter, xylophones and chimes. Real? Try telling the guys at the end of that stint that it wasn't. All of them heard it, and none of them ever mentioned it again.

"Sometimes what you make up is truer than truth," says O'Brien. "All I remember, in reality, is sitting in the darkness. Not hearing that stuff, but my imagination is going—what's out there? Just floating: an exotic sense of peril. If I ever told the 'truth' about those nights, I'd say, 'Boy, what a long dark night. Boy was I scared.' While invention allows the strange particulars that can get at this stuff: This is a mysterious place, the rocks are talking. It's Nam—this place talks." He smiles. "That's the truth."

"Sweetheart of the Song Tra Bong" is the eeriest story in *The Things They Carried*. A soldier flies his young girlfriend from the States into a remote outpost. She takes up with a group of Green Berets, goes native (to put it mildly), and is last seen on night patrol, wearing a necklace of human tongues. "It's the only thing in the book I ever really heard," says O'Brien. "Guy came up to me and said, 'Hey, see those mountains out there? This guy flew his girlfriend in . . .'

"It was the beginning of the end of my tour, and I just laughed at him, said you're crazy, and walked away. And he came back a couple of days later—I think he was embarrassed—and said, 'I didn't witness it, but I swear to God, it's the story.'

"It's been with me, as a kind of story power, ever since. Who knows what happened? The odds are probably one in a thousand. But it intrigued my storytelling nature.

"Here I am in Vietnam, trying to write about truly incredible things and make them credible. Almost always, the events of fiction are incredible. But why tell stories about the ordinary? I wanted in this book to write about storytelling—about rendering the incredible credible, and the frustration of doing it.

"Some of the events that stick to my memory—the real events of Vietnam—you wouldn't want to write about them." O'Brien laughs softly. "Because no one would believe you."

Sometimes the prose of *The Things They Carried* can have an almost King Jamesian urgency to it, and it's clear from spending time with O'Brien that the book has been a watershed for him. Generally self-effacing, he talks about language and the act of writing with the same open-eyed delight that other people use to talk about their kids. He loves this book—loves the men in it, whoever they are—and says about the title story that "If I die, and God says, 'You got one piece of work we'll let you keep,' that's the piece." The book has his lifeblood in it, and it was a long time in coming.

O'Brien went to graduate school in government at Harvard after he came home, but never finished his dissertation; he had other things to write. He let go of Vietnam, so much as he was able: no leftover horrors to speak of, no demons to exorcise. He still speaks about the war as though he made the wrong choice in going, but it's more an observation of history and compassion than regret.

"It's a blur now," O'Brien says about coming home. "All I remember is feeling happy, and glad to be alive. Full of guilt, that I'd done the wrong thing. But the war made me a writer. I was writing in Vietnam, and all through graduate school, and I've been writing ever since. I wrote in *The Things They Carried* that for years I felt smug about how easily I'd made the adjustment—I'd never written for therapy, or consciously for catharsis, or any of that stuff. It was just that the stories were so wonderful, and the literary possibility seemed so rich.

"And it wasn't until this hour thing I talked about with you earlier that I thought, 'My God, you've been writing about this stuff'—and I recognized the obvious, which any moron could've told me decades ago. You've been doing this all your life. No wonder you're not screwed up; you haven't been getting it out."

"Insight, vision," thinks Paul Berlin on night watch, in *Going After Cacciato*. "Where was the fulcrum? Where did it tilt from fact to imagination?"

O'Brien got his hands on the fulcrum, and the memory and imagination have come full circle into the work. "Absolutely," he says now. "Absolutely. My Vietnam is essentially what's between those covers"—he points to *The Things They Carried*—"and *Cacciato*. And most of all of it was invented. But that's the Vietnam that I remember."

An Interview with Tim O'Brien

Steven Kaplan/1991

From *Missouri Review* 14.3 (1991): 93–108. Reprinted with permission of the *Missouri Review*.

Tim O'Brien is the author of the critically acclaimed war memoir *If I Die in a Combat Zone*, the novel *Going After Cacciato*, which won the National Book Award in 1979, and two other novels, *Northern Lights* and *The Nuclear Age*. His most recent work of fiction, *The Things They Carried*, was chosen as one of the ten best books of 1990 by the *New York Times Book Review*.

Steven Kaplan received his Ph.D. in comparative literature from the University of Tuebingen, Germany, and is now an associate professor at the University of Southern Colorado. He is working on a full-length study of Tim O'Brien's fiction. This interview was conducted in January of 1991 at the Charles Hotel in Cambridge.

Kaplan: You've said that you differ from Paul Berlin in *Going After Cacciato* in that he is more of a dreamer than you are. How do you differ from the narrator Tim O'Brien in *The Things They Carried*?
O'Brien: Everything I've written has come partly out of my own concerns as a human being, and often directly out of those concerns, but the story lines themselves, the events of the stories, and the characters in the stories, the places in the stories, are almost all invented, even the Vietnam stuff. If I don't know it I just make it up, trying not to violate the world as I know it. Ninety percent or more of the material in the book is invented, and I invented 90 percent of a new Tim O'Brien, maybe even more than that.

Kaplan: The chapter "On the Rainy River" describes in great detail how close Tim O'Brien came to fleeing to Canada after he received his draft notice. You've depicted this kind of flirtation with draft evasion in almost all of your books. How closely does this particular story reflect your own life?

O'Brien: It's a dramatization of what I felt during the summer of 1968: a kind of moral schizophrenia. Like the Tim O'Brien in the book, I believed the war was wrong and thought that the morally correct thing to do was to flee, to run from it, or else go to jail. But another side of my personality, like the character in the book, felt a kind of gravity pulling me toward the war. The drama of the story, the facts about that character going to the river, meeting somebody, and almost crossing into Canada, were all invented. It was kind of a dramatic enactment of what had been an old, old daydream on my part.

If I were to tell you the truth about the summer of 1968 it would be that I worried a lot. I also played golf and ate hamburgers, but all of that would have been a dramatically empty story. It wouldn't have had the emotional quality of the Rainy River story, where I put a character right on the edge, how I felt psychologically, on the edge.

Kaplan: Many critics said that *The Things They Carried* is a great book, but that it can in no real sense be considered a novel.

O'Brien: Novels have a kind of continuity of plot or of narrative which this book does not have. But it would be unfair for me to say that it's a collection of stories; clearly all of the stories are related and the characters reappear and themes recur, and some of the stories refer back to others, and others refer forwards. I've thought of it as a work of fiction that is neither one nor the other.

Kaplan: Several chapters of *Going After Cacciato*, like much of *The Things They Carried*, were initially published as short stories. Did you think of *Cacciato* as a novel while you were working on it?

O'Brien: Almost from the moment of conception. It's a matter of feel. It's also a matter of how you're going to work with the materials.

Kaplan: In all of your previous books there is at least one strongly delineated character, someone who sticks in the reader's mind for a long time, such as Cacciato, or William Cowling. I don't know, however, if I would say the same thing about *The Things They Carried*. Has your focus somehow turned away from character?

O'Brien: No, not really. To me there is a dominant character in *The Things They Carried* in the Tim O'Brien character, but he's rendered more as a teller of the story, I guess in the same way Marlow is used by Conrad. I can't picture much about Marlow. He's a voice and a commentator. He analyzes, and at times he behaves in his own stories. He explains, for example, at the end of *Heart of Darkness* what he did when he returned to London—that he visited the fiancé and told her what had happened. He's not a judging figure, but a consciousness, both telling the story and vaguely participating in it.

Kaplan: Is that how you use O'Brien?

O'Brien: Yes, although the O'Brien character is much more a participant. He gets shot, and he plans revenge. He does a lot of things in the story, both in the present and in the past.

Kaplan: Were you more interested in the issues of storytelling than in the storyteller?

O'Brien: In part. I can see that young girl in her shorts. I can see little Linda. And I can see Mitchell Sanders and his yo-yo. I can see these things. But because it is interrelated fictions and not a novel, one can't have beyond that O'Brien consciousness a dominant figure who is going to stay with you through it all. Rat will tell a story, and then Mitchell Sanders will tell another. The girl dancing will be another. This kind of form precludes a typical, dominant character.

Kaplan: In both *The Nuclear Age* and *The Things They Carried* a female character undergoes a transformation from a kind of cheerleader/hometown sweetheart to a terrorist/guerilla warrior. Are you somehow trying to comment through your female characters on the nature of the man's world in which your novels take place?

O'Brien: I am. The materials in the stories are what they are. I'm a man, and I write about things. I often write about war, and war in our culture has been historically a man's milieu. Yet it seems to me that it is unfair to half of the population to unnecessarily exclude female participation in male events. It would be more fun, it would be more instructive, it would be more artistic, more beautiful, to include as much as possible the whole of humanity in these stories. Also, it's interesting to test in one's imagination, almost as one would test a hypothesis, the actions and reactions of a female heart to situations to which they are not accustomed.

Kaplan: Do you think there are differences between the way men and women react to situations of extreme stress?

O'Brien: I don't. I think that too much has been made of gender, way too much has been made of it, by both sides. Under situations of stress and in situations of incredible danger and trauma, women are capable, as men are, of great evil, of great good, and of all shades in between.

What I am trying to show, what I am trying to open the door to, is the possibility that we aren't that different. We're different, yes, but we're not that different. We all experience anger. We experience lust. We experience terror. We experience curiosity and fascination for that which repels us. All of us.

Kaplan: Many of your female characters seem to be exaggerated embodiments of stereotypical characteristics, such as innocence—the cheerleader—and tenderness—the hometown sweetheart. Aren't you somehow saying that they are in fact different from men?
O'Brien: No. I do the same thing when I portray men. My chief male characters have been almost prototypes of innocence. I think of Paul Berlin, a Midwestern kid, and I think of Tim O'Brien in *The Things They Carried*. I also think of my Montana guy in *The Nuclear Age*, William Cowling.

All of my characters are shaken out of a state of stasis—a kind of innocence, a kind of belief in the world that's grounded in a thoughtless traditionalism, and by thoughtless I mean that it is accepted or taken for granted—by some kind of outside, global event. In all of the books except maybe *Northern Lights* some outside event intrudes on that innocence. The characters, like Rip Van Winkle, are shaken awake and forced to confront their own naïveté, their own jejune acceptance of an order.

Kaplan: Critics have frequently compared you to Hemingway, but what you just said sounds a lot more like Fitzgerald.
O'Brien: I also have a lot in common with Conrad in many ways, especially when I think of *Lord Jim*. Good stories somehow have to do with an awakening into a new world, something new and true, where someone is jolted out of a kind of complacency and forced to confront a new set of circumstances or a new self. You know, the father dies, or a ship is wrecked like in Robinson Crusoe, or a new order has to be established, or an effort to establish a new order has to be made. Fiction, storytelling, has to do with those kinds of crucial changes in a character's life.

Kaplan: That might be true of characters in conventional fiction, but I don't know to what extent that formula could be used to describe some of your more absurd characters, such as Ebenezer Keezer and Nethro in *The Nuclear Age*, who don't seem to develop at all. When you created these two characters did you consciously distort their personalities?

O'Brien: Sure. *The Nuclear Age* in general was meant to be a big cartoon of the nuclear age, with everything heightened and exaggerated. William Cowling's own fears are way beyond the ordinary quiet terror that most of us have lived with over the last fifty years. Sarah, as a character, is blown way out of proportion. Events in the story are blown way out of proportion, the way Trudeau does it in Doonesbury. It's got kind of a Popeye feel. You know, the muscles are bigger.

Kaplan: You did a parody of Hemingway's first novel, *The Sun Also Rises*, in your own first novel, *Northern Lights*. Could you talk a little bit about the similarities and differences between these two books.

O'Brien: I tried to make fun of Hemingway. I respect Hemingway's work, and some of it I love. But sometimes I find myself being irritated by a kind of macho simplicity and by the way women are treated almost as little pawns to be moved around from place to place. That's not always true of his women, but often it is true, I think. There are approximately forty pages in *Northern Lights* where I parody Hemingway, though I probably would not have done so if I had known at the time that good fiction is not ordinarily the place for parody. I wish now I hadn't done it, though I must admit that it was really fun. I don't think I've ever enjoyed writing so much as I enjoyed the month or so I spent on those forty pages.

Kaplan: Like Hemingway, you seem to be preoccupied with the question of courage. Many of the incidents in *If I Die* appear in a new form in *The Things They Carried*, as do themes of desertion and courage.

O'Brien: Some of the events are the same in the roughest, narrative kinds of ways. I don't know what else to say. I guess I go back to material in the way that every writer goes back to his or her concerns for the world. My concerns as a human being and my concerns as an artist have at some point intersected in Vietnam—not just in the physical place, but in the spiritual and moral terrain of Vietnam. They intersected there in the way that the Midwest-Princeton linear flow of Fitzgerald's life intersected with the aftermath of World War I. There was an intersection of values, of what was and what was to come, that I'll always go back to, and I'd be crazy not to.

Conrad kept returning over and over again to the same venue, which was the sea, and the microcosm aboard a ship frames his work. Shakespeare kept writing about kings, to eternity. But one tries to wrestle new meanings and new stories out of the concerns of one's life. One has to care about the material. I care about issues of courage, and I care about issues of storytelling, and I care about issues of mysteriousness, and I care about cyclical patterns of plot. In *The Things They Carried* the events of the war are kind of recycled over and over again, and so are my characters' histories and thoughts. I try to make those things I care about as a person interesting.

Kaplan: Unlike most of the other writers and filmmakers who have dealt with the war, you devote very little space in your books to war crimes. Why is that?

O'Brien: Most war crimes, in my experience, are little episodes of war, little fragments of war. Something such as shooting one innocent human being for fun, let's say a farmer in a rice paddy, is to me in its magnitude of evil as bad as, say, firebombing Tokyo. Quantity is not a measure of evil, in my opinion. The shooting of the water buffalo in *The Things They Carried* is an act of evil. It's a little thing, the death of a water buffalo. And yet my hope as a writer is that those accruing acts of evil will touch a reader's heart more than a grandiose description of the firebombing of a village, or the napalming of a village, where you don't see the corpses, you don't know the corpses, you don't witness the death in any detail. It's somehow made abstract, bloodless.

Because it is such a horrible and huge event, war in general is seen abstractly by most of us. Even the declarations about war, such as war is hell, war is evil, and so on, are bloodless and abstract because they're so broad. The only way that the horror of war can mean anything to us is through small detailed vignettes or episodes of evil. Finally, I guess I should also say that as a human being I have never witnessed any large-scale atrocities. I think that by and large, large-scale atrocities are a rare phenomenon of war, unless one includes things like the bombings of cities, which are, at least in my way of thinking, atrocities. But I have never seen My Lais. I have never seen concentration camps. I have never seen any large-scale murder. I've seen the trappings of it, and I've seen the surface of it, but I've never seen anyone die in those kinds of situations. As a writer you almost have to trust in that, not which you have necessarily witnessed, but to which you feel some kind of proximity, and I've never felt that kind of proximity to large-scale, blatant atrocities.

Kaplan: How do you react to scenes like the one in *Apocalypse Now* where a village is attacked and destroyed so Colonel Kilgore can hold a surfing contest?

O'Brien: I could almost imagine that thing being staged, with people shouting through megaphones. It looked artificial, although parts of *Apocalypse*

Now looked absolutely wonderful. That scene in particular, however, struck me as gimmicky. It didn't seem very horrible to me either. It seemed a little bit like World War II movies where there was no sense of real gut-wrenching savagery and horror, much of which the rest of the movie does have. The end of the movie seems to be much more horrible, the killing of that calf, the butchering of it.

Kaplan: One of the problems with films like *Apocalypse Now* is that they tend to emphasize the craziness of the war without coming to terms with the suffering of the Vietnamese people. Do you feel you have dealt with the Vietnamese people as closely as you would have liked to?

O'Brien: More closely than I would have liked to. I didn't know them. They didn't know me. One can't pretend to know what one doesn't. One can use one's imagination and try to identify with villagers and with particular human beings, soldiers who are Vietnamese. But to do it successfully you have to somehow be grounded in that which would somehow fuel their imaginations. One can't simply impose a Western imagination on those people and come up with anything meaningful. If I were capable of imagining the Vietnamese I would do it. But I'm not.

Kaplan: A speaker at a conference on the literature of the Vietnam War called the Vietnamese people the great lost factor of the Vietnam War, and he said it was the obligation of American writers to deal with them. Do you agree?

O'Brien: No! The natural responsibility for telling the Vietnamese side of the story should and does rest with the Vietnamese themselves, with the Vietnamese writers. At a conference here in Boston last summer this very issue was discussed with three Vietnamese. All of us, all of the American writers, said to various degrees and in various ways that we've been criticized for not giving the Vietnamese point of view and the Vietnamese writers just laughed and said, "That's *our* job." I think, by and large, in American fiction the Vietnamese people have ended up as stereotyped cartoon figures or as puppets.

Kaplan: What are some of the other ideas and issues that concern you?

O'Brien: My answer to that has to do with the book I am working on now. Do you remember the story about Judge Crater, the guy who in the 1930s in New York City went out of his house and just disappeared? That's an earthly representation of a larger mystery. What happens when we die? Where do we go? We'll never know. In this world we'll never know.

What we don't know is inherently intriguing to the human spirit. That includes big metaphysical things like death and God, and it includes little discrete daily things like, what is she thinking now as I'm having this drink at this bar? There is always that mystery because one can't read other people's minds. What fascinates us in part about character, about other human beings, is that we just will never be that person, live that person's life.

The mystery of what we can't know is what's dominating the novel I'm working on right now. It's structured in a sense as a mystery, I suppose. A man wakes up and his wife is gone, no fights, no notes, no explanation at all. She's just physically, forever gone, with no reason. The book is a series of hypotheses about what might have become of her. He imagines her saying, "I got on a train and went to Seattle. I drowned." So it's the man trying to enter his wife's imagination, looking for explanations.

Kaplan: There are several elements in both *Cacciato* and in *The Nuclear Age* that are strongly reminiscent of detective fiction. Do you see similarities between what you have done in your writings and what some of the masters of crime fiction, like Poe and Borges, have done in theirs?

O'Brien: Not really, no. I don't read much detective fiction. I've read some, now and then. To me great crime fiction would be stuff like *The Brothers Karamazov, Crime and Punishment, Les Misérables*, or a great short story by John Fowles called "Poor Cocoa." Ordinary detective fiction as I know it is kind of inconsequential in its concern for the surface: for "who did it?" and "how was it done?" Those are the kind of practical, mechanical questions, which are interesting, but ultimately forgettable. Once you know who did it, you don't care who did it, because you know. But in the story I'm trying to write, and in the stories I've told, the ultimate mystery of the mystery story has to do with the unknowable.

Kaplan: What you just described could also be applied to Conrad's method in *Heart of Darkness* and *Lord Jim*. The narrator is a kind of detective looking for answers to things that cannot be answered, for answers to the unknowable.

O'Brien: Exactly. Those are good examples. He's asking himself in *Heart of Darkness* about Kurtz as he tells the story. There are all kinds of statements such as, "This may have happened," and there's no opportunity to really know the facts about Kurtz, because by the time Marlow reaches him, Kurtz has become unknowable. All he can do is mutter "the horror." He doesn't say much else.

Kaplan: You talk a great deal in *The Things They Carried* about storytelling. What psychological and social functions do you think storytelling has?
O'Brien: That's a tough one, a big one. There are all kinds of answers, but the answers that matter to me, personally, are those I talk about in the book itself. Good stories can be true or untrue. It doesn't really matter too much, provided that the story does to the spirit what stories should do, which is to entertain, but entertain in the highest way, entertain your brain and your stomach, and your heart, and your erotic zones, and make you laugh.

Kaplan: Ebenezer and Nethro are definitely among your funniest characters. They remind me of the characters in Harold Pinter's plays. Have you ever written a play?
O'Brien: I wrote a radio play for public radio called *Your Play* about ten years ago based on a chapter from *Cacciato*.

Kaplan: Do you think your novels or your characters would come across well on the screen?
O'Brien: Fiction relies more on a reader's participation in the development of character. You're not presented with concrete embodiments of a character's face. Film seems to be a little bit more passive as a medium.

I guess what I am trying to say is that I've felt a bit disappointed in seeing, say, Huck Finn's face in a film after having made up my own. To that extent I'm not sure I want any of my books made into movies. I'm certainly willing to take the money that they've been paying me for years, and I'll keep taking it, while still hoping that they'll never make one. That's the ideal world.

Kaplan: You have said that the purpose of writing fiction is to explore moral quandaries, that the best fiction has a character who is confronted with having to make a difficult choice. How does this apply to Tim O'Brien in *The Things They Carried*? Outside of the Rainy River segment, how does it apply to the book as a whole?
O'Brien: Well, there is the Rainy River section, and one can't deny it. It explains so much, and it also determines so much of why the O'Brien character behaves as he does in the book. But in the course of the book, the O'Brien character makes all kinds of choices. There's the "Ghost Soldiers"

chapter, with the decision to get revenge. And there is Kiowa's death, all kinds of choices are made there—choosing to live and let Kiowa die. There is also the choice of what one does to come to terms with a whole history.

I can't think of a story that isn't structured around choices, except maybe for a couple of Flannery O'Connor stories. I'm thinking of "A Good Man Is Hard to Find," which is difficult to talk about in this way. I mean, who chooses what? Something just happens to those poor people. They go out and they're massacred. Yet what makes the story come alive are the things that those characters choose to say and do in the course of this horrible, inexplicable thing. They didn't choose for this to happen to them, but they do choose how to behave as it happens to them.

The reason choice seems to me important as a word and as a way for me to think about stories is that it involves values. It's most interesting when the choices involve things of equally compelling value, when you say, God, I really want that, but I also want that. Or I really don't want that, and I don't want that either.

Kaplan: When I first proposed writing a book on you, you said that it might be premature since you are still in the middle of your career. Where do you hope to be in the next five to ten years?

O'Brien: I don't know. That's another tough one to answer. You learn something every day, and what you learn is particulars, little tiny things that have to do with sentences. Is that a rotten sentence, and why is it a rotten sentence? It could be rotten for billions of reasons, and you learn new reasons every day. Sometimes when you first write a sentence you don't realize there is something wrong with it, and it might be a week or it could be a second before you realize, oh that's the reason why it's not a good sentence. It's the particular things that are sparked in my mind, and if there were one important thing I could say in the whole interview it would be that my attention is more on this stuff that we're talking about right now than it is on grand things. The grand things float. They're around you all the time, and if you try to pay too much attention to them you kill the mentality of the writing itself. And so you kill the grand idea. One's attention as a writer is on trying to put down one word after another with a kind of grace and a kind of beauty that's a constant, never-ending balancing act of billions of variables.

Artful Dodge Interviews Tim O'Brien

Daniel Bourne and Debra Shostak/1991

From *Artful Dodge* 22/23 (1992): 74–90. Reprinted with permission of Daniel Bourne.

Since the appearance of his war memoir *If I Die in a Combat Zone* in 1973, Tim O'Brien has been widely regarded as not only a major new voice in American writing, but also as an important witness to the day-to-day realities of the Vietnam conflict and to war in general. His novel *Going After Cacciato*, set in Vietnam, won the 1979 National Book Award; and more recently, *The Things They Carried* (1990), a novel composed of interlinking stories about a group of American foot soldiers on patrol, was nominated for the National Book Critics Circle Award and was selected by the *New York Times Book Review* as one of the best works of fiction in 1990. The recipient of awards from the Guggenheim Foundation, the National Endowment for the Arts, and the Massachusetts Arts and Humanities Foundation, Tim O'Brien has published two other novels, *Northern Lights* (1975) and *The Nuclear Age* (1985), and is currently at work on his next book of fiction, an excerpt of which appeared in the January 1992 issue of the *Atlantic* under the title "The People We Marry."

The following interview, however, contests the classification of Tim O'Brien as solely a war writer. Instead, O'Brien's choice of dramatic landscape provides "a way to get at the human heart and the pressure exerted on it," for instance, how in *Going After Cacciato* fear and desire open the door to imaginative possibility, or how stories can save us, as O'Brien writes in *The Things They Carried*. As the latter example shows, O'Brien is deeply concerned with the many faces of storytelling itself—the relationship between fact and fiction, the creation of what he calls "happeningness," the way language is incommensurate with reality, the way form shapes belief. Tim O'Brien's gift is to explore these questions through lyrical, deceptively spare, casually immediate prose. His fiction puts a spin on human experience to reveal the unexpectedness in our most intimate feelings. Fear and love, longing and guilt, violence and the urge for vengeance—all these are landmarks on the terrain of our common humanity: glimpsable, but not necessarily knowable. Addressing a gathering of writing teachers a few months after the interview with *Artful Dodge*, O'Brien explained the openendedness of his exploration this way: "The purpose of writing is to enhance mystery, not solve it."

The following conversation took place on October 2, 1991, during Tim O'Brien's residency as a Lila Wallace–Reader's Digest Writing Fellow at The College of Wooster.

Daniel Bourne: Do you think you would have been a writer if you had not gone to Vietnam?
Tim O'Brien: No. At least I don't think so. These things are always mysterious and so any answer has to be equally enigmatic.

Debra Shostak: But had you thought about writing before you went?
O'Brien: I'd thought of it, but never as a career, never as a profession. It wasn't the material that Vietnam presented me with so much as it was a revolution of personality. I'd been an academic and intellectual sort of person, and Vietnam changed all that.

DB: After the war, when you did start to write about your experience, did you make a conscious decision to start writing about Vietnam through non-fiction, through a war memoir as in *If I Die in a Combat Zone*?
O'Brien: No. At the time, and to this day really, I couldn't care less that the book was nonfiction. It is presented in this way, but any person with an I.Q. over 84 knows that any narrative has to be—at least in part—invented. That is, who's going to remember every scrap of dialogue? Most of that speech has to be made up. And events get reordered in the course of writing, recounting. Also, reality did not come at me the way it comes at you in the book: in the war, back at home when still a little boy, then in basic training, back to the war. There's a scrambling of the chronology which isn't totally real to the world as I lived it. Also, parts of the book, although it's technically nonfiction, are utterly invented, in the same sorts of ways as in *The Things They Carried*. Not a lot of it, but now and then in the course of writing I took a scrap of event and put it together with another scrap, or I took something from an account, when I wasn't personally present to witness it, or sometimes I would take a conflicting account and choose it over my own,

blending everything together to make what seems to be a convincing and coherent story about things I hadn't borne witness to in their entirety. By and large the book is a representation of the kinds of reality I lived through, but the picture is also changed by the dialogue, the storytelling technique, things I wasn't aware of at the time. I did this intuitively, sort of saying, "I think basically that this is true," but knowing, at the time, I had to do things that weren't strictly nonfiction to make the account possible.

DB: Was there any point in Vietnam where you woke up as a writer? Do you remember saying, "I need to write about this," or "There is no way I can write about this?"
O'Brien: There was one incident I wrote about while I was still there. Something may have happened inside of me that said, "Tim, you have to write about this," but the voice there was a mute one, speaking in gesture to me, through my genes or something. I guess something just happens when one day a guy hits a land mine and he's a friend of yours. The horror brought me to put some words down on paper, and having written those words, new words came to me, and having written new words other words, until I had a six or seven page piece that went beyond this one man's death and the death of those around him to death in general, almost outside of Vietnam, and I was examining myself essentially, my own terror inside.

DB: I was really struck with the story "Step Lively," that it had for me the feeling of something actually written there in the field. Again, I realize it was indeed fiction . . .
O'Brien: Well, part of it was fiction. As a matter of fact, that was the story I'm referring to, the death of a friend by a landmine. I wrote some things down, and then the story was put aside for some time, and subsequent events—when I became the radio guy for the squad and had to call for medical evacuations and deal with this stuff head-on—actually made me go back to the story. Later on, after I got out of the field, I began rewriting it, adding more things to it. So it was written over a course of three months, four months. But it was written mostly in Vietnam, almost entirely in Vietnam. Just a couple of lines were added afterward. It's one of the few things in *If I Die in a Combat Zone* that was written there.

DB: You mentioned the other day that while you were there you hated the idea of writing out in the field, that you were paranoid you would be killed and there would be this writing discovered in your pockets.

O'Brien: I did hate to write, and by and large I didn't. Writing those six or seven pages was one of the very few times. Words didn't seem adequate to the experience. I had this thing with drowning and gore and blood and terror, and words seemed superfluous. I didn't want to write about it. I also felt a kind of superstition that if I were somehow to write about these things, they would happen to me, to me personally. I'm not sure why I felt that way. It might have been some old movie I'd seen where a body's lying there and they find the guy's diary and it's Joe Schmoe bending over the corpse, and he's reading these sad, self-pitying journal entries. I don't know what the source of my superstition was, but I know I felt a pretty strong sense of "I don't want to be writing now." But now and then I was overwhelmed and did start writing. What I'm trying to say, though, is that there was nothing conscious going on. I wasn't looking for literary material.

DB: Now that you are looking at the war in that way, how have you found this terrain of Vietnam a convenient metaphor?

O'Brien: That's mostly how I look at it—though I'm not sure I'd call it a convenient metaphor. I'd say an essential metaphor or a life-given metaphor that, for me, is inescapable. And I'm grateful for it in a sense. I've used it in the way Conrad writes about the sea, life on the water, stories set on boats, from *Heart of Darkness* to *Lord Jim*, from *Nostromo* to *Typhoon* to *Youth*. But Conrad is no more writing about the sea than I am writing about war. That is, he's not writing about marine biology and dolphins and porpoises and waves. He's writing about human beings under pressure, under the certain kinds of pressure that the sea exerts, life aboard vessels, the discipline of living aboard a ship at sea, the expectations of behavior that are a part of a ship's life. *Lord Jim* and his act of cowardice and so on. Conrad uses the sea the same way I use Vietnam, as a way to get at the human heart and the pressure exerted on it. He's not writing literally about sailing and sailors. At the same time, this life aboard vessels carries with it a framework for storytelling that he uses beautifully. My content is not bombs and bullets and airplanes and strategy and tactics. It is not the politics of Vietnam. It too is about the human heart and the pressures put on it. In a war story, there are life and death stakes built in immediately, which apply just by the framework of the story. There is a pressure on characters that in other kinds of fiction one would have to meticulously build. So, in a way, using the framework of war is a short cut to get at things without having to engage in some of this mechanical work that I don't particularly like, to get bogged down in plotting. I don't like reading heavily plotted stories. I like a situation to have an instant sort of pressure.

DS: Is that why *The Things They Carried* is anecdotal, not a sustained, plotted narrative?

O'Brien: It is. In any case, that's the form of the book, anecdotal. But the anecdotes have a kind of pressure on them which is automatically there. If two guys are sitting in the middle of a war, talking about their girlfriends, that's not the same as two guys sitting in a cafeteria at a college talking about theirs. There's a sense of the unexpected or the unanticipated happening at any second, a sense of one's own imminent death being just beyond the next word that's uttered. But that's a metaphor that goes beyond war. It has to do with our own mortalities we aren't always aware of. When we lead our lives, when we fall in love or our fathers hurt us or our mothers forget to feed us, by and large we forget that we're going to die pretty soon. But in a war story, when the mortality is right on you every moment, those subplots of our lives take on an added resonance and an added existential tension. And that's part of why I like writing war stories.

DB: I was going to ask what you thought about that old adage that a writer has to suffer, but what you've just said pretty much answers my question—that writing war stories isn't so much about theme but the fact that dramatically you're almost immediately on this terrain of life and death.

O'Brien: Yes, that's true, a writer does have to suffer. As we all do. We all stub our toes, we all have people who don't love us enough. There are all kinds of suffering; life is a bunch of suffering. There are a lot of other things too, of course, but we all suffer. And stories are ordinarily made out of suffering. I'm trying to think of one that isn't, and I can't. *Bambi*? Well, Bambi loses his mommy, right? Burned up in a forest fire? I think that's what happens. All the fairy tales we grow up with, these little things we think we treat our kids to are just filled with suffering. Goldilocks, lost in the woods. What could be more terrifying: a little girl lost in the woods with a bunch of bears? That's essentially what stories are about. That is not to say it's the suffering alone; but it's the premise of a certain way of storytelling, how we deal with conflict and with struggle and tensions in our lives.

DB: Were you aware at any time of particular images from the war taking on significance in your writing, becoming larger than life?

O'Brien: Sort of yes and no. All my answers are kind of yes and no. I feel funny analyzing things I can't quite remember and at the time didn't even understand because they were happening. I didn't understand these things at all—and still don't, in a way. All I can do is talk about examples, and I'll only mention one. A recurring image, not only in the books about Vietnam, but in other stories and books I've written, has to do with the death of animals. The kind of raw, up close, detailed butchery of animals, of water buffalo in particular, though in *Northern Lights* there's the death of the deer up close, a dead deer examined closely. Why I'm doing this, why I did this, in part I don't know and in part I do know. In part I know it has to do with a kind of human fascination with mortality. What is it, what does it look like? What does it feel like to be dead? Well, I know on one level, biologically, it probably feels like nothing, right? A nothingness. But questions then occur to me like what were the last thoughts of the dying animals; do animals think? What kinds of flashes occur in the brain as things dissolve? What I'm trying to say here is that these questions get increasingly philosophical and increasingly perplexing. Is death purely a biological thing or do spiritual things happen too—an awareness of one's own demise or pending nonbeing? But to represent these questions in a feeling way requires a proximity to death, a kind of looking at death occurring now or having already occurred. There's a kind of wonderment.

DS: You talk generally in your stories about death, but your images are also specifically violent. Some of the most memorable passages in *The Things They Carried* involve really horrific violence: Curt Lemon, scattered in pieces up in the tree; the face of the Viet Cong warrior who has a star-shaped hole where his eye should be. How do you avoid turning those images, that material, into a sort of pornography? Do you worry about that?

O'Brien: No. I think that violence itself is pornographic in a way, and this pornography has to be described in raw, physical, truthful terms. If one's subject matter, as mine often is, has to do with the taking of life, it would be an act of obscenity and pornography even more to try to describe it in anything but the most horrific, detailed and graphic terms. For me, one of the objects among many in writing about violence has to do with reaffirming the truth of the clichés that "war is hell," or "death is horrible," something we all so often tend to forget. Body counts, casualty rates, our politicians have made it all so abstract. And this isn't to say that I'm trying to prevent war exactly, though I'd love to do that, but I know I never will, I don't think any writer will, at least not any one writer. But my writing is a reminder that war is hell for a particular reason. That star-shaped hole where an eye ought to have been is something pretty ugly, and, hopefully, the image shows that ugliness ought to be, by and large, in our lives avoided. And I also think that this detailed portrayal of the horrors of violence is a reaction to the myths I grew up with as a kid: John Wayne movies and Audie Murphy movies and the little GI Joe comic books I used to read where death was inconsequential because it didn't seem very horrible at all. No blood, they'd all just "drop" dead. War and violence didn't seem all that horrible as it was portrayed back then. My object is not to wallow in blood and gore. The object is to display it in terms so that you want to stay away from it if possible.

DS: In "Sweetheart of the Song Tra Bong" you describe Rat Kiley, an inveterate liar, as a man for whom "facts were formed by sensation, not the other way around." Do you work like that?
O'Brien: Yes.

DS: Are there aesthetic risks?
O'Brien: No, but I'm willing to hear what they may be. In general, though, for me one of the fundamental things to be accomplished in fiction is to convince. That is, to convince the reader of the stuff that is happening in the now that it's occurring, whether it's a fairy tale, something fabulous, or something realistic. No matter what it is, fiction requires a sense of underlying credibility. And so when one's inventing fact, and the so-called invented facts aren't convincing, then there's a problem. But, when you're inventing things, what you try to do is to make them seem as if they are truly occurring. I guess every fictional writer runs the risk of invention all the time. I'm sure Mark Twain ran into it, writing about trout or a kid going on a raft down the Mississippi. Much, almost all, of that story is invented, though Twain does draw on remembered images, remembered dialogue. *Connecticut Yankee in King Arthur's Court?* That stuff can't happen at all. You can't go back in time that way. Here especially you have to develop this sense of things happening, and that requires good technique, that requires keeping the dream alive, the way dreams are alive when we're truly dreaming, a state that we're constantly at risk of disrupting if we lose the sense of credibility. This disruption can be done in a million ways. You can lose your readers' faith by putting a stone here rather than there, or by having a comma in the wrong place. You can do it by melodrama, by making your stuff seem too cartoonish. You can lose the sense of credibility in all kinds of ways. And what one tries to do is not to make those kinds of mistakes.

DS: Speaking of credibility, in *The Things They Carried* there are numerous devices—come-ons, enticements, snares for the reader—such as starting out stories with "It's time to be blunt" or "This is true," having one story supposedly give the facts about the evolution of another story, or naming the narrator after yourself. It seems to me that an appropriate metaphor for talking about this aspect of the book would be that you're seducing the reader, and that obviously the reader can have ambivalent feelings toward such a seduction. Do you see that?

O'Brien: I'd say that maybe it is an appropriate metaphor, probably not one I would use, but it's certainly appropriate. I guess that's what I was trying to do, to make the reader feel those sorts of ambivalences. Hearing a story, being seduced, then having the seducer say, "By the way, I don't love you, it all isn't true." And then doing it again. And then saying, "That also isn't true, just kidding," and doing it again. It's not just a game, though. It's not what that "Good Form" chapter is about. It's form. This whole book is about fiction, about why we do fiction. Every reader is always seduced by a good work of fiction. That is, by a lie, seduced by a lie. *Huckleberry Finn* did not happen, but if you're reading *Huckleberry Finn* you're made to believe that it is happening. If you didn't believe it, then it would be a lousy work of fiction. One wouldn't be seduced. And I'm trying to write about the way in which fiction takes place. I'm like a seducer, yet beneath all the acts of seduction there's a kind of love going on, a kind of trust you're trying to establish with the reader, saying, "Here's who I am, here's why I'm doing what I'm doing. And in fact I do truly love you, I'm not just tricking you, I'm letting you in on my game, letting you in on who I am, what I am, and why I am doing what I am doing." All these lies are the surface of something. I have to lie to you and explain why I am lying to you, why I'm making these things up, in order to get you to know me and to know fiction, to know what art is about. And it's going to hurt now and then, and you're going to get angry now and then, but I want to do it to you anyway—and for you. That's the point of the book.

DS: It strikes me as interesting that your first book is a real memoir, while your last is a pseudo-memoir. How do you see that development, the relation between the way you want to accomplish those seductions in nonfiction and in fiction? Would you write nonfiction again?

O'Brien: There are all kinds of things that occur to me in answer to your question. One is that I don't form my career, my writerly interests, consciously. I don't outline a novel and say, "Here's where I'm going next" in terms of form and so on. The language just takes me there. A scrap of language will occur to me that seems interesting. And one of the first scraps of language that occurred to me in writing *The Things They Carried* was the line, "This is true." When that line was written—"This is true"—the form of the book wasn't present by any means, but the thematic "aboutness" of the book was there in those three words. "This is true." I had no idea what I was going to do with it, or where it would take me, but I knew in my bones as well as intellectually that this was important, these three words are important words. I didn't know important in what way or how I'd be exploring them, but I knew they were important. In the way I'm responding to your question, I guess I'm not trying to evade it exactly as much as I'm trying to speak in terms of heart. In terms of heart I don't think about these things much, and don't want to think about them. I prefer to look at writing as a heroistic act, finding out what I care about through writing stories. "Why do I care about truth? I don't know why I care about it!" And I'll write a story like "Sweetheart of the Song Tra Bong," for example, in which the guy Rat Kiley is telling the story and within the context of the story the matter of truth gets talked about. All along I've cared about this, but now in writing the story I wanted to know how I cared. That is, I always wondered, "Why am I making this stuff up? Why am I writing these stories?" But I never pursued it intellectually. I just said, "Well, I am." But I always wondered, and by writing those words down I began to realize there's a way you can begin to ask yourself a question seriously, methodically.

DB: So you are talking with yourself, then, while you're writing, especially with the stories in *The Things They Carried.*

O'Brien: In a way I am talking to myself, although it doesn't feel like that. The way it feels is as though I'm composing a story. It feels as if something else is talking to me. I'm not sure what it is. The characters? I'll write a line, fully believing in it. Then, once it's written, I'll believe it's been uttered by this person, Mitchell Sanders or Rat. They would say to someone else, "You guys are sexist. What do you mean you can't have a pussy for president?" Meanwhile, I've just written this line and I'll say, "What pussy? Where did this come from?" Then I'll think, "This guy said this!" He accuses these other guys of being sexist and then he himself uses language like that and it jars a little in my head, but in a good way. Here's a guy talking about being sexist while he's doing it himself. It shows me the complexity of the material until I don't feel I've written it, though I know I have, and so I consciously keep the word "pussy," knowing it bounces off the "You guys are all sexist." But, at the same time, I don't feel as though I've written these words, as though the phrase had been directed toward me. Instead, I ask what some character in the story might say in response. Once a story is underway I no longer feel in complete control. I feel that I'm at the whim of my creations. I'll be pulled by them as much as I'll be pulling them. It sounds mystical, probably too mystical, but that's really how it feels. I think you can understand why I feel that way. Your questions here, for example, are tugging me, while I'm partly responsible for these enquiries because of the consequences of the things I've written. But I no longer feel in control of your responses to the things I've written.

DB: Given your statement that everything in *The Things They Carried* is fiction, can we believe "Notes" is nonfiction, when at least the surface assumption is that here you're giving us the truth about what went on in the composition of another story?
O'Brien: You ought not to believe it. In fact, it's utterly and absolutely invented. It's an example of one more seduction on top of the rest. No Norman Bowker, and no mother. It's a way of displaying that form can dictate belief, that the form of the footnote, the authority that the footnote carries, is persuasive in how we apprehend things. We think once again we're locked into a factual world by form, and that process is a great deal what the book is about, including the next little note called "Good Form," which is sort of the same thing. It says, "Well, I'm going to confess something to you. It's time to be blunt. None of this stuff happened. I'm going to tell you no guy ever died, and here's what really happened." And then the next paragraph is going to say but that story too is invented. Here's the real story. Of course, that one's invented, too. I just don't say so in the story.

DB: In some ways I am reminded of Borges and how in a story he will cite a book and give extensive bibliographical information about it, but he's made the entire thing up.
O'Brien: I thought of using that device in fact but didn't, because I realized that I'd be copying Borges too closely, but I sure wanted to. Forms of things determine the things we believe. For example, the form of a memoir determines one's belief in a book. General fictional techniques do the same thing. Dialogue is a way of making us believe. Putting words in quotes is a way of representing reality: "These words were once spoken." It's the same way with narrative, characterization, the sense of setting, despite whether something's invented or stolen from reality. Fiction is a compilation of ways of making things believable. And belief, as I began by saying, is one of the fundamental aspects of storytelling. One wants to develop a sense of vivid, continuous dreams. It's not an abstraction; it's a vivid continuous dreaming. But it's not enough just to tell a continuous dream. I wouldn't say, "Hey, I had

this dream last night," and just tell you what happened. I could make it very vivid for you, but it would be boring, probably with no thematic weight to it. It wouldn't matter to you much. It might be very vivid to you but you'd say, "Ugh, blah. I'm bored silly."

DS: But maybe once you provided the context for it . . .
O'Brien: It may well become an interesting story.

DB: Have you found yourself consciously influenced by your reading knowledge of war? Say Stephen Crane, Tolstoy, etc.?
O'Brien: Not really. But when I read the best things by Crane or Tolstoy, I feel a sense of confirmation. That is, Vietnam happened to me twenty years ago, or more, and I wonder sometimes what did happen then. Was it real? Am I writing bullshit? Are my memories accurate? And when I read a good piece of literature, it reminds me of what I've been through and what civilizations, not just people, have gone through—that in fact all of us, in all our lives, whether we're personally serving in a war or not, have gone through the threat of war, the threat of annihilation, the threat of human violence. Good writing about the subject shows me that I'm not utterly mistaken, that I'm not wandering off alone, down this silly path. It tells me I'm not mistaken to pursue these emotions. But it's not war so much I'm thinking about here. It's violence, which is around all of us. It's in our genes, this sense that we're all going to die someday.

DS: Had you read those things before you went to Vietnam or did you find yourself seeking them out after you came back?
O'Brien: Some I'd read before going. Others not. I was so young when I went to Vietnam. I'd read *A Farewell to Arms*, and I'd read *The Iliad* and *The Odyssey*, *War and Peace*, probably some others as well. Today if I hear there's a wonderful book about war I'll read it, but I'll also read a good book about anything. By and large, I don't seek out books about war. As a matter of fact, I try to avoid them. They're all so terrible, filled with melodrama, stereotypes, cartoons, predictability, clichés.

DB: I'm struck with how you've said writing—specifically your own writing—deals with a pondering of one's own dying. There's one episode in *Going After Cacciato* where a smoke bomb goes off and the whole platoon falls to the ground and instantly Paul Berlin feels like shit. His stomach hurts, his teeth hurt and so on. But he's okay, because he's in so much pain. It reminded me of a passage from Tolstoy's *Sevastopol Sketches*, where during a cannon attack a bomb falls next to these two guys and both of them fall. One guy is going, "Oh my God, I've been hurt, I'm in pain. I'm going to die, I know it." Right next to him, this other guy is going, "Boy, I'm so glad it missed me. I'm feeling fine. Everything's so light and breezy." Euphoria. What has really happened, though, is that the one who is in agony has only been grazed by the bomb, while the one who is feeling no pain has been mortally wounded. He's in shock, dying.

O'Brien: Interesting, but I don't remember ever reading it.

DB: I was very much fascinated with how you set up point of view in *Going After Cacciato*. While describing Vietnam, everything seems to be precise, authentic, at least to someone like me who wasn't there. But when the imagination of Paul Berlin launches out onto the road after Cacciato, on the road to Paris, the details, although rich and deep, begin to seem like *National Geographic* information, self-consciously so. For instance, you even refer to Bob Hope and Bing Crosby, *The Road to Mandalay*, and so on. Basically, it seems like the sort of information an intelligent guy who had not actually been to these places might hold, someone like Paul Berlin—or the author. Was this point of view conscious?

O'Brien: Yes, entirely conscious. I was trying to represent these places the way they'd be represented by someone who hadn't in fact been there, but with all the details that a person who hadn't been to a place might know if he were an intelligent, reasonably educated guy like Berlin who has had two years in college. Because, essentially, that is how we think. That is how we do our daydreaming, on the basis of what we know about a place. So I took this *National Geographic* India and particularized it in the way we do the landscapes in our dreams. That is, through unique events occurring against a predictable backdrop. Hence the Jolly Chand character. Berlin says bluntly, "This is the world I'd seen in photographs, in my imagination." Bolts of cloth, cows roaming the streets of New Delhi, all these general images. But, in the midst of this, suddenly there's a strange Americanized Hindu who studied at the Johns Hopkins School of Hotel Management, something unpredictable, which gives everything a unique, strange quality. In each of those cases, throughout the way to Paris, it started with a kind of standard backdrop, and then a character superimposed on this stereotype that changes everything. Iran is an example. If I had to choose a character in the book whom I'd most want to meet in the real world, it would be this man, Fahyi Rhallon. I'd want to have with him the discussion that goes on about purpose and how purpose guides our lives and drives us to do things, while the absence of purpose is awful. I love that. I'm not sure I believe a man like this exists. But, nonetheless, a man like this is not someone whom one would pick out of a *National Geographic*. In any case, that's how I wanted to do those scenes. Start with the standard, ordinary, all-American knowledge of these places. Then impose on it a uniqueness as a consequence of the human imagination.

DB: You've talked a lot about how your experience in Vietnam has affected your literature. What about your rendering of the Midwest? It seems as if your landscapes of small towns in Iowa or Minnesota are as important in your fiction as the landscapes from Vietnam. Do you think readers have neglected this part of your writing?

O'Brien: No. In a way I suppose it has been neglected in terms of quantity. Not a lot of reviews or critical articles have centered on that stuff. But I don't worry about it. I know that this Midwest stuff is important, and I know why it's important. It's backdrop material. I could talk about—if that's what you're getting at—what it means for me to use that sort of thing. One aspect is my sense of bitterness about small-town Republican, polyester, white-belted, Kiwanis America. The people who vote and participate in civic events, who build playgrounds and prop up our libraries and then turn around and send us to wars, oftentimes out of utter and absolute ignorance. And I'm bitter about it. I'm bitter about people who say with a knee-jerk reaction, "Let's go kill Satan." The Middle America I grew up in sent me to that war. And it's the same thing now with Saddam Hussein. He was portrayed by Bush with demonistic qualities, and right into the guts of bourgeois America it was digested. That know-nothing attitude really disturbs and angers me. The Midwest for me is not just a sweet background I naively grew up in full of innocence and romanticism. I have a real bitterness towards it that lasts to this day. As a result, it was very difficult giving that talk yesterday to the Kiwanis club here in Wooster. I was full of anger towards their pancake suppers and the singing of their little fight songs and the reading of their little stock market quotes for the day, all these little rituals they went through. And, just to finish this little tirade of mine, above all my bitterness has to do with my hatred of Middle American ignorance. These people didn't know— in my case, in the case of Vietnam—Ho Chi Minh's politics from those of the governor of Arizona. They didn't know Bao Dai from the man in the moon. They didn't know the first thing about SEATO. They didn't know the first thing about French colonialism, about basic history. One of the questions

I was asked at the Kiwanis club yesterday after I finished my little talk was, "How many Chinese did I fight?" Chinese! This person knew nothing about the history of Vietnam and China and their antagonism. It's true, China supported the Vietnamese, but anyone who goes to a voting booth and whose rhetoric is belligerent and bellicose—"Let's go kill the Commies, let's go kill Hussein"—should know certain basic things. And the ignorance in these little towns is overwhelming. There's a laziness and a complacency, a kind of Puritan sense of pious rectitude, that you can tell really pisses me off. So when I write about the Midwest, I'm writing about it in part out of a sense of real rage and anger, justifiable rage and justifiable anger. I'm certainly not portraying these people as holy and pious. Of course, I'm engaging in such all-encompassing statements partly rhetorically. There are some people out there who do read their newspapers carefully. But in my experience, by and large that is not the case, and I'd like to nail the bastards. In fact, in one of the stories in *The Things They Carried*, there's a passage about a Kiwanis Club, a guy daydreaming how he'd love to go up to one of these people who do not know shit from shit and give them a piece of his mind. Remember that little fantasy: "I'd like to go talk to the Kiwanis and lay it all out?" I sort of lived that here in Wooster the other day.

DS: Does that make you feel rootless, then? Writers often write out of connectedness to a past.

O'Brien: Writers are connected. I'm connected to my past, but we're connected to bad things, too. There were things about the Midwest that I liked. But my dominant recollection about growing up in this part of the country, in the Midwest, is one of a kind of seething, contained rage. Even as a kid I felt that way. Small town gossip and the values of these places. I don't feel these things, this kind of rage, in my ordinary life when I return to Massachusetts, but when I return to the Midwest these feelings of resentment and rage do resurface.

DS: You mentioned in one of the classes you visited how you came to a number of writers, that some writers you saw as influential; others you just admire. You talked about Borges and García Márquez as being influential, but you also mentioned Toni Morrison, Anne Tyler, John Fowles. How do you see yourself writing among this company of writers? Who's influenced you the most? Are you willing to say what you don't like?

O'Brien: How do I see myself? As myself, I guess, that I can't be mistaken for Toni Morrison or for Fowles, nor for any of the others, yet I've learned a great deal from each of these writers you mentioned. I've culled all sorts of different things. I can mention Morrison, for example, especially in her book *Song of Solomon.* Mystery and myth are intermingled in a way that I very, very much admire. We love the impossible, the mystery of things. People are flying, but it happens mythically. It doesn't matter that it's impossible—they just are. The key phrase here is that it doesn't matter. You can do those sorts of miracles and not have to explain. That's a little thing I learned—relearned, I guess—from reading Toni Morrison's *Song of Solomon* and obviously applied it in my work. It's something I'd done before, yet not taking the risks in the same way as after reading that book. But I don't think I thought about *Song of Solomon* as I was composing any of my own work. I think it soaked in the way my father's alcoholism soaked into my life. I'd never written much about it directly. But it soaked in and was distilled, transmuted. I could say the same things about the other writers. But they're not conscious lessons. They're tucked away far into the cells of my brain, then joined with other things.

DS: It seems to me that often in contemporary writing you see an immediacy in first person narrators, like that in your pseudo-autobiographical framework for *The Things They Carried.* Narrators who encourage the reader to think that there's little or no distance between the first person narrative voice and the writer—for example, a whole slew of Philip Roth protagonists whom readers have confused with the writer. They seem to differ from the first person narrators of, say, Dickens or Faulkner, where there's no question that that they're characters. It looks to me like a new convention in writing. Do you see yourself participating in it?

O'Brien: In other books of mine, though, I've done the third person, and I've done the first person obviously not me, the Dickens thing, which I like trying, I guess, like any writer. I don't fall into one stream. I can't imagine myself, for example, writing another book like *The Things They Carried* using that form, but I think *The Things They Carried* takes the form beyond what others do. Even with Roth's first person narrators, I feel more of a distance between the author and narrator than I do with my book—the explicit naming of a name, the explicit use of material from one's own life—the name of the college, hometown, particular events. Somehow it makes me feel that *The Things They Carried* is very different because of its audacity in going for the full memoir form, or pseudo-memoir, I should say. But I wouldn't do it again. That's a convention I would try once only. I can't imagine a sequel to

The Things They Carried. The Things They Put Down? *The Things They Married*? Not a bad idea.

DS: Have you ever been accused of writing about war so that you don't have to write about women?
O'Brien: You can't accuse me of that, because that would obviously, transparently be wrong. I have written about women.

DS: Right, you have. But the ways you have written about women, at least in war books, seem to make them rather peripheral.
O'Brien: They're minor characters; is that what you mean? That's true, they are in supporting roles. When one chooses a point of view to tell a story, say, from the point of view of Paul Berlin or the O'Brien character—this technical thing that one does—it means you're locked by the rules of art, you're locked into that point of view throughout. And I could have chosen, for example, an omniscient point of view to tell these stories, or I could have told *The Things They Carried* from the point of view of, say, a Vietnamese soldier thinking back on the war, or a Russian advisor thinking back on the war. Why didn't I choose those things becomes the next question; why did I choose the point of view I did? That has to do with one's sense of personal passion, one's sense of knowledge. To choose to write things that I care about from the point of view of a Vietnamese soldier would be a horrible mistake. In fact, I have been accused of ignoring the Vietnamese in my fiction, ignoring their concerns and so on. It's not a question of ignoring, though, but of not knowing. It involves the question of point of view. The books I've read that try to show how everyone feels—like in *The Winds of War* where the point of view is everywhere, first in the Pentagon and then at the battle front—strike me as melodramatic and stupid. Another thing that occurs to me when talking about representing the Vietnamese is that to try to represent them seems to me presumptuous. An experience that means a lot to me was when I met three Vietnamese writers in Boston a couple of years ago. This issue came up of American literature about Vietnam, of complaints about American writers like me not representing the point of view of the enemy, or what we called "the enemy." I mentioned this to one of these guys, to Lei Lu, one of their most well-known fiction writers. He gave me a funny look and he laughed. He said, "Leave it to us. You don't know what we felt any more than you know what your wife feels at this moment." And the way he said that made me stop and think. "What was she thinking

now?" I didn't have any clue what she was thinking at that moment, and I realized that even beyond that I don't know what she's thinking lots of times. This whole problem is compounded with the basic problem of otherness. "What is Dan thinking now?" I have no idea, I really don't. This problem of not knowing the other is compounded even more by problems of culture, problems of language, compounded by problems of not knowing the history behind this culture. With all the kinds of ignorances that were present in Vietnam, it would be more than presumptuous for me to jump into another's psyche and personality on a large scale. On a small scale, now and then, yes. I did make this jump in *The Things They Carried*, jumping into the head of that dead man, for example, but only just to touch on a kind of humanity. Here's a human being who had a history. I wasn't trying to represent this history as factual, however. It's imagined by the Tim character who has killed this guy. This Tim character is imagining a history for the dead man, knowing it probably wasn't that way, but still he's imagining it, and so to him it really was this way. That to me is a problem of presumption, but it's the Tim character's presumption, not the author's. Then, another problem with having these broad points of view is melodrama. As I started to say before, books like *The Winds of War* tend to take an omniscient point of view. Oftentimes they don't succeed because of a diffuse, less-than-intense, stereotypical feeling that comes from trying to represent everything from all sides. The great masters have gotten away with it. They've done it beautifully. But a contemporary writer would find it extraordinarily difficult to write about things the way Tolstoy did in *War and Peace*.

The same principles I'm talking about apply to writing about women—which is how your question got started. First there's the problem of fact, that with the kinds of stories I'm telling it would be historically odd to have two or three women walking alongside, playing the roles of Henry Dobbins or the others. Much like in Conrad's stories. By and large the people in Conrad come from the particular story he's telling. On a sea vessel, there aren't many people named Mary. Similarly, if one were to write about Smith College, there would be women. The possible subjects in a story are constrained by choice of material—you can't have Albanians in a story that takes place in the Bronx. I could think of a zillion examples. You get the point, right? My choice of material is sort of limiting, but it's not in order to exclude women in general. This type of writing just requires that they play peripheral roles, except when one can do things as in "Sweetheart of the Song Tra Bong," where one can obliquely refer to the absence of women. And I've tried to do that not as obliquely as well, sometimes directly. For example, "How to Tell a True War Story," where there's a simmering anger and resentment on the part of this Tim narrator toward women. Remember the Rat Kiley story, where the sister never wrote back, "the dumb cooze," the language used throughout, the reference to the wife lying in bed at night, the "older woman of kindly temperament and humane politics" who "hates war stories" and "all the blood and gore." There's a rage that goes through that story that was entirely intentional, but doesn't represent my own rage necessarily, but the rage that could be the consequence of men doing all the fighting and women being excluded from it. Not a political rage, but a sense of "well, here we are in the war and there they are back home." It's a rage I saw exemplified on a lot of occasions. You can see it in the lingo in which women are talked about in the military. The language is pretty coarse. Women are treated in language, in conversation, as aliens, and in some ways women are aliens to that combat milieu. Exploring these issues is important to me, and even without having the lead characters be women, I can explore this.

DB: It's interesting that in "Sweetheart of the Song Tra Bong" a woman actually comes from America to Vietnam.
O'Brien: Right, that story is an example of a woman's presence, but this is striking only because women are so rare. The story's also one of the few cases in the book that is based on reality. A woman did in fact come to Vietnam, an ex-cheerleader, just out of high school, pretty much as I described it. But the rest of the story I invented. I had fun doing it.

DB: The source of authority at the end of the story is legend. By the end the narrator is only reporting hearsay, that supposedly the woman did this or that. It's a nice sort of fade.
O'Brien: It's more than just a fade. It goes to what stories are, in a way. Stories, retold, carry the force of legend. There's a sense of legend in that the story is still going out there somewhere. Huck is still going down that river, Ahab is still chasing that whale. Legends have to do with the repetition of things. Though there's a narrative end to *Moby-Dick*, there's a sense, as in all stories, that everyone is still out there, still doing these things, forever and ever. Mary Anne Bell is still out there in the dark, chasing masculinity, an obsession with this stuff forever. She's still wearing that necklace of tongues. I'm fascinated by the fact that every time this story is read, the whole thing happens again and again and again. I chose that ending for that

reason. Again, the book itself is about stories and this one story is about storytelling. Rat is telling the story and is being interrupted: "This can't happen; a woman can't do those things."

DS: Given that, as you say, you've used the images and material of war in your work as metaphors, are you interested in using other metaphors to talk about those same things?

O'Brien: Yes. The novel I'm writing now, for example, is set in peace time, but some of the issues that I've written about, that I always will write about because they're things I care about, will be present in these other dramatic situations. For me, the intersection of story line and abstraction, a set of concrete events against abstract values, is what moral fiction is about, what storytelling is about. A guy loves his wife. His name is Ed. One day he finds her dead on the carpet and the maid, someone he's been having an affair with, is holding the gun. What does he do? That's a story line: there's Ed, there's Mary dead, and the maid holding the gun. That's concrete stuff, sort of hokey, but the question what does he do next is what's important. Does he turn her in, does he beat her up, does he marry her, does he cover it up? The events of the story intersect with value questions. They have to do with love and rectitude and law, and that's what makes storytelling interesting. I wanted to find different kinds of stories to get to the same value issues. For me those value issues are stable. The story line is put up against them, but the values are there, always floating around.

DB: You said that your new novel started with a sentence that "came" to you. How did you know that was the right sentence?

O'Brien: Because a whole bunch of other sentences preceded it that weren't the right one. I put those aside, the same way you might do when you're writing a poem, until a sentence like "This is true" occurs to you. I guess a sentence like that came to me with the new book. On one level it seemed simple. On the storytelling level it seemed directional—as well as full of mystery. The word "unhappy" is in the sentence. But at this point the thing isn't formed enough. It's only eighty or ninety pages. If I were at two hundred pages, I'd be more sure. That's really all I have to say about it, though. What I've found as I'm getting older is that when you start talking too much about a thing—I'm not superstitious about it, but you find yourself locking yourself in. "I told Dan and Deb that the book is going to be about this." And it's not. Then I have to force it to be that way. You find yourself telling your publisher this and telling other people that, and then you feel especially locked in. So not talking about present work is not superstition so much as it's a fear of being confined. You start thinking it's about this or that, rather than discovering more and more and more. When I tend to abstract or analyze too early on I find myself locked into connecting the dots. I try to avoid that.

DS: But did that sentence come to you before anything else did?

O'Brien: Yes. I had this general sense of "stuff," but it was nothing formed. I'd been writing sentences for three months, until a sentence came that lasted. Each of the sentences I had done before attracted me a little bit, but then I'd cast it aside after an hour or two and try another possibility. Like fishing. I don't know if I was fishing for tuna or carp or minnows. I had no idea what I was fishing for. I just wanted to fish for a little bit. Then I came up with something that's a possibility.

Responsibly Inventing History:
An Interview with Tim O'Brien

Brian C. McNerney/1994

From *War, Literature, and the Arts* 6.2 (1994): 1–26. The interview has been edited for this volume.

This interview took place at the Kellogg Center on the campus of Michigan State University in East Lansing, Michigan, on April 7, 1994. It was the third day of O'Brien's visit as a guest speaker and the day before he had read from *The Things They Carried* and discussed his Vietnam experiences, as well as his experiences as a writer, to a class of students in the course on the war.

One of the principal issues I discussed with Mr. O'Brien during his visit was his reaction to his recent visit to Vietnam—the first since he served there as an infantryman. Because my own interest focused so heavily on the relationship between historical reality and the way O'Brien's combat experiences appear in his fiction, we spent considerable time discussing copies of his military unit's Daily Staff Journal logs. Mr. O'Brien reviewed the same logs at the National Archives in Washington, D.C., prior to his return visit to Vietnam.

Catherine Calloway, who has compiled the most complete bibliographic record of works by and about Tim O'Brien, participated in the interview and provided selected questions. She is a professor of English at Arkansas State University.

McNerney: During a recent trip to Vietnam you got to go back and look at the ground where you served during the war. Were there surprises?
O'Brien: The geography of Vietnam is sacred ground to me in the way that for any of us our backyards, our front yards, are sacred in memory—where our sandboxes and swings used to be. Those memories we carry with us

for the rest of our lives, because of the important events that occurred on such ground. When I returned to Vietnam [17 February–4 March, 1994], I found a few backyards and a few front yards and a few places where I spent my adult-childhood, and the terrain, in its way, hadn't changed. The paddies were shaped as they were by events which occurred twenty years before. There's nothing left on my firebase in terms of barbed wire or buildings, not a scrap. But the outline of the hills on which the firebase was placed is the outline as it was a long time ago, minus all the buildings. In a spooky way, it looks as if ghosts are inhabiting the place now. It's not used for anything because it's heavily mined. The ARVN took it over after we left, and they mined the place. None of the villagers use it for anything now. It's not tilled; it's just there, preserved in a vacuum. And I have a feeling it will be that way for a long time to come.

Twenty years ago, when I wrote *If I Die in a Combat Zone,* I penned a line somewhere in it like, "years and years from now, some veteran will take his wife, or girlfriend, or children over here, then walk the same soil and I'll bet the mines will still be here. The earth will not yet have swallowed and disarmed them." It's a kind of bitter statement saying that this stuff is still here and if you think this war is right, come over and walk this land and see how you like it. That prophecy was in a way fulfilled when I returned. The ghosts are still there. It's as if you close your eyes, you can see the paddies and villages and firebases and so on; you can almost hear the soldiers laughing and drinking. It makes you believe in a spirit world.

McNerney: In "Field Trip" in *The Things They Carried,* you wrote about your vision of what it would be like to go back to Vietnam on an imaginary trip with the character Tim O'Brien's daughter Kathleen. In what ways did your trip confirm the expectation you portrayed in that story?

O'Brien: Pretty much identically. The human imagination is a powerful faculty. We use it all the time in our lives; we live our lives by it. It has to be powerful. You imagined the questions you were going to ask today, for instance, and you imagined the answers. If I were to say I saw a Martian with a green head in Vietnam, you would be surprised, because you expect to hear a different answer, the answer you imagined. When we take a sip of coffee, and we've taken a lot of sips before, the next sip is going to taste pretty much as the sip before it. In all kinds of little ways we use our imaginations to live our lives. We worry about smoking because we imagine dying of cancer. This doesn't stop us from smoking, but it makes us worry—we imagine death—that worry, that bad feeling we have now and then when we take that drag on that cigarette is based on the imagined event for the future: our own death, our own suffering, our own pain. We imagine it more or less fully at times. Sometimes not so fully, other times more fully.

Writing my fiction, I was basing my imagined chapter or story on prior events, what Vietnam had meant to me, what it had been to me, what I had seen there. My knowledge of how geography operates is that it changes very slowly. My imagination of what I would want to do when I got to Vietnam in actuality was to find hallowed ground. The spot where Kiowa died is the made-up event in the "Field Trip" story. And when you imagine these things, then you act on your imagination, you are bound to find some correspondences, including emotional ones. And the emotional correspondence was very precise. A kind of quietude—that sense of ghosts I just talked about. There is something just out there, the sense that things just hadn't changed a lot geographically. I could find places, a sense of barely heard voices in the background. In the case of "Field Trip," it was the interpreter and the daughter laughing and the guy showing her magic tricks. In my own case, it was a camera clicking—the *Time* photographer took pictures. And although the villagers' voices were the present voices, I was hearing the voices of yesterday, voices of twenty-five years ago. So in a large way, the feeling of going back to Vietnam was exactly the way I'd imagined it. That's the power of human imagination. That's why I think we love stories so much. They are future predictors.

McNerney: You reviewed your unit records at the National Archives before you went back to Vietnam. What were you looking for specifically and what did you find?

O'Brien: First, I was looking just to jog my memories, to recall the names of people who'd died. You remember faces when you don't remember names, and you certainly don't remember whole names. I remember a lot of nicknames, for example. We had so many of them. So, first, to jog my memory as to who died, just the names of people. In some cases, I had forgotten entirely people who had died, because I didn't know them very well. You get a company of guys and they rotate in and out. They are just bodies essentially. So that was one reason to go to the archives, to jog my memory.

The more important reason for going there, though, was to find military coordinates, six-digit numbers where events occurred, so I wouldn't go to Vietnam and hump blindly around looking at hedges and paddies and villages, not knowing what was what. I knew that would happen and it would have happened if I'd have gone there without these coordinates—you know, here's where *this* occurred, or *that* occurred. Here's where the tracks ran over us; here's where I was wounded; here's where this guy died, that guy died. By compiling a set of coordinates I was able to go to Vietnam with a map. Once there, I was escorted around by a former VC soldier—a retired army Colonel—who was taking me to places and, by and large, he hit it. In a few cases he said, "You're there." And I looked around and said, "No." I would get the coordinates out and say, "This is where I want to go, *here*." And he would say, "Well, you're here," and I would say, "I know I'm *there* and I don't want to be *there*, I want to be *here*." The coordinates helped. I was able to find a couple of villages that I really had to find.

A third thing happened in going to the archives that I should mention. This is important in terms of your research. As far as I know, you are the first researcher to have gone back to find some of the primary stuff, including myself. I had never gone back to it. It seems to me that this is an important thing for someone to do—to find the soil that literature grows out of. I had forgotten, as we all do, a great deal of my own history. And to recover some of that history, some of that ground—to see it freshly, to see it anew—invigorated me as a writer. It gives you courage to go on and it brings new stories to mind, things you've forgotten. And it makes possible another five years or ten years of writing for me in a lot of ways. So that is a third purpose for visiting the archives. It was a purpose I didn't intend, but that occurred anyway.

McNerney: One thing I found when I looked at the archival material was the name Richard Cacciato, who arrived in country on July 31, 1969, and assumed the duties of battalion adjutant. How, if in any way, did this individual affect your character Cacciato in your novel?

O'Brien: The actual Cacciato did not affect the character, nothing like him. All I did was steal the guy's name. I liked the sound of the name. I remember the first time I saw it, I was out in the field and some document had come in. I was the RTO [radio-telephone operator) for the company commander and the document came to me and I saw the name printed, and I said, "How the hell do you pronounce this?" And I went *catch-chee, cache-shee-ah*, we were joking about it. And then somebody said *Cacciato*—somebody who knew him.

The name stuck partly because we laughed at it, thinking this is not much of a soldier's name. It sounded like the guy should be cooking spaghetti somewhere. And also because when I did learn to pronounce the name I loved the way it came off my tongue. Sort of like "catch." I was already probably thinking that I would be going back to the States if I survived and trying to write about this thing, and the name stuck with me.

The real Cacciato discovered I'd used his name in my book and assumed that I was trying to portray him as a deserter running for Paris. He let me know in no uncertain terms that he wasn't any fucking deserter. And he wasn't. He was a great guy. He was an adjutant in a firebase. We got attacked and mortared often. He was a good soldier. He later became a company commander out in the field and acquitted himself well. So I want to make it clear that the real Richard Cacciato was a terrific officer. All I did was swipe his name because I liked the sound of it.

McNerney: Let's talk for a moment about the officers. We were talking yesterday about how some officers emphasized mission. Sidney Martin comes to mind in *Cacciato* and maybe Smith in *If I Die*. And there are other officers in your novels who have more of a connection with their men than with the mission—a Lieutenant Corson or a Captain Johansen—who don't make the fellows go out, but allow them to report events from a safe haven. How did you respond to your officers in Vietnam, how did the soldiers make distinctions among how these officers emphasized mission or men?

O'Brien: The enlisted men—the common grunts—preferred an officer who put the emphasis on man over mission. That is to say, if we were in a situation, a village, let's say, and we discovered a bunch of tunnels, we wanted an officer who would say, "Look, the mission here is to find weapons, find the VC, and here are these tunnels . . . but let's just blow the damn thing." It's an example I use often in my work because this command dilemma occurred on a regular basis in Vietnam, almost daily. There were tunnels everywhere, bunkers everywhere. If you were to search them all—and they were generally very heavily mined and trapped—pretty soon you'd have no men left. There would be no men left to do the searching.

For me, though, my intellect told me that it was a war and that you are supposed to *win* a war. That's what the Army's objective is supposed to be and I understood intellectually why some officers said, "Let's search. Let's follow the book and search these things. It's SOP [standard operating procedure], we're supposed to do it." I understood why, I just didn't like it. Just like I understand you are supposed to stop smoking. I don't like to stop smoking. Your intellect can know one thing, but your emotion can prefer something else—but I'll tell you this, soldiers preferred the "man over mission" approach.

The officer I most remember, however, emphasized mission over man.

I wrote about him in *If I Die*. I called him Daud. His actual name is Julian Barnes. He died. He was a black Colonel. He was our battalion commander, and he was killed on LZ Gator in an attack one night in May 1969. I think it was May 12th or so. We were out in the field at the time and saw it from a few miles away, saw the firebase all night long. It was a bad attack. Not just Barnes died; I believe four others died, Americans. I discovered in my trip back to Vietnam, in talking to some of the villagers and to the VC, that this particular attack was a planned attack to target that man alone—to kill Barnes. The VC knew where to find him, where his bunker was, where his hootch was. *Because* he was such a good officer. *Because* he emphasized mission so much. That is to say, he was an ass-kicking officer. We lost a lot of men that May, because of the things Barnes was making us do, but the VC were losing a lot of people, too—and they didn't like it.

I remember the day Colonel Barnes gave us a speech. We were in stand-down in Chu Lai for three days before going on to Pinkville for an operation where many people died and were wounded. I was wounded myself in this operation. We all knew we were going to Pinkville. We didn't want to go. We had heard about it from some other soldiers who had been there.

Barnes's speech went something like this: "I'm Colonel Barnes, you guys are going out to Pinkville. It's going to be bad. We are going to lose men. I know that in advance and I don't like it, but I'm going to sacrifice you. Some of you guys are going to die and be wounded. But I have to do it. And I know you don't like it and you probably don't like me. I'm sorry, but you're in the Army and when you are in the Army, you have to do things you don't like."

The guys sort of snorted at him during this speech, yet it was a hell of a good speech. In any case, he wasn't lying to us. I think we respected him while also hating him. In some way, though, we hated him more than we hated the VC, to be honest. The night he died—we heard about it over the radio—we began to sing, "Ding-dong, the wicked witch is dead." I started it. I knew the song to sing. I admit it's a horrible thing. I'm embarrassed by it now—was embarrassed by it then—yet did it anyway, knowing it was an evil thing to do. *A man was dead*. At the same time, I said to myself, "I may live now if the next Colonel isn't quite so gung-ho." That was a long answer to your question, but I had to get it said.

. . . .

McNerney: You were recently singled out in a Vietnam War literature journal for your work, in the way that it was perceived as possibly antifeminist.

You have also had to defend yourself at times from accusations in which you use the words of the Vietnamese themselves, saying that you have not presented the Vietnamese perspective. Does this bother you?

O'Brien: It bothers only insofar as it would bother any human being who has something negative said about his or her person. You don't want to have bad things said about you. It's like being called a shitball, and you'd prefer not being called a shitball if you don't think of yourself as one, and, even if you do think of yourself as one, you don't want to be called one. To that extent it bothers you. The question then becomes one of fairness. You have to ask yourself in a quiet moment if the criticism is valid or not.

Let's do the Vietnamese question first. I haven't pretended to present a Vietnamese viewpoint in my books, except on one or two occasions. In *Cacciato*, I present a character Li Van Hgoc, who is a fable-like character, living down in the earth. I try to imagine what it would be like, in a grossly distorted, almost cartoonish way, to be a Viet Cong or NVA soldier living in the earth. Besides Li Van Hgoc, there is the Vietnamese man I kill off in *The Things They Carried*. There I tried to imagine what it would have been like to have been a scared, young VC draftee. Except for these two occasions, I haven't attempted to present a Vietnamese viewpoint. Why haven't I? Because I don't know it. I don't know the life of the VC and the life of the Vietnamese. I know only a smattering about what Buddhism and Confucianism are. I know only a smattering of the culture. I don't know the language at all. I'm not going to deign to speak for people who can speak very well for themselves.

When I was recently in Vietnam, I talked over this very issue with five or six Vietnamese writers at a literary magazine I visited there. I said, "Other American writers and I have been criticized for not presenting your point of view enough." They laughed and said, "Well, we don't present *your* point of view." It was obvious among us writers that you can't. They said to me and I said to them: *You are capable of speaking for yourself, and I am capable of speaking for myself.* To don the mantle of an alien culture and to pretend to speak for that culture as if you knew it seems to me hubris. I don't want to write for the Vietnamese. They are capable of writing for themselves, and have done very well. Even though a lot of their stuff hasn't been translated yet, they have a thriving literary community that is under incredible pressure from the Vietnamese government. They are always being blackballed and so on, but nonetheless they are speaking for themselves.

The feminist issue is more difficult. It is hard to talk about because things

I say may sound antifeminist, but are, in fact, not. Put another way, I think I often am much more a feminist than the so-called feminists criticizing me.

One fact we live with—and like all facts, there are layers—is that women don't serve in combat in western societies, much. And so in my stories, I don't have women soldiers walking around. Just as an environment, women are excluded. The question then becomes what do you do when women are by nature excluded from participation in events? What do you do with women? Which view do you take? And what role do they play dramatically in the making of a work of art? If to place a woman in a combat setting would be to violate the rules of credibility that rule verisimilitude, then you end up having characters talk about women.

There are a couple of lines—I'll just take a couple of examples—one is in *If I Die* where a soldier says, "She's sort of pretty for a gook." Well, on the surface it seems like an utterly misogynistic statement, and racist at that. Which it is. But my role as a writer is not to make up a world that is better than it is. My role is to report the world as it is. And that statement is a very delicate way of saying something that is said in much stronger language and much more offensive language every day by men in a war. I wouldn't have a character say after being shot, "Oh, poop, I've been shot!" instead of "Oh, shit!" Similarly, you wouldn't have soldiers talking about women or making comments that they wouldn't ordinarily make in the real world. What I'm trying to say is that while I'm recording a thing, I'm not necessarily endorsing it. When Dostoyevsky writes about murder in *Crime and Punishment*, he's not endorsing the acts of Raskolnikov. He is thinking of the complications of a man pretending he is superman. You don't blame the messenger for the news. What are some of the statements made about my work in particular that would make it seem antifeminist?

McNerney: There is, for example, the business at the end of "How to Tell a True War Story," where the woman comes up and says that she doesn't like war stories. And I guess some critics have said that this implies that women are not smart enough or not intuitive enough to understand a war story. As you have said before, "Sweetheart of the Song Tra Bong" is a kind of answer to the depiction of women which may present them as less understanding or less in contact with the emotional force of what's going on in your war stories.

O'Brien: I believe that, by and large, women in America don't like war stories. That is, if you asked a cross-section of women demographically selected, "Would you read a war story?" or "Would you prefer war stories to love stories, father stories, mother stories, son stories," I believe you are going to find the dominant statistical answer being, "Women don't like war stories." It doesn't mean that women are not perspicacious. It doesn't mean that they are not smart. It doesn't mean that they are not intuitive. It means that women prefer not to read war stories. The question then becomes *why*? And my answer to that is a cultural one. It is that because women are excluded by law from serving in combat, and up until recently were really discriminated against from serving in the armed forces in general. I believe they still are to some extent. This exclusion explains, I think, why women would prefer not to read about something with which they cannot identify. Beyond that, another reason that women may not like war stories has to do with how war stories oftentimes are bad stories—full of cliché, blood, death, bullets, bombs, purposeless stereotypes, glorification of war. All these are valid reasons not to like war stories. And so when the woman at the end of "How to Tell a True War Story" says, "Ordinarily I don't like war stories, this one I liked," it is supposed to be a backhanded compliment to that woman. This war story she liked because, I hope, it isn't stereotypical, isn't predictable, isn't melodramatic. It touches a woman's spirit the same way it would touch a man's spirit.

What I'm criticizing is the culturally caused statistical propensity on the part of women to not give war stories the same open-minded consideration that I would give to a story about a feminist and a professor in a college. If it is expected that I should be able to read *Madame Bovary*, a book about a woman written by a man, I can expect that a woman, through acts of the imagination, acts of cultural identification, acts of socialization, would someday write a war story as good as any I could write. What I'm doing is criticizing a culture that unfairly has excluded women from the responsibility of taking part in a social phenomenon: war.

There is another level to my response to feminist criticism of my work that is a little angry. And that level is that it seems to me that women are going to have to acknowledge that men are being treated unfairly when they are sent to war. I don't think women have thought about it much. I think women, by and large, in western society take it for granted that they don't have to serve in combat, and it's not even thought about much. It's just a given. It's as if God has somehow granted a divine right to women: *You don't have to die in combat. You don't have to go through this horror.* Well, God didn't mandate this privilege, man did. Law did. Tradition did. Culture did.

It seems to me that excluding women from combat is a clear violation of the equal protection clause of the Fourteenth Amendment to our Constitution. We should all be treated fairly. Why not only draft blacks, or only draft Albanians, or only draft Italians? There would be a revolution in this country in any of those cases. "How to Tell a True War Story" is meant to call attention to a fundamental inequity. Half our population is excluded from the horror of serving in combat. I want to call attention to that fact.

I want also to say that I think there is an unsubstantiated belief that gender determines bellicosity. Based on people like Lizzie Borden or Catherine the Great, I can't say that women are absolutely and utterly nonviolent creatures. It seems to me to be a kind of denigration of women to contend such a thing. To say "We are not capable of belligerence, we're not capable of anger, we're not capable of this" seems to me to denigrate women. The so-called feminists who say, "We, the women, are the nurturers; we are the lovers; we are the child-bearers of the world; we are endowed with a God-given goodness that men are not endowed with" is to violate a fundamental humanity about women. The experience of the human race is that women know what sin is, know what evil is, and have participated in both in their own ways. I'm rebelling against a stereotype. I would think a feminist would be applauding me for this. I would think a feminist would be saying, "You are right!—our gender doesn't make us less than human."

. . . .

McNerney: Can the nonparticipant understand the combat experience through literature? Is there even such a thing as an essential quality of war?
O'Brien: No, there's not. War is everything. In "How to Tell a True War Story" I make a long list: war is adventure; war is holiness; war is pity; war is longing; war is love; war is ghosts. The list is long. War is a multiplicity of events. Maybe always, but certainly now, for me, the environment of war is the environment of life, magnified. That is, instead of mortality pressing on us twenty years from now—the possibility, say, of cancer—it is pressing on me now. The stakes of living in a war are enhanced only because of the awareness of the proximity of death. That is to say, I'm almost dead with every step I take in a war as opposed to fifty steps to the day I get cancer or have a first heart attack. We are all living in a war. It's just that the wolf isn't quite at the door. The wolf is sort of baying in the woods, in the lives we live in the ordinary world. The wolf is out there baying, but it's a ways away. Whereas in a war, the wolf is right at the door scratching and the door

is unlocked and partly open and you're trying to keep it closed. The enemy is right there; death is right there. We just don't recognize it in ordinary life, but with every breath we take, we are one breath closer to the grave.

I hope that my work will ultimately have its effect in understanding the war of living. The stakes are always high. We are always almost dead in our lives—we just don't know it. The problems and dilemmas presented in a war setting are essentially the problems and dilemmas of living itself. It's hard to be brave in the ordinary world. It's hard to know what bravery is in the ordinary world. It's hard to know what rectitude is in the ordinary world because we are often put into situations of paradox. In the daily world you are in these situations constantly, trying to adjudicate that which is ultimately insoluble. I love her but I also love *her*. What should I do? I love them both. Who are you going to live with? Who are you going to marry? Who are you going to be faithful to? That is just one example which should hit home to women, men, Martians, Albanians. It should be specific to nothing except to humanity itself. Those paradoxes which war presents with the wolf at the door are there all the time. I hope that when my books are read, they'll reverberate for those reasons, for those who have never experienced war and never will, but experience daily, a different war: the war of life itself.

I receive a lot of letters about my work. I would say that at least 80 percent of the letters I receive are from women. Maybe more. The letters are from the mothers of soldiers who served in Vietnam and Desert Storm and other wars. They are from sisters. Women married to these guys. All say essentially the same thing. "Thank you for writing this book because now I feel something in terms of identification, and in terms of participation that I didn't feel before. My husband can't talk about it, but now I sort of understand why he doesn't, why he can't." There is a joy that you get receiving that kind of a letter as opposed to a letter from a vet saying, "I read your book and thank you for writing it; it echoed my experience." I don't have to echo his experience. He knows what his experience was. He's been there. It's nice to have an echo, but he doesn't need it the same way that a child of nineteen needs it before trying to make up his or her mind whether to join the army. Or the citizen needs it when it comes time to enter the booth to vote. Or that a woman needs to be able to give comfort or counsel to a husband suffering or a child trying to decide to join the military or not.

What I'm trying to say is the joy I get is probably the same joy Conrad got when he would get letters from people who weren't sailors, saying, God, you know, thank you for that experience of going through that typhoon. Now I've had an experience I couldn't have otherwise. That's the joy. The joy is not the joy of touching veterans or touching people who have lived what you have lived. The joy is just the opposite. Maybe that's what hurts me when I hear that articles are being written by women saying I am an antifeminist. The whole creative joy is to touch the hearts of people whose hearts otherwise wouldn't be touched. That's why it hurts to have these things saying I am antifeminist. It hurts me badly because the purpose of art is to touch the human heart in its solidarity and solidity. Art has very little to do with the differences among us, more to do with the similarities we share.

Calloway: You mentioned yesterday that you don't want to write another novel.

O'Brien: What I want to do is write short stories. A novel takes so much out of your life. How many years do I have left? I am forty-seven and let's say I live to eighty. Well, I haven't got a lot of years left. It takes me five to eight years to write a novel, give or take. They used to take less, but now they're taking that long. That's not many more books. I'm aware of the limits of my life now as we all are when we get older. I would prefer to be able to do fifty stories about different facets of the world as opposed to just three or four more books, which is all I probably would be able to finish. There are so few gratifications that come to the writer. And to have to wait eight years to receive the gratification of a book coming out is too long for me to wait now.

You should never trust what a writer says about his goals because they are so fluid, but given the way I feel now, I can't imagine writing another book. And if I can't imagine it, the odds are slim that I'll do it. I have to be able to imagine a thing before I can do it. What I can imagine is writing stories. Maybe forty-page, fifty-page stories. But still just stories.

Tim O'Brien Interview

Tobey C. Herzog/1995

Excerpted from *South Carolina Review* 31.1 (1998): 78–109. A version of this interview also appeared in *Writing Vietnam, Writing Life* (U of Iowa P, 2008). Reprinted with permission of Clemson University Digital Press.

This published interview with author Tim O'Brien is based on approximately seven hours of conversation I had with the author on July 9 and 10, 1995, in his apartment in Cambridge, Massachusetts. My purpose for the interview was to gather biographical and literary information for my book on O'Brien (*Tim O'Brien*, Twayne's United States Authors Series, 1997). As a result, I divided my questions into those related to O'Brien's roles as a son, soldier, and author. Within these categories, we discussed a wide range of subjects including O'Brien's childhood, adolescence, and college years at Macalester; his tour of duty in Vietnam and his attitudes toward this war; his years as a graduate student at Harvard; his development as an author; his process and goals for writing fiction; and key underlying themes in his books. Although we discussed all of O'Brien's six books and a few of his essays and short stories, my particular focus was on his most recent novel, *In the Lake of the Woods* (Houghton Mifflin, 1994).

For this condensed version of the interview, I have eliminated dated information, O'Brien's off-the-record comments, some information appearing in other published interviews, and exchanges unrelated to the focus of this published version of our conversation. Also, in a few places, I have shortened some of O'Brien's responses and altered the order of questions during the two days to create a greater unity and coherence for this published interview. My purpose is to illustrate the intimate relationship between O'Brien's life and his writing, the significant thematic and structural interconnections of his works, and the underlying mystery and ambiguity in his life and writing.

Preface

H: One of the central metaphors in your most recent novel, *In the Lake of the Woods*, is that of the author as magician. In the "Evidence" section of this novel you include an excerpt from the *Magician's Handbook* that states magicians should never explain their tricks to an audience. Do you believe authors explain their "literary tricks" during interviews?

O'B: I suppose in a way, but I wouldn't call a piece of literature a "trick" exactly. It is a work of art, and to explain a work of art is ultimately to kill a work of art the same way to explain a trick is to kill a trick. Works of art are not explicable, in my opinion, any more than a human life is explicable. Human lives are, like books, mysteries, combinations of circumstances and what's said and what's done. To explain away the flesh and blood of a work of art is a kind of murder.

Son

H: Let's move to this first section of the interview on your role as a son. What are some details about your family life that give people an insight into your development as an author?

O'B: I think the fact that my mom was a school teacher, an elementary school teacher, had a lot to do with my interest in books, reading, grammar, and things like that. She cared about where commas, apostrophes, and dashes go, things that in the long run make a huge difference to a writer. Without a command of the code, which is English, you cannot fulfill yourself as a writer. You can't make full use of the English repertoire. I think, too, that my father, who was on the library board and an avid reader, was a huge influence, bringing books into the house—stacks of them—from the time I was very young until the time that I left home to go to college. There were always books around, and I would pick them up and read them.

H: What are some of the books that you read as a young person?

O'B: As a very young person I was big on *Grimm's Fairy Tales*. I read *Tom Sawyer* when I was very young. I read *Huckleberry Finn* when I was very young, not reading it the way that you read it in college, but just reading it as a story. I remember reading little *Wonder Books*, those tiny books for kids, from the time I was six to about nine. *Timmy Is a Big Boy Now* was my favorite *Wonder Book*. The book is still around: I saw it in a friend's house whose son's name is Tim. *Larry of the Little League* was influential. I played little league as a kid in Worthington, Minnesota, and that book really caught my attention and made me try my hand at my first work of fiction called "Timmy of the Little League." I think I was ten or eleven when I wrote this little thirty-page piece, what I called a novel.

H: As you were growing up, did your family spend a lot of time discussing books, politics, ideas, religion, values?

O'B: Yes. Discussion was constant around the dinner table. Those things came up constantly. Their reference points usually were such things as movies, TV programs, articles in magazines, books, and so on. And then the discussion would move from the particular to the general: from an article on the hydrogen bomb to a discussion of whether we were up against a nuclear war or not or whether Worthington would be hit and what the consequences might be from fallout. I remember this issue being a continuing one at fourteen, fifteen, sixteen years old. Politics was discussed a lot, especially during the Kennedy and early Johnson years. Religion was discussed in a fully heated way. My father was a lapsed Catholic. My mother was a Methodist. My father certainly scoffed at religions of all sorts, scoffs to this day at the trappings of religion—especially Catholicism. The genuflection, the modern Popes' positions on social issues. My mother was a staunch defender of "meat-and-potatoes" Midwestern religion. You go to church every Sunday.

H: During your childhood and adolescence, did you have any particular heroes, other than Timmy and Larry from the children's books?

O'B: Oh, sure. There were all sorts of heroes—heroes out of the imaginary world. Huck Finn getting on that raft was a hero, escaping the social conventions of small town Missouri. And I wanted to get the hell out of small town Minnesota. There were no rivers to float away on, so I imagined other means. But, nevertheless, Huck was a hero of mine. As a youngster, I had imaginary heroes like every young kid: Roy Rogers, Gene Autry, the Lone Ranger—cowboy heroes. They were the kind of hero who knew right from wrong and was willing to act on this knowledge to the point of risking his life. There was another sort of hero: Lash LaRue, Hoot Gipson, Tom Mix. I'm going way back to those black-and-white B-movies that I would watch on Saturday mornings on television. . . . I also had real-life heroes. Those were sporting types. Ted Williams was a big hero of mine, also a first baseman for the New York Yankees named Bill "Moose" Skowron because he played once for the Austin, Minnesota, Packers and I was born in Austin, Minnesota.

H: Any political figures as heroes?

O'B: President Kennedy was a hero of mine as a high school student. I actually went to Minneapolis to listen to a speech he gave. So I wasn't just a long-distance worshipper. I really admired his politics, but I'm not so sure that I'd be such a fan today. Back then, notions like the Peace Corps meant a lot to me. His seeming elegance of style meant a lot to me, the way that he carried himself, his wit, his intelligence. All those qualities impressed me and still do. I'm not so sure some of his politics impress me as much now as they did back then.

H: In your books an important theme related to growing up has to do with father-son relationships. Did you have a close relationship with your father? Was he a model or hero for you?

O'B: It was a difficult relationship, like everything, complicated. On one hand he was a model—his intelligence, his wit, his grace in public, an extremely stylish guy. A charming man. His capacity to devour books and to understand what he was reading impressed me and does to this day. His judgments about literature impressed me then and to this day still do. His judgments are ordinarily pretty black and white, but they are firm; they are heartfelt, not wishy-washy. They are not complicated sometimes, but firm. And he has good reasons for them. Those things impressed me.

We had a lot of problems, too. I was picked on a lot as a kid. For reasons that I still don't understand, I was teased relentlessly, at least it seemed to me, from the time I was nine years old until I left for college. I felt that I was never good enough for him, could never please him no matter what I had accomplished. And to this day I still don't understand what it was that didn't please him. I wanted desperately to win his love, affection, and esteem but never seemed to be able to do it, no matter what I did in the world. He was an alcoholic, bad alcoholic, institutionalized a couple of times. His alcoholism hurt me deeply. That is, it changed his personality so radically that it made him very hard to be with. That had a lot to do with his taunting of me and his nonstop teasing. He could detect how much I despised the change in personality that he would go through, and because he could detect it, he would call me on it.

Dinner would be especially difficult because he would sometimes begin drinking after work, and by the time dinner came around, he would be sullen and way inside himself. And the man that I loved and adored, the charming and stylish guy, had vanished. That was a horrible, horrible time in my life, all through junior high and high school. He would vanish into institutions, and I would wonder when he was coming back—if he was coming back and in what condition. I was always hoping for some radical change that never came about.

H: You mentioned your father teased you at the supper table. What were some of the things he teased you about?

O'B: Weight was one thing. He would taunt me about my response to his alcoholism in a sense. He could feel my disgust at his drinking and would turn it on me in a funny way: "What's wrong? What's wrong with you?"

I want to say a couple of things, though. I hope you downplay some of this information as much as you can. I don't mind you using this stuff, but I don't want to make it appear as if this guy is all foul. He had many, many virtues and to this day still does. And I want to make sure that those virtues balance the negative aspects of my Dad's problem. Among his virtues is his intelligence; he's also well read. He was extremely supportive of me in things like Little League and managing the team. Played ball with me all the time. Taught me to golf. Took me golfing with him all the time. Took me on trips with him when he would go out and sell insurance. A lot of times when he was sober he was a terrific father. And I want to make it real clear that his influence on me was probably dominantly affirmative as opposed to dominantly negative, but coming across in our conversation, because we are spending so much time on it, is the dominantly negative. It was the opposite. It was a dominantly positive influence.

H: You have mentioned elsewhere that you performed magic tricks when you were a youngster. How and why did you get involved with magic?

O'B: Books again, through the library. I remember checking out a number of books on magic from the Worthington Public Library. I don't remember the titles of any of these books, but I can picture the covers. One author that I do remember is Bruce Sevron. . . . In any case, when I was ten or eleven years old, I began practicing the hobby fairly rigorously, every day. On trips to New York that we took periodically for my dad, insurance conventions that my dad would go to, I visited Lou Tannon's Magic Store in New York City, which was a mecca for big-time magicians where real illusions were sold, expensive illusions. And I would always end up getting a twenty- or thirty-dollar trick. My father would buy it for me.

Magic for me was a way of escaping the world at that time. It was a terrible time at home—my sense of not being loved, my father's alcoholism, my feeling lonely. So I think that it was a form of escape, of trying to change that world, that mad world, a little bit—making miracles happen, a way of earning applause.

H: As a child, were you interested in world events and politics?

O'B: Well, I was interested in only the way a small-town kid is. Not until high school did I develop a serious interest. Through grade school and junior high school I was interested only so far as the world had a direct impact on my life. I remember, for example, in Worthington, an American prisoner of war returning from Korea. And there was a big hoopla, a parade in Worthington. That interested me.

I played war games out on the golf course as a kid. Sort of war games based on war stories I heard from my dad and stories I heard from adults who had served as foot soldiers in Germany or the Pacific. Games based on comic books and on movies. Audie Murphy's *To Hell and Back* was a movie that impressed me a lot. *Pork Chop Hill* was another movie that impressed me a lot. And as a kid I played these games. I was the American hero, and there were Germans and Japanese to be killed out on that golf course. There was an Army surplus store in Worthington that sold relics from WWII and Korea—ammunition belts, helmet liners, canteens, and the like. I would buy these things and strap them on. In that way, the history of earlier wars influenced the games I played as a kid. Also, the games I played as a kid in some respects reflected my self-image: "Tim the Hero" and just like the Lone Ranger—"Tim the Lone Ranger." That whole constellation of imagination and history, those heroes from both sources, combined in my head to form a self-portrait of sorts that suggested when the time came I would be physically brave and morally brave.

H: How did this period of your life—growing up in Worthington—contribute to your development as an author?

O'B: In myriad ways, so many ways that it's impossible to articulate anything more important than another. The threads are not only numerous, but they are also incredibly important in my work: the father theme, the theme of heroism, the theme of history and war. There's the theme of loneliness and alienation. There's the theme of the importance of imagination in our lives as a way to escape and to change the world. There's also the theme of magic that runs through all of my work, even the most realistic of my work like *If I Die*. That is to say, artistry is a kind of trickery or a kind of illusion building. Those are just big chunks of my books that have their sources in childhood.

H: At Macalester College, which you entered in the fall of 1964, you were involved in campus politics and served as student body president during your senior year. Had you set a goal for yourself of being well known and popular in college?

O'B: No. It wasn't a glory sort of thing. It was back in the era when student politics mattered in a way that I don't think that they matter so much today. The Vietnam War was raging. A lot of what I tried to do as a student politician had to do with the war. A lot of it had to do with social issues. This whole in *loco parentis* business was then at the forefront of the students' and administration's attention: visitation rights, coeducational dorms, things like this that are taken for granted today that open up the social life of students and lead to their being treated not as wards, but as human beings. You have to remember that the war was going on and people were dying at age eighteen. They might be sent over there, and they were being treated on campus as wards of the school. It was not a happy combination. And it wasn't treated happily by the kids on campus, myself included. That too was an important part of my awakening. I don't think today that sort of political activity is seen the way it was back then.

H: In a couple of other published interviews you mention that there weren't many organized war protests at Macalester, just a few antiwar activists. What were your own views about the war at the time?

O'B: I was opposed to it. There were active campus debates. Macalester wasn't a radical school. That is to say, it wasn't full of Communists and SDS [Students for a Democratic Society] types. But it was an extremely politically conscious school, partly because of the [Walter] Mondale and [Hubert H.] Humphrey connections to the school and partly because some of the professors at the school were well known in Minnesota politics. A fellow named Ted Mitau had written numerous textbooks that were well known and are still well known today. He later became Chancellor of the Minnesota State University system. It was a highly politicized school, and the war was debated in campus forums. I personally took part in many of these debates, stood in peace vigils, and rang doorbells for Gene McCarthy when he ran for president.

H: Why did you become so actively involved in the Eugene McCarthy campaign?

O'B: I can't say that I was all that active. I wasn't an everydayer. I was a weekender. Why involved? I guess because the war seemed ill conceived and wrong. At the time, McCarthy was the only candidate who had taken a political stand against the war. I remember right after he announced for the presidency, he spoke in Macalester's fieldhouse, and it was jammed with supporters. It was a heady occasion. I was full of hope. I was a children's crusader in my soul. I wanted that war ended so badly. But I wanted it ended through legitimate political means, a view that separated me in that year, 1968, from the years that followed, '69, '70, '71, when more and more violent means were both advocated and used by students and by the [Jerry] Rubins and the [Abbie] Hoffmans and the Yippie movement, whom I had no sympathy for and had no relationship with. My attitude was an old-fashioned liberal attitude; change is effected though legitimate political means: caucuses, elections, and so on.

H: How did this period of your life at Macalester contribute to your development as an author?

O'B: In a couple of traditional ways. One that we haven't touched on was that I took some terrific courses in English [although a political science major] at Macalester, taught by wonderful professors: Roy Swanson, Harley Henry, Roger Blakley. Courses in the modern novel and American Colonial literature. I remember going through *Ulysses* in a study group indexing the book, bit by bit by bit, mapping that book out. I had my first exposure to Faulkner and *The Sound and the Fury*, to Hemingway and *The Sun Also Rises*, to Dos Passos, and to Fitzgerald. I also read a lot of Hawthorne and the American Colonial period writers. I was excited about literature in a way that I hadn't been prior to taking these courses. I had read a lot as a kid, was interested in books in general, but I liked them for story and for what they would do to me emotionally. But the technical aspects of fiction excited me in college for the first time. I have a feeling that had I not taken those courses and not had the great professors I wouldn't be a novelist today.

Soldier

H: Let's move to the next section of this interview—your experiences with the Vietnam War. Had you been accepted into Harvard graduate school when your draft notice arrived in May 1968?
O'B: Yes, I had been.

H: With a possible graduate school deferment in mind, did you talk with the draft board?
O'B: No. I didn't. I suppose I should have. But didn't. I assumed that it was hopeless. I had no grounds for appealing the 1-A classification or getting drafted. There just weren't any grounds for it. I wasn't a conscientious objector—no history of it, no religious background to call upon. My thoughts were centered on one of three possibilities: go to the war, go to Canada, or go to jail. Those were the three possibilities that seemed feasible.

H: Did you think about securing draft counseling about options to avoid the draft?
O'B: No, my thoughts were thoughts of the imagination and fantasy. I would fantasize that I was going to Canada, crossing the Rainy River. I'd fantasize getting in my car and just driving away. They were fantasy kinds of thoughts. They were elaborate fantasies. They were waking fantasies. I would imagine what I would have to pack, what documents I would have to bring, what clothes I would bring along, where I would leave the car, and the note I would leave for my parents. I mean they were elaborate heuristic exercises.

H: You spent so much of your young life playing war games on the golf course and encountering war stories and acts of heroism, but when you came face to face with the Vietnam War, you were against the war. Was your opposition strictly political?
O'B: From a political, humanistic ground, not just politics. It seemed a barbarous, inhuman war, a war fought for uncertain reasons. War, in my opinion, having read a lot of Aquinas, requires some sort of just cause, like WWII. . . . My thoughts were that Vietnam did not have a clear, just cause behind it. It was a war that contained a myriad of ambiguities: legal, philosophical, moral, historical, and ambiguities of *fact*—pure fact. What happened in the Gulf of Tonkin [August 1964] on those two separate nights? What really happened? There was so much ambiguity reflected in the national response to that war. There was ambiguity of support for the war. That

ambiguity grew more and more gray as time went on, to the point where it became really conspicuous that there wasn't a lot of political support for the war. My thought then, and it remains to this day, is that you don't kill people and you don't die when everything is so ambiguous. There wasn't some sense of consensus on the side of rectitude for that war.

H: Paul Fussell in *The Great War and Modern Memory* analyzes World War I memoirs and comments on their basic three-part structure of prewar innocence, battlefield experience and disillusionment, and then a postwar consideration stage. Other soldier-authors from other wars also adopt this tripartite structure for their books. In your war memoir, *If I Die in a Combat Zone*, you definitely portray the experience stage, and you obviously have a consideration stage. But the innocence stage is missing.

O'B: There's not an innocent stage. I didn't go to war as an innocent. I went to war knowing, at least convinced, that the Vietnam War was ill conceived and morally wrong. That was my conviction. I didn't go to war an innocent. I went to war a "guilt," that is to say "guilt" being a sort of weird noun. I was not an innocent; I was a "guilt." I knew that the war was wrong. I wasn't a Henry Fleming. I wasn't a [Philip] Caputo or a Ron Kovic. I wasn't a Paul Baumer. My situation was different, and it separates me from a lot of veterans to this day. It doesn't make me better or worse, but different, in the sense that I believed that the war was wrong and I went to it anyway. I didn't go to the war with a sense that I was going to prove my own courage or for reasons of glory, for reasons of adventure, for patriotic reasons—a lot of the variables that send men off to war and that are so conspicuous in most literature about Vietnam and other wars. In my case, these didn't apply.

H: In the Audie Murphy movies you watched as a child, a standard of heroism and courage appears that resembles the unthinking courage you describe in *If I Die*, a courage without wisdom or understanding—the "charge-up-the-hill" courage.

O'B: Yes. And I despise that. That is to say, I learned it as a kid and practiced it on the golf course. It was a childhood value that changed through junior high and into high school and into college. I thought it was ridiculous and stupid [in Vietnam] to die for glory, to die for honor, to die for reasons that seemed to me less than fully human.

H: When you were visiting a class at Wabash College in November 1994, you reluctantly talked about receiving a Purple Heart for wounds you received two months after arriving in Vietnam and being awarded a Bronze Star for rescuing a fellow soldier. Tell me more about this last event.

O'B: It was just a common thing; it was nothing. I think I told the class that it was nothing that wasn't done every day by somebody. A guy was wounded, and I ran out and pulled him back. That's all there was to it.

H: Was it an unthinking act of courage?

O'B: No, thinking. I was scared shitless, but also thinking, "The guy's hurt." Partly, I was calculating the odds. "What are the odds that I'm going to get shot?" It wasn't a huge firefight. The odds of getting shot were not that great. I think that if it had been a full-scale sort of Okinawa battle, you know just grease [weapons fire] all over the place, I would have calculated my odds of being hit, and they would have been a lot more severe, maybe on the side of just waiting ten minutes. There was a slight calculation, but the odds seemed pretty slim that I was going to get hurt. It was over in twenty seconds.

H: Tell me a little bit more about your writing activities while you were in Vietnam. You didn't keep a journal but wrote vignettes. What was the reason for writing these pieces?

O'B: I don't know why, preferable to writing letters in some ways. A letter seems so personal that you cannot get the full truth out. Writing vignettes instead of letters, I could be more objective, slight distance. My letters tended to be full of self-pity and terror.

H: At what point did you know that when you returned to the United States you were going to try to publish some of these vignettes?

O'B: I did publish a couple of them when I was in Vietnam.

H: You sent them to your local newspaper?

O'B: The Minneapolis paper, two or three pieces that appear in *If I Die.* I think two pieces were in the *Minneapolis Star* and one or two appeared in my hometown newspaper the *Worthington Daily Globe.* All of these were rewritten for the book. And then I sent a piece into *Playboy* that was accepted after I got back from Vietnam and appeared July of 1970, called "Step Lightly," about land mines.

H: The hamlet of My Lai and its surrounding area called "Pinkville" by American soldiers, as well as the My Lai massacre (which occurred almost a year prior to your arrival in Vietnam) obviously have had considerable impact on you personally as well as on your writing. Why?

O'B: Probably the physical place of Pinkville, how beat up it was and scarred and mangled. How hostile the remaining villagers were. There weren't many left, but those who did remain in those villages, My Khe and My Lai, were hostile; you could smell it and taste it in the air. As a company, we were terrified whenever we were sent into this area. It was full of land mines, just littered with land mines. The odds were very very high that somebody would hit a mine when we were out there. You prayed to God it wouldn't be you. There was no strong enemy to fight. That is to say, we never faced any battalion, even though we were searching for the mythical 48th Mekong Battalion. We never found them, never even saw them, as far as I know. We never had any fire from them. We were getting a lot of sniper fire, a lot of short little firefights. Mostly it was just mine after mine after mine after mine after mine. The land just blew us to smithereens. We were afraid of the physical place the way kids are afraid of closets or darkness under the bed. The bogeyman feel of that place still haunts me. I still dream about the physical place. I don't dream about events that occurred, but I dream stories that happened in that hell—devastation and ghosts, the ghosts being the ghosts of My Lai. But they are not just from My Lai. The ghosts are from what happened prior to my getting there in terms of the bombing of the place, the wreckage of this area, the dislocation of all the villagers. They were taken out of the villages and put into little tin huts, concentration camp villages. My Lai was a place where evil had occurred, conspicuously had occurred. You could tell by the wreckage all around, even prior to the My Lai thing breaking. . . . These acts caused among the populace that we were trying to save, not just anger, but incredible sorrow and grief that was palpable as we walked around this place. And the response to all the savagery on the part of the enemy was to litter the place with land mines and blow the shit out of us. The place was blown to shit anyway, so why not blow some more?

H: In *If I Die*, you mention that one of the things that emerged from your Vietnam experiences was the vow you made to yourself to return to the United States and crusade against this war.

O'B: That I've done, haven't I? I haven't kept many promises. That one I did keep.

H: But obviously yours is not a crusade against all wars. It is more a crusade against *this* war.

O'B: *This* war and wars that are analogous, which there are some. I'm thinking of the Spanish-American War, or what we did in the Philippines during the Spanish-American War, before and after. What happened in the Crimea or in South Africa, the Boer War. My crusade is against an ignorant imposition of one nation's will on the aspirations and desires of another nation. I guess I should say the "legitimate aspirations and desires of another nation." That excludes, for example, Hitler's aspirations and desires. I can't say this is a true crusade, but a literary expression of disgust and anger about what can happen when a nation goes to war out of ignorance and inflated will.

H: Tim, we have been talking about your Vietnam battlefield experiences, but I want to discuss briefly the few months after you returned from Vietnam [March 1970]. At this time, did you write about your war experiences?
O'B: If I did, I don't remember it. I do remember writing when I got to Harvard. Once I got there and began graduate studies, after a day's work of studying and going to classes, I'd sit down for two or three hours a night and write the vignettes that later became part of *If I Die*.

H: In 1970 veterans' protests were occurring in Washington, including those organized by the Vietnam Veterans Against the War (VVAW). Did you think about joining that organization when you returned from the war?
O'B: I was in absolute sympathy, but I wasn't a joiner, and in a way regret it. That is, I wish I had taken a stand then in a way that was political—gone to Washington and thrown my medals at the White House or at the Capitol steps, wherever they were demonstrating. On the other hand, I'm pretty sure I was doing the same thing through my writing. I took my writing seriously. At that point, I really did want to get a book out [*If I Die*] about the realities of the war. It seemed that a lot of the literature about Vietnam coming out at that time, which was 1972 and '73, was of the patriotic grunt experience—sort of the "we did our best, came home disillusioned, but disillusioned only because we couldn't win the war." I wanted to write a book about the infantryman's experience through the eyes of a soldier who acknowledged the obvious: that we were killing civilians more than we were killing the enemy. The war was aimless in the most basic ways, that is, aimless in the sense of nothing to aim at, no enemy to shoot, no target to kill. The enemy was among the people. As a consequence, the fire put out was put out in massive quantities against whole villages, whole populations. I wanted to write a book that got at that. So I felt that I was doing something.

H: Have you ever thought why, upon your return from the war, you seemed, perhaps, more well-adjusted compared to other Vietnam veterans who were having problems?

O'B: I think it was because I acknowledged from the beginning, even before going to Vietnam, that I was a coward, guilty. I have never changed this opinion of myself. I've been urged to, billions of times by billions of people at billions of readings: "Oh, you weren't a coward. You did the right thing. You did what you had to do." All of which is bullshit. None of which I believe about myself. To believe that about oneself is to forgive oneself for the un-forgivable. Or to lie about oneself. Or both. And I'll be damned if I'm going to lie about myself. I did the wrong thing. I shouldn't have taken part in the war, given what I believed. That is to say, others can do what they want to do, follow their own conscience. In my case I committed an act of unpardonable cowardice and evil. I went to a war that I believed was wrong, and I actively participated in it. I pulled the trigger. I was there. And by being there I am guilty. And the issue then becomes what do you do afterward? To me, acknowledging the guilt helped me, from the start, helped me adjust, as opposed to kidding myself and finding out later.

H: Are you suggesting that some returning Vietnam veterans had adjustment problems because of their great disillusionment about their war experience?

O'B: They had fantasies of themselves as one thing and discovered later they're not. When one discovers months or years later that one is wrong, there is bound to be a horrible aftershock. In my case, I didn't need to have that discovered. It had been discovered prior to my going. In a way, this realization makes my sins worse than theirs.

H: Is too much attention given in books, magazines, and newspapers to Vietnam veterans suffering from posttraumatic stress disorder (PTSD)? Is this attention unfair to well-adjusted veterans?

O'B: Mostly unfair to the Vietnamese more than anything. There hasn't been enough written about the impact of the war on those who suffered most, the millions of Vietnamese who died or who were wounded. We had 59,000 American deaths, God knows how many wounded. But nothing comparable to what the Vietnamese suffered. I'm not talking just about the enemy soldiers, I'm talking about babies, women, and teenagers. The devastation in terms of human life that the war caused the Vietnamese hasn't been faced by America. It's sort of been acknowledged in a general abstract sense, but not in a visceral sense. A lot of visceral suffering of Americans has been examined in our writings about the war, a lot of hand wringing, a lot of psychological second-guessing and third-guessing. Confession about the suffering of Americans and American soldiers. But that stuff is way out of scale to what we ought to be looking at from the other side.

H: Finally, regarding this Vietnam War period of your life, what did it contribute to your development as an author?

O'B: Well, it's impossible to answer. In one respect it's like asking Toni Morrison, "What has being black contributed to your being a writer?" Well, it contributes a lot. More particularly, it's like asking Conrad, "What did your time at sea contribute to your being a writer?" A lot, that is, in terms of memory and material, event, dialogue, situation, setting, smell. All of that stuff. I couldn't have written the books that I've written without war. I wouldn't have had that material any more than Conrad would have had all the ocean experiences to write *Nigger of the* Narcissus, *Lord Jim*, or *Victory*. He couldn't have done it. At the same time, the things we talked about earlier in the interview—way back to those childhood events, influences, and interests—are of equal importance, that is, issues of imagination, fantasy, background in the English language and its uses, fathers-sons. All that stuff is equally important.

About Tim O'Brien: A Profile

Don Lee/1995

From *Ploughshares* 21.4 (Winter 1995/96): 196–201. Reprinted with permission of *Ploughshares*.

The good news is that Tim O'Brien is writing fiction again.

In 1994, after his sixth book, *In the Lake of the Woods*, was released, he distressed his many fans by vowing to stop writing fiction "for the foreseeable future." Then, a few months later, he published a now famous essay in the *New York Times Magazine* that described his return to Vietnam. With his girlfriend at the time, he visited My Lai, where on March 16, 1968, a company of American soldiers massacred an entire village in a matter of four hours—women, children, old men, chickens, dogs. The body count ranged from two to five hundred.

From 1969–70, O'Brien had been an infantryman in the Quang Ngai province, and his platoon had been stationed in My Lai a year after the massacre. Then and now, he could feel the evil in the place, "the wickedness that soaks into your blood and heats up and starts to sizzle." In the *Times* cover story, O'Brien elaborated on the complex associations of love and insanity that can boil over during a war, almost inevitably exploding into atrocity. But he went a step further, drawing parallels between the "guilt, depression, terror, shame" that infected both his Vietnam experience and his present life, especially now that his girlfriend had left him. Chillingly, he admitted, "Last night suicide was on my mind. Not whether, but how." This time, his fans were not the only ones concerned. Friends and strangers alike called him: shrinks to sign him up, clergymen to save his soul, people who thought he had disclosed way too much, others who thought he had disclosed too little.

Today, O'Brien has no regrets about publishing the article. He considers it one of the best things he has ever written. "I reread it maybe once every two months," he says, "just to remind myself what writing's for. I don't mean catharsis. I mean communication. It was a hard thing to do. It saved my life, but it was a fuck of a thing to print." After taking nine months off and pulling his life back together, O'Brien started another novel, intrigued enough by the first page to write a second, propelled, as always, by his fundamental faith in the power of storytelling.

Born in 1946, O'Brien was raised in small-town Minnesota, his father an insurance salesman, his mother an elementary school teacher. As a child, O'Brien was lonely, overweight, and a professed "dreamer," and he occupied himself by practicing magic tricks. For a brief time, he contemplated being a writer, inspired by some old clippings he'd found of his father's—personal accounts about fighting in Iwo Jima and Okinawa that had been published in the *New York Times* during World War II. When O'Brien entered college, however, his aspirations turned political. He was a political science major at Macalester, attended peace vigils and war protests, and planned to join the State Department to reform its policies. "I thought we needed people who were progressive and had the patience to try diplomacy instead of dropping bombs on people."

He never imagined he would be drafted upon graduation and actually sent to Vietnam. "I was walking around in a dream and repressing it all," he says, "thinking something would save my ass. Even getting on the plane for boot camp, I couldn't believe any of it was happening to me, someone who hated Boy Scouts and bugs and rifles." When he received his classification—not as a clerk, or a driver, or a cook, but as an infantryman—he seriously considered deserting to Canada. He now thinks it was an act of cowardice not to, particularly since he was against the war, but in 1969, as a twenty-two-year-old, he had feared the disapproval of his family and friends, his townspeople and country. He went to Vietnam and hated every minute of it, from beginning to end.

When he came back to the States, he had a Purple Heart (he was wounded by shrapnel from a hand grenade) and several publishing credits. Much like his father, he had written personal reports about the war that had made their way into Minnesota newspapers, and while pursuing a doctorate at the Harvard School of Government, O'Brien expanded on the vignettes to form a book, *If I Die in Combat, Box Me Up and Ship Me Home*. He sent it first to Knopf, whose editors had high praise for the book. Yet they were already publishing a book about Vietnam, *Dispatches* by Michael Herr, and suggested that O'Brien try the editor Seymour Lawrence, who was in Boston. "He called me at my dormitory at Harvard," O'Brien recalls. "He said, 'Well, we're taking your book. Why don't you come over, I'll take you to lunch.' It was a big, drunken lunch at Trader Vic's in the old Statler Hilton, during the course of which we decided to fire my agent. Sam said, 'Look, you're not going to get much money, there's no way, might as well fire the guy. Why give him ten percent?'"

If I Die in Combat was published in 1973, just as O'Brien was being hired as a national affairs reporter for the *Washington Post*, where he'd been an intern for two summers. "I didn't know the first thing about writing for a newspaper, but I learned fast," says O'Brien, who never took a writing workshop. The job helped tremendously in terms of discipline, which, O'Brien confesses, was a problem for him until then. "I learned the virtue of tenacity."

After his one-year stint at the *Post*, O'Brien simply wrote books. In 1975, he published *Northern Lights*, about two brothers—one a war hero, the other a farm agent who stayed home in Minnesota—who struggle to survive during a cross-country ski trip. *Going After Cacciato* came out in 1978. In the novel, an infantryman named Cacciato deserts, deciding to walk from Southeast Asia to Paris for the peace talks. Paul Berlin is ordered to capture Cacciato, and narrates an extended meditation on what might have happened if Cacciato had made it all the way to Paris. The novel won the National Book Award over John Irving's *The World According to Garp* and John Cheever's *Stories*.

The Nuclear Age, about a draft dodger turned uranium speculator who is obsessed with the threat of nuclear holocaust, was released in 1985, and then, in 1990, came *The Things They Carried*, which was a finalist for both the Pulitzer Prize and the National Book Critics Circle Award. The collection of interrelated stories revolves around the men of Alpha Company, an infantry platoon in Vietnam. The title story is a recitation of the soldiers' weapons and gear, the metaphorical mixing with the mundane: they carried M-60's and C rations and Claymores, and "the common scent of cowardice barely restrained, the instinct to run or freeze or hide, and in many respects this was the heaviest burden of all, for it could never be put down, it required perfect balance and perfect posture." A central motif in the book is the process of storytelling itself, the way imagination and language and memory can blur fact, and why "story-truth is truer sometimes than happening-truth."

In his latest novel, *In the Lake of the Woods*, which is now in paperback, O'Brien takes this question of how much we can know about an event or a person one step further. John and Kathy Wade are staying at a secluded lakeside cottage in northern Minnesota. He has just lost a senatorial election by a landslide, after the revelation that he was among the soldiers at My Lai, a fact he has tried to conceal from everyone—including his wife; even, pathologically, himself—for twenty years. A week after their arrival at the lake, Wade's wife disappears. Perhaps she drowned, perhaps she ran away, perhaps Wade murdered her. The mystery is never solved, and the lack of a traditional ending has produced surprisingly vocal reactions from readers.

"I get *calls* from people," O'Brien says. They ask questions, they offer their own opinions about what happened, they want to *know*, missing the point of the novel, that life often does not offer solutions or resolutions, that it is impossible to know completely what secrets lurk within people. As the anonymous narrator, who has conducted a four-year investigation into the case, comments in a footnote: "It's human nature. We are fascinated, all of us, by the implacable otherness of others. And we wish to penetrate by hypothesis, by daydream, by scientific investigation those leaden walls that encase the human spirit, that define it and guard it and hold it forever inaccessible. ('I love you,' someone says, and instantly we begin to wonder—'Well, how much?'—and when the answer comes—'With my whole heart'—we then wonder about the wholeness of a fickle heart.) Our lovers, our husbands, our wives, our fathers, our gods—they are all beyond us."

O'Brien feels strongly that *In the Lake of the Woods* is his best book to date, but it took its toll on him. He is a meticulous, some would say fanatical, craftsman. In general, he writes every day, all day. He does practically nothing else. He lifts weights, watches baseball, occasionally plays golf, and reads at night, but rarely ventures from his two-bedroom apartment near Harvard Square. He'll eke out the words, then discard them. It took him an entire year to finish nine pages of *The Nuclear Age*, although he tossed out thousands.

Always, it will begin with an image, "a picture of a human being doing something." With *Going After Cacciato*, it was the image of a guy walking to Paris: "I could see his back." With *The Things They Carried*, it was "remembering all this crap I had on me and inside me, the physical and spiritual burdens." With *In the Lake of the Woods*, it was a man and a woman lying on a porch in the fog along a lake: "I didn't know where the lake was at the time. I knew they were unhappy. I could feel the unhappiness in the fog. I didn't know what the unhappiness was about. It required me to write the next page. A lost election. Why was the election lost? My Lai. All of this was discovered after two years of writing."

But when O'Brien finished *In the Lake of the Woods*, he stopped writing for the first time in over twenty years. "I was burned out," he says. "The novel went to the bottom of the well for me. I felt emotionally drained. I didn't see the point of writing anymore." In retrospect, the respite was good for him. He likens the hiatus to Michael Jordan's brief leave from basketball: "He may not be a better basketball player when he comes back, but he's going to be a better person."

Of course, the road back has not been easy, particularly with the loss of his editor and good friend, Sam Lawrence, who died in 1993. "Through the ups and downs of any writer's career, he was always there, with a new contract, and optimism. Another of his virtues was that he didn't push. Sam didn't give a shit if you missed a deadline. He wanted a good book, no matter how long it took." For the moment, O'Brien has yet to sign up with another publisher for his novel in progress, which opens with two boys building an airplane in their backyard. He prefers to avoid the pressure. "Maybe it's Midwestern," he says. "When I sign a contract, I think I owe them X dollars of literature."

And in defiance of some editors and critics, who suggest he should move on from Vietnam, he will in all likelihood continue to write about the war. "All writers revisit terrain. Shakespeare did it with kings, and Conrad did it with the ocean, and Faulkner did it with the South. It's an emotional and geographical terrain that's given to us by life. Vietnam is there the way childhood is for me. There's a line from Michael Herr: 'Vietnam's what we had instead of happy childhoods.' A funny, weird line, but there's some truth in it."

Yet to categorize O'Brien as merely a Vietnam War writer would be ludicrously unfair and simplistic. Any close examination of his books reveals there is something much more universal about them. As much as they are war stories, they are also love stories. That is why his readers are as apt to be female as male. "I think in every book I've written," O'Brien says, "I've had the twins of love and evil. They intertwine and intermix. They'll separate, sometimes, yet they're hooked the way valances are hooked together. The emotions in war and in our ordinary lives are, if not identical, damn similar."

The Heart under Stress: Interview with Author Tim O'Brien

James Lindbloom/1998

From *Gadfly* March 1999. Web. http://chss.montclair.edu/english/furr/Vietnam/timobgad-flyinterviewo399.html. Reprinted with permission of Gadfly Productions.

After a notorious 1994 *New York Times Magazine* essay that was tantamount to a suicide note and a breakdown during a reading in Ann Arbor, Michigan, writer Tim O'Brien began, slowly, to confront his demons. If he made good on his promise of retirement, his stature would be assured; he has received the National Book Award for *Going After Cacciato* and the Prix du Meilleur Livre Étranger for *The Things They Carried*. Happily, it was a promise he couldn't keep.

Tomcat in Love is a book that Tim O'Brien thought he'd never write. Although his previous novel, *In the Lake of the Woods*, was a critical and popular success, O'Brien announced that it was his last. The flashes of humor in O'Brien's earlier works are given free rein in *Tomcat in Love*. An outrageous black comedy, the book is a portrait of a sexist, self-deluding linguistics professor who attempts to work through the anguish of a failed marriage by sabotaging his ex-wife's new relationship. Though a comic novel may seem a departure for an author best known for his masterful fiction about combat experience, O'Brien insists that it is not. His subject has remained the same throughout all his books: the human heart under stress. *Gadfly* spoke to him at his home in Cambridge, Massachusetts, shortly after the promotional tour for *Tomcat in Love*, his newest novel.

James Lindbloom: The critical reception of your new novel has been wildly polarized; some reviewers have loathed it, while others have called it a masterwork. What sort of reaction did you see on your recent book tour?

Tim O'Brien: Well, people don't talk in terms of critical responses; they just laugh, or they don't. They laughed, and that's what I wanted with the book. Essentially, you want books to generate not just intellectual but visceral or emotional responses. In this case, you gauge it by the laugh-o-meter, sort of like the Ted Mack Amateur Hour, where they had that little meter going. And, for a change, that's what I wanted to do with this book: to make people laugh at themselves, at the characters in the book, and at the human condition. So it was a good response.

JL: At the two readings in the Twin Cities, the reaction was quite positive. I saw a few arched eyebrows and shakes of the head in response to some of the more outlandishly misogynistic statements made by Thomas Chippering, the narrator of *Tomcat*. But there were no irate walkouts, and during the question-and-answer sessions that followed, no one seemed to have difficulty making the distinction between the flesh-and-blood author and his fictional creation. So no one read you the riot act at any of the readings?
TO: No, it went well.

JL: Your seven novels have established you as part of the canon of twentieth-century American literature, yet your second novel, *Northern Lights*, has been out of print in the United States for some time. Is that your decision?
TO: Yeah, it is. Dell has asked several times to reprint it, and I've said no. I want to rewrite it. If I could cut fifty to eighty pages out of it, I know I could make it a better book. As it is, it's just overwritten. I think that's a project that I'll do some time in the next four or five years. It would take me a good six months to do it right, and it would also require some rewriting. But I think it could be a good book, if I were to put it on the Jenny Craig diet. I keep putting it off, because it's something you can do when you've kind of lost your juice, and I haven't lost it yet.

JL: The question of memory—its veracity, its accuracy, and the role it plays in shaping our personal histories—has been a principal theme in your work, particularly *The Things They Carried* and *In the Lake of the Woods*. How do you see the relationship between truth and memory?
TO: Well, I think one has a little to do with the other. To put it conversely, they have everything to do with each other. It depends, like I guess all things do, on your angle of vision. One could argue, as Plato does, that truth is something abstract, just floating out there. Whether we remember a thing, imagine it, or know anything about it, is irrelevant; it's just out there. There

are others who would argue—as I guess I do; I'm not much of a Platonist in that sense—that the human being shapes and determines what we call truth. Truth is ultimately a statement. It's an issue of language. You make declarations and then you judge them. The word "truth" is dependent on the kind of declaration we make about the world. You could declare that the world is flat. It's a linguistic statement. Its so-called "truth" is determined by evidentiary standards, whatever you can do to determine flatness. I guess I fall into what is philosophically called the camp of the idealists, as opposed to the realists. I think the truth is really a function of the statements we make about the world. Witness Clinton, with this whole business about the truth of what's sex and what's not sex. Witness Chippering, the character in my book, with his equivocations, hairsplittings, and so on. Ultimately, the truth of things is what we say about things; what we say about things determines the way we think about truth.

JL: The style that you use when describing war experiences is very elliptical, very fragmentary, with a moral compass that doesn't always point due north, so to speak. What do you think of something like *Saving Private Ryan*, which takes the opposite tack in its linear, "clear-eyed" representation of wartime?

TO: I didn't buy it. I found the first twenty minutes compelling, partly because it was fragmentary, with this and that happening, and everything sort of confused, which is not only how war strikes me, but how life itself ultimately does. This doesn't always tie in with that, and if it does, you sure as hell can't tell where and how. The rest of the movie I found . . . boring, I guess is the best word, because it was linear. It was a story that I'd seen before, or read about before: you know, going off to save a guy, and every little dot connects with every other dot in a perfect way. It just seemed to me to be syrupy, sentimental, predictable, and kind of stupid on top of it all. I don't know; I mean, many veterans of the war loved the movie, and I hate to bad-mouth it. But I have no choice, because I think it's just a shitty piece of art, except for those first twenty minutes. I found the characters predictable. I even turned to Meredith [Baker, O'Brien's girlfriend] at the beginning of the movie—right after that very first scene, where they go to the cemetery—and I said, "That old man is not going to be Tom Hanks. That's a red herring. Tom Hanks is gonna die, and that's going to be Matt Damon. I promise you." It was just so predictable as to be not very interesting to me, finally.

JL: On the eve of the publication of *In the Lake of the Woods*, you wrote an essay for the *New York Times Magazine* ("The Vietnam in Me," 2 October 94) that was the literary equivalent of a raw nerve. It's not often that a major novelist muses so publicly about wanting to kill himself. Can you talk about how things have changed for you since then?

TO: Writing *Tomcat* helped a lot. Fortunately, when I began writing the book right after the *In the Lake of the Woods* tour was over, I found myself laughing at the first few pages that I wrote, and thought, "Well, this is an improvement over the way things were a few days ago." The more I wrote, the more I laughed, and the more I laughed, the better I felt about the world. That's just an example of how literature has an effect on not only our critical and intellectual capacities, but on our lives. It can really help the soul and help us heal.

JL: In the press you did for *In the Lake of the Woods*, you adamantly stated that it was your final book. Yet, you began work on *Tomcat in Love* almost immediately. How did the reversal happen so quickly?

TO: Well, it wasn't almost immediate. It was nine months or so before I really began writing again. I took a long time off. I had intended to take eternity off, and it turned out to be nine months. But I did take a pretty substantial break. I'm not even sure now what it was that brought me to start typing sentences again. I can't recall the day I did it. All I remember is that laughter I mentioned earlier. I remember just kind of giggling, sort of laughing at myself, and at obsession, love, and all these sorts of things. But what it was that actually brought me back to the typewriter, I really don't know. I initially started to write a book of nonfiction, with *Tomcat*—that first section about Herbie [the sister of Chippering's childhood love, Lorna Sue], when they were kids. I really thought I was writing a memoir. Over the course of the first month or so, slowly—as always—the fiction began creeping in. With dialogue, I thought I could make things up that were an improvement over the way things were. And by the time the first month was over, I was writing a novel again.

JL: I remember reading that first section of *Tomcat* in the *New Yorker* ("Faith," 12 February 1996). You've said that the reason you've written so few short stories is that they wind up being the seeds for future novels.

TO: That's the truth.

JL: With that in mind, I'd like to ask you about any plans you might have for two recently published short works: "Loon Point" (*Esquire*, January 1995) and "The Streak" (*New Yorker*, 28 September 1998).

TO: I'm of two minds about that. Right now, I'm working on stories, on conceiving them. I had talked and thought a lot about turning "Loon Point" into a novel, but I haven't done that yet. Now I'm just doing a bunch of stories, and that's going to be one of them. But you never know when you may say, "Well, God, with each of these stories that I'm doing, if I just changed the names, they could all be one and the same person." It could be a novel, but as it stands now, I'm just working on a set of discrete stories. But I do have a novel in mind. It's probably going to be a book away from this book of stories. I'm thinking of doing a novel with the title of *May '69*, which would—basically—be a novel about the month of May in 1969.

JL: Are the stories you describe going to be another set of interconnected short works, like *The Things They Carried*?

TO: Yeah, I think they will end up being that way. There are already characters appearing who have appeared in other stories. I had a piece in the February '98 issue of *Esquire*. It's very short, only one page long in the magazine. It's called "Class of '68," about a class reunion, meeting thirty years later. Already I've done two other stories about that same reunion. I've started thinking of all these other characters that I've been writing about in other stories who are all appearing at the same reunion. So, yeah, I think that may be the way it goes. Again, you don't know until you get farther into it. I know they're going to be interconnected; I just don't know quite what the framework will be.

JL: The framework will appear at the end, I guess.

TO: It always does.

Journeying from Life to Literature: An Interview with American Novelist Tim O'Brien

Lynn Wharton/1999

Originally published in *Interdisciplinary Literary Studies: A Journal of Criticism and Theory* 1.2 (Spring 2000): 229–47. Reprinted with permission of Lynn Wharton.

Lynn Wharton's informal interview with Tim O'Brien occurred at the Durrants Hotel, George Street, London, on Sunday, 11 April 1999.

LW: I know that some of your characters are based on real people—the character Curt Lemon, for example, in *The Things They Carried*, who is blown into a tree by a mine, was based on a comrade, Alvin Merricks. Could you talk a little about how you metamorphose your personal experience into fictional form?

TOB: The death of Chip Merricks—he's a real human being. I didn't have exactly the experience that I wrote in the book—no climbing up trees, no peeling off body parts, and in fact I didn't even see Chip's body in person. I was a hundred yards away, looking in a different direction. I was busy on the radio, calling for helicopters to, you know, get him out of there. But he was a friend, and the emotional impact of his death was very great. The idea of sudden death was brought home to me very quickly in my tour—that is something I'll never forget. I begin the Curt Lemon death out of my own life and experience and memory but, as I write, it is transformed into something new and different—even I don't know how it will turn out. When I begin writing, I'm not sure what I'm looking for or working toward. I'm finding things out as I go along—in *The Things They Carried*, for example, where there's a paragraph an inch or two long, which is discussing seemingness—

what it must have seemed like, both to Chip and to Curt Lemon, that instant of death. The booby-trapped artillery round—it must have seemed as if the light itself were killing them. Who knows what they were really feeling, but one tries through an imaginative act to explore what it would be like to die in such a light as this, and we go on beyond that, of course, to issues of dying in general, and beyond that again to what stories are about, of the ultimate unknowns that haunt all of us. So my writing goes beyond my own experience, which is kind of limited, to an exploration of others' experience, in that instance to an exploration of death in general.

LW: Stories such as "Lives of the Dead" are, in a sense, about how stories resurrect dead people.
TOB: Yes—and they resurrect not only the dead, they resurrect those who never even lived—like Huckleberry Finn. Here's a creature of Mark Twain's imagination and he's dead up on a library shelf and you pull the book off the shelf, you open the book and begin reading and there's Huck Finn alive, floating down the river again. And there's personal experience of death as well, that I might remember—my father might have died and then, I'm lying in bed at night, before sleeping, so there he is, winking, from the past, a memory. I see him opening the refrigerator door, looking for a carton of milk, and he's back with us again, he's no longer dead. Stories have a way of encouraging that process—the process probably of memory, probably also of imagination. This is a primary function of stories, to keep the ghosts with us. Stories allow the dead to say, "Hello guys," I suppose. Ultimately, also, as writers, we ourselves seek a kind of immortality in what we do. Of course it's not physical—but *Ulysses* is checked out, and there's Joyce and we imagine him sitting in Trieste or somewhere, and he's no longer dead.

LW: Can we talk a little bit about *Tomcat in Love*? Did you feel you were going in a new direction with your new book?
TOB: No, not at all. I was writing about pretty much the same things that I've always written about. Not Vietnam, but then I've never felt I've written about Vietnam.

LW: Nevertheless, Vietnam is a very real element in *Tomcat in Love*.
TOB: It is very real and, yes, it's part of it. It's a book like *In the Lake of the Woods*. It's about things people will do for love. In the case of *In the Lake of the Woods*, this man was lying to keep this woman—doing outlandish things. People go to war for love, they do all sorts of things for love. With

Tomcat in Love I was really on familiar terrain. The primary change in the book lies in its comedic tone. But the subject matter itself, that's to do with the human spirit, how we try to win and sustain love—it's an enduring subject for me. The draft to Vietnam, for example—it was the love of my family and so on that sent me off to a horrible war. That's not romantic love, but it's still love. I'm the kind of person who always finds it hard to say no—yes, yes, yes, just constantly, because that's just the kind of person I am, I want everybody to like me. It's caused trouble in my life but it's also brought good things as well. So love hasn't just been a subject in my books, it's really been the center—probably more than Vietnam itself. Vietnam is really just an aspect or a reflection of the central driving focus of my life, which has been to win love. I'm sure it goes back to things in my childhood—what exactly, I don't know, but I'm sure it does.

LW: Can we go on now to your more conventional first novel, *Northern Lights*?
TOB: *Northern Lights* was a kind of training exercise for me. My publisher called me up after the publication of *If I Die* and said, "Do you want to write a novel?" I said, "Well, sure!" I was just a kid, so I thought writing a novel would be marvelous. So I wrote this book. That was one of the things my editor and I were just talking about today. They reissued that over here and they'll soon be reissuing it in the States, over my objections. That is a book that I really need, when I'm an older man, to spend a year cutting, essentially. If I can cut it by a hundred pages, or eighty—somewhere near a lot! When I read it I saw the Joycean and Faulknerian influences a little bit, and the constant repetition. Everything comes at you in couples—if there's a nail on page one there'll be a nail on page thirty-five, just for sure! It's a book that's hard for me to talk about because it doesn't seem mine anymore and it's unfortunate that it got published. All I can say about it is that I do believe that if I had six months to eight, I could turn it into at least a readable and fairly decent book of fiction—that's not to say very great, but I could make it at least decent, so that a person could read it and not be embarrassed every other sentence or two by the clutter of language.

LW: I've read that book two or three times and I think you're a little over-critical! I understand what you mean, though, maybe it takes a little more effort from the reader to make it roll along easily.
TOB: I think you could be right. I think once the two brothers are lost in the snow, it radically improves, it's far more me writing than, say, me trying

to be Faulkner or Joyce. I don't know, there are clumsy phrases throughout the book where—probably as a writer you'd say these are language issues. Mostly I think it means throwing away probably ninety percent of all those adjectives, the verbiage that surrounds what in essence is a simple story. In *Northern Lights* I try to pay homage to, in this case, Hemingway along with Faulkner. I do everything, in a way, as a kind of nodding. I grab people by the throat and say, "Here is Hemingway!" Well, it could be done a bit more delicately!

LW: There's a tremendous sense of place in that novel.

TOB: Place is accurately grounded, that's true. But it's accurately rendered one time too many, two times too many. In a way, I think that was a good experience for preparing me to write *In The Lake of the Woods*. I do know Minnesota and am in a way entranced by the place. It's on the one hand starkly beautiful—lakes and woods, a true wilderness—on the other hand it's starkly terrifying, a very terrifying place. I think I tended in *Northern Lights* to overdo the descriptive stuff which, in *In the Lake of the Woods*, I handled somewhat more delicately.

LW: I have an anthology of Midwestern writing which seems to try to place you as a Midwestern writer, even though you no longer live there. I wonder whether you'd go along with that kind of categorization?

TOB: I don't like being "placed" in any category, any more than Conrad would, or anybody. You can actually rebel against that kind of compartmentalization, because your whole goal as a writer is to be idiosyncratic, yourself. At the same time, of course, I am from the Midwest, many of my characters at least grew up there, some of my stories are set there—but I don't think of myself as a Midwestern writer, I think of myself as a writer-writer! I draw on the Midwest when I have to, I draw on drowning when I have to, I draw on Vietnam when I want to, on love, whatever. Living in a literary world can be mayhem, it can be anywhere. I certainly hope that my tombstone does not bear the word "Midwest" on it.

LW: It's obviously a significant journey that the two brothers make in *Northern Lights*. Each of them undergoes a kind of personal developmental journey, which seems to be facilitated by the real, physical act required in making a journey. Significant journeys are sprinkled throughout your entire corpus of work. Is journeying important to you, to the way you write and what you write about?

TOB: It's a storytelling thing that I'm wedded to, and always will be. I've always loved stories that involve journeys of some sort. *Ulysses* is an example, I suppose . . . I can't think of a favorite novel that doesn't involve a journey—I've mentioned Huck Finn in our talk already—that physical component of a route you can follow in a geographical sense. But for me, more importantly, is the sense of spiritual destination. We're all of us in our lives on journeys, in the "boats" of our bodies, and we know ultimately where we're headed—our boats will end up at the bottom of the sea, or lying in a shipyard somewhere—but for now, the water's still buoyant, waves rolling along, and we're riding them trying to find some destination. For some of us it's a very romantic and idealized destination, a Fiji of the soul—you know, I'll find a nice exotic island and live there with my lover until I die. For others it's a journey toward God. For me it's always been a journey for an understanding—understanding myself. Who am I? This little shy boy growing up in a tiny godforsaken town in Southern Minnesota—how did he become a writer? What is it I want out of writing? Writing itself is a kind of journey. There are things I learn through each book, so the books are journeys. Not just the plots, but the books themselves represent journeys—for me, journeys into the unknown. One of the challenges I've given myself with every novel and every story I've written is that I never know the end. I won't write something if I know the conclusion, because there's no sense of destination. The journey's already over if I know the ending. So when I began *Tomcat* or *If I Die*—all of them—none of these books had an ending, none could conclude itself until I'd written those final lines. So that journey was over but the big journey was continuing when I started the next novel. The books are organized as journeys—walking to Paris is a journey—they're all, for me, organized—*If I Die* is a journey from childhood to Vietnam and back home again. It isn't true as a memoir but it's organized that way. I just had a story in the *New Yorker* a few weeks ago . . .

LW: "Nogales"?
TOB: Yes, a journey in New Mexico. Quite creepy, macabre. But it's a journey.

LW: Did you have Flannery O'Connor in mind when you wrote that story?
TOB: A little bit, yes. There's just a tiny shade of Flannery in there. But it actually grew out of an episode that happened to my mom and dad. My parents are in their eighties now but they used to vacation in Arizona and one day they went into a restaurant. When they first arrived, this twenty-

four-year-old kid befriended them. He'd buy them drinks and meals. My parents thought, "Why is he doing this?" But they liked him. He was a very nice, polite, well-mannered guy. He invited them eventually, "Let's go down to Mexico, to Nogales for a day, I'll show you around." My parents said yes initially. The next time they met in the restaurant he said, "Let's use your car. We can't use mine." They actually set a date, on the Sunday. My dad felt, though, that something was wrong. The story came out of my question, "What would have happened to my mom and dad if they'd gone?" That's why I had the old folks in the back of the van. So it's a little tip to Flannery but basically it's one of those investigations of "what if . . . ?" But again, that was how the story began, but it turned out to be more about the girl's need for love, and about the lengths she'll go to get it.

LW: There seems to be, not so much a telescoping of time, but a simultaneous existence of different timespans in your books. There's a sentence in *Tomcat in Love*—"The world sometimes precedes itself"—where Tom feels cheated by not having seen Lorna Sue being nailed by Herbie—he felt he was entitled to see that because of what would happen to them together in the future, as though the payment for now would be made in the future.
TOB: That's a nod to Joyce, the time focus in his literature, the kind of circulatory aspect.

LW: Also, the sense of the Vietnam War, in time terms, is very real. I didn't read the Vietnam veterans who are allegedly chasing Tom in a literal way. Rather I saw them as representing a specter of Vietnam in time, somehow chasing behind all veterans.
TOB: Yes! And in my initial drafts it was actually written that way. The way it was written, there was a big section toward the end in which, when I turned the book in, I tried to say pretty much that. In this section, which I later took out, Tom was saying to himself, "I'm not even sure whether these people even exist. Maybe they're everybody. Maybe the war itself is chasing me." But my editor thought—and I thought, too—that too many readers would go, "What? We've been believing in these guys all along!" So I took it out, hoping that there'd be some readers who would get that sense of unreality anyway—because I tried to create that in such a way that made it murky and cloudy and more surreal. The way that Spider, for example, appears in the garage and they float down the sidewalk together and he vanishes. It's almost as though a ghost is visiting Tom, as opposed to a real person. That,

by the way, is how Vietnam feels to me all these years later, as though I'm being revisited by people I knew, and villages, and whole events from the past.

LW: I wonder whether any traumatic experience would do that—although
war is of course so much more dramatic.
TOB: I think so. I think a really terrible divorce would do it, or losing a lover.
There are all kinds of things that occur in our lives besides war, it's kind of
similar.

LW: I'm very interested in the themes of magic, trickery, and deception in
your books. I wonder if you could say something about that.
TOB: A couple of things I could say about that. One, it comes from loving
magic as a kid, as a hobby. That's a short, practical answer—I was a would-be
magician as a kid. The more interesting issue, though, is why I liked magic
as a kid and still today like performing magic tricks with my fiction. As a
kid, I think it was a means of escape from—this is theoretical, hypotheti-
cal—escape from the constraints of a small town, a kind of boring Midwestern upbringing, where no miracles happened, nothing out of the ordinary.
There was a sense probably of my own powerlessness as a kid, an alcoholic
father. You know, that life was bad, but in this life miracles were wonderful
and possible, things could happen. I think partly, too, it was a way of winning applause from people, just being able to do it. Gaining affection—I
think that's a big part of it that people don't realize. I've read about a lot of
magicians—including people who became movie stars, Johnny Carson was
a magician, for example—you know, people crave the applause of others,
the wonder of others. Maybe that's the kind of person I was as a kid. But my
interest has gone beyond mere Freudian stuff now, it's gone to interesting
questions about the fluidity of truth. Someone says, for example, "I love you"
and it may be true now but won't be true tomorrow or the next day. Love
is fluid, as is the world of magic. It seems to me that my interest in magic
grew out of practical things in my youth and a general philosophical interest
and speculation regarding the fluidity of things around us, the mutability of
things around us. By "things" I mean physical things partly, countries and
people—how we age and how our bodies and souls are transformed through
life. That, coupled with an instinctual human desire to change it all. How
can we not die, how can we sit up and say, "I'm alive again"? Doing fiction
is a kind of magic trick, you know, it really is very much like magic. You can
make the dead talk, you can make tigers appear and disappear as if they're

on a stage, you can do it in a few words. There's a very close similarity to what I was doing as a kid and what I'm doing now, in a more intelligent kind of way. They're very close. If not identical, they're close.

LW: I wonder whether you have any thoughts on the nature of ideas. I'm thinking of what happens to ideas when we no longer think them—for example, a philosopher such as Iris Murdoch gets Alzheimer's Disease and "forgets" everything she thought before—what happened to those ideas she used to "know"? If we believe something today, but we're going to believe something different next week, how valid are the ideas we have today?
TOB: Oh, these are really neat questions, they really are!

LW: Maybe the ideas exist of themselves and we pluck them out of the ether.
TOB: Yes, that's the old Platonic question, isn't it? He used to believe that ideas flowed around—they were out there. It's a seductive thought that Iris's ideas are somewhere out there floating—but in a way they're in the library. That's where her ideas really are. We can pick up a book and there's the old Iris.

LW: Can we talk about the motif of drowning in your books?
TOB: It certainly occurs in my work, you're right.

LW: It's the physicality of drowning in your books that interests me. That sense of being engulfed by the water, but in order to drown you've also got to engulf the water with your body.
TOB: That seems close to what I'm getting at, what I'm writing about. The whole business of drowning for me comes out of a couple of personal experiences, where twice in my life I came within a whisker of drowning. Once I was only a toddler, this tall, and I was fishing and fell into a pond. The pond was extremely shallow—if I'd have stood up I'd have been fine. Instead I sat down. A kid who was with me, ten years older than I, sort of looked at me and said, "Why doesn't the kid stand up?" He just reached down to pick me up by the arm. I was under water and my eyes were wide open. I was so young that I didn't even know I was drowning. I didn't know what was happening. I was aware that I couldn't breathe and it wasn't entirely terrifying, it was partly magical. I had my eyes open and could see the water-bugs, little tiny bugs walking along on the water. I knew something was terribly wrong but I was also entranced by this strange murky show going on before me. The second time was much more terrifying. I was older—in Germany, at

college—and I jumped into the deep end of a pool thinking it was the shallow end. I'm a poor swimmer and I just panicked. I managed to claw myself to the edge of the pool. That was absolutely terrifying. Why these things stuck with me, who knows? I know why the first episode did, but the second I don't know. As a literary matter, though, those experiences of life—like I guess all experiences: lovers, wars, everything else—are the material I have to make stories from. Hence I draw on those—when I had no knowledge of the literary traditions, I just drew on my personal feelings. Drowning, as opposed to say electrocution, is a kind of slow process, a fading out as opposed to a—[snaps fingers]—gone. Cognition is involved—you're aware, at least for a time, of what's going on. Certainly the second time I knew, I was aware that I was dying and that dying took a long time. In a sense of being in a medium, of not breathing air but water—all the water around me and in me, you're absolutely right—that's something that just stayed with me. That thing that happened in Germany was more terrifying than anything in Vietnam, because I couldn't take breaths.

LW: There's a sense of terror, but also of powerlessness and a kind of acceptance . . .
TOB: It's a fatalism—this is how it is. There's utter chaos, too, you're surrounded by this foreign "thing."

LW: And you don't get normal sound . . .
TOB: I remember that terrible sound, a kind of buzz in my brain, an electric buzz went through my head—words were kind of imprinted—you can't speak but words like "Dear God" come to mind. You have them but you can't say them—so even words are failing you, you just can't talk.

LW: You use the image of a lake very often. Is that an image that holds significance for you?
TOB: Yes, it is. It appears and reappears in my work. In the Vietnam books there's fishing in a bomb crater, and in *In the Lake of the Woods* and *Northern Lights* there are lakes everywhere—driving around lakes, the Bowker character—just a few off the top of my head, but I'm sure there are many more instances. The question of what it represents or is meant to represent, I think, varies by case. Two things I can say to give you information. One is that I grew up on a lake—my home town was situated on a lake called Lake Okabena and the lake was the focal point of the town. It's a place where, because of my near-drowning experience, I was a little afraid. I stayed away

from the place. Yet it was still a focal point and we'd drive around it—so the Norman Bowker character has its roots in my own memory, my own life, this water we've been talking about. But the meaning of the lakeness varies a little bit. I think that the stories vary from book to book but, in general, it represents for me—for example, Pliny's Pond, this kind of algae-filled place—that comes from the pond when I was a little boy—that bug-filled, dark and soupy water, and that near-death experience that's been with me for so long. Hence, for example, Kiowa's death in *The Things They Carried*. The lake has been partly tempting and largely, for me at least, as a writer and human being both, a scary place, that comes to represent that immersion in death, that giving up, that fatalism we talked about. In all my work, the lakes are about: "Well, here's where we go, it's where we all go." Kiowa, Kathy Wade, they've all gone there, which is I suppose a kind of eternity of death, of some sort. Which is odd, because it's a reverse use of the lake—water in much literature is a symbol of life, a symbol of refreshment. But I use it in the opposite kind of way, probably because of my life experience.

LW: Yes, your lakes are so often the opposite of fecund, aren't they? Even the woman in "Speaking of Courage," the woman fishing—she never catches anything.
TOB: No. Nothing to catch. Empty lake.

LW: Speaking of "Speaking of Courage," can you tell me about the disembodied "confessor" voice that Norman Bowker talks to when he's buying a hamburger? Is that a reference to God?
TOB: The voice over the intercom? I didn't mean that to represent God. I don't know what it represented. Maybe it does, now that I think of it. I don't know what it was. It's partly a play just on military radios in Vietnam where you are desperately calling for help. When I was in Vietnam, I was an RTO and there was this disembodied voice always coming at me, when they were incapable of giving help until twenty minutes later, and I need it now. I want help! I want out of there! You know? And I could never attach a face to these things, to these people at the other end of the radio. But it may well stand for God. In *The Things They Carried* there was a section called "On the Rainy River" where I make a kind of—it's likened to how I perceive God's presence, looking over my shoulder and watching me fail, but I'm not very religious. I don't think of God speaking to me, giving advice, saying, "Do this—you'd better do that, or this . . ." He's sort of just there, neither a he nor a she, just a presence, like a dead parent watching my behavior—never commenting on

it but there as a kind of witness. Similarly, with the radio imagery—I use it in *In the Lake of the Woods*, at the end of that book, where John Wade uses the radio, talking to God, basically transmitting his pleas for salvation to a mute universe. No one's listening to him.

LW: Can we go on, then, to the use of what might be termed sacred relics in your books: Henry Dobbins's stockings, Mary Anne's necklace of ears. Even when Dobbins's girlfriend has rejected him, her stockings, for him, still keep their power.
TOB: Yes. Sometimes that's all we have left of people, stuff that they've given us, and those little scraps of memory that we're left with. Many of us will cling to them, certainly in that situation of war. You'll keep a pair of stockings sent by your girl, something tangible to hold onto.

LW: So in the same way that perhaps an idea exists in itself, does perhaps the significance of an object exist in itself, regardless of what you do with it?
TOB: I haven't thought theoretically about this subject, although I feel instinctively that I know what you mean. I'm not quite sure what to say. Firstly, I could talk about T. S. Eliot's objective correlative—it's not just the stockings that are important; what's important is that the stockings are a correlative of this guy who's in love with this woman—or peace—or maybe both. In that sense, every object—every significant object that appears in my work—has that quality. I don't put things in for no reason—everything, the radios, for example, are in there for a reason—maybe I'm not sure what they are! To explore that moment of life in there as well—myself, and the heightened sense of what the radio means—it's what the thing will become in the text, as well as what it is of itself. I guess my answer is that all the objects that appear in my work have been of significance. They're there for reasons beyond their mere decorative presence. I won't, for example, when describing a room, mention the color of the wallpaper unless the color of the wallpaper really matters to me. I won't even mention it. The things that you've spoken about, you see, I've only mentioned for a reason. The icons in *Tomcat in Love*—for example, the household of Lorna Sue—it's there for a reason—religious artifacts. It's a comedy, but to talk about it seriously— it's about oppressive Catholicism in a family that's been warped by conventional religion. The crucifixion scene is about how the lives of some people are really warped by it—really badly warped. And about how civilization itself I think has been, in some ways, hideously affected by those kinds of conventions. People have gone on crusades, wars, because of it. So it's kind

of comedic in that sense, but I also meant it seriously: watch it, folks! I have a kind of love-hate relationship with organized religion. I have a sarcastic, cynical side—I've brought all my artillery to bear on religion.

LW: The power of abstract ideas again.
TOB: Yes.

LW: Does that notion—the power of ideas—have anything to do with why there's no overt sex in your books? It all happens in characters' heads.
TOB: True. It all happens in the head. There's very little there! I don't know why I don't write it. It's not as though I'm afraid of it or anything. I just don't know how to have it happening—I mean, it happens, so what? Stories for me ordinarily involve some kind of conflict going on—well, with sex, it's hard to have a lot of conflict—I mean, you're both aiming at the same end, and it's hard to argue while . . . ! Someday I might think up a story where I've got conflict going on and some kind of . . . I don't know what to say about that! It's like a conversation I had with my editors in New York. They looked at some stories I've been working on lately and said, "Why do they all have to be so bleak?" My response is, all stories are bleak! Even comedy has a bleak aspect. That's what a story is—I don't tell a story about how happy I was yesterday morning and I had lunch and slept well that night—God's in his place and the world's all fine. That's not a story. At some point in a story, something happens that's off, slightly dangerous, some kind of tension or struggle—definitely not sex—sex is too nice a thing, I don't have anything interesting to write about it!

LW: I've read interviews with you before, about the way you view story-writing, and I wonder whether you find stories in a way "easier" to write, as stand-alone pieces, rather than constructing them as chapters to fit into a specific novel form.
TOB: That's a question I like to be asked, because it's a good practical literary question! Well, "easy" is not an easy word, but in some ways yes, a story is easier. If we only talk about the time it takes to write, for example—I can finish a story in three months, but a novel takes three to five years. So in that sense I could almost say yes. But that question intrigued me when I read it in the plane coming over—my thought was, well, for me—and I suspect virtually any writer—nothing seems easy, if you're trying to do serious work. It all seems hard. I'll struggle for three days, four days sometimes, with a

single sentence. It's not really the sentence I'm struggling with so much as what's going to follow it in terms of story, and the rolling sentence technique—that is, whatever the sentence might end up meaning will determine what the next sentence is and therefore the rest of the story. So you have to be so careful, especially with a story, to have sentences that guide you to the proper shape of the novel, but at the same time to have sentences that will eventually lead you somewhere and eventually strain the story back down to a short story. Because it's limited in terms of space, one doesn't, for example, have the luxury of inefficient sentences. And I kind of like that challenge—I must say I'm probably temperamentally the kind of person that likes making short, efficient things instead of big fat things. You know my novels aren't very long. In one sense, yes, stories are "easier," but in another sense, they're like making a nice little watch: extremely challenging—in some ways more challenging than a novel. It's a kind of yes and no answer, I'm afraid. Another thought that occurs to me with respect to that question is that I think I'm better as a story-writer than as a novelist—because I like it better, I think I'm better at it. It's as a novelist that I'm best known, but my novels essentially all begin with stories—even the thing that I'm doing now.[1] I guess it's been that way all along—the chapters that I like best in my novels are almost always those that were published first in magazines. As a kind of aesthetic principle, I believe that a chapter should be a chapter for a reason in a novel, a kind of mini-story—there should be a kind of mini-resolution to the end of each chapter. And I like to leave a chapter aside in terms of time, to jump to it in a slot in time, and leave that connective time-space out. Most novelists laboriously put in—you know these are questions that really get my blood going as a writer! My ideal would be to write whole stories that become a novel without any of the connective material, because in life that stuff often bores me. When I'm watching movies or seeing television shows, I see the connective stuff and think, well, here it comes, they're getting from A to B, they're going to walk into a room and you know they're going to meet. I can almost watch the writer pushing them together, with sentence after sentence, and dialogue. My preference would be there's she and there's he—and now they're talking to each other. Without that connective thing. My memory often works that way as well. My memory of events in the world comes at me in sort of blobs of things—this face, and then that face, and then that event and then that event, but not in chronological order, they just come. If

---

1. *July, July*, which would be published in 2002, two years after this interview took place.

I think of my father as one example, now he's an old dying man, now he's a young guy who took me to baseball years ago, and I'll go back and forth with no interconnection, no slow aging process. I think most people's memories operate in much the same way.

LW: So you rely on the reader's imagination to connect . . .
TOB: I do—to do that connective work. I really rely on it—I think writers do rely on it; we have to, finally, because we can't put everything in, no matter how much detail we try to put in the story. Ultimately it thins out—you're in the bathroom, you're drinking a glass of water, you're taking a nap—you can't describe the whole nap. If you did it'd be a very boring book! It'd take as long to read the book as to lead the life! You couldn't do books that way.

LW: I was asked by a veteran to explain whether I felt I could have an experience of Vietnam or understand anything about Vietnam by simply reading a book written by you. My answer was really that your memory has to combine with my imagination and I'll then get some sense of a basic "truth." But it depends upon terminology—what we mean by "know" and "truth" and "understand."
TOB: I understand intuitively what you mean, and I think you're absolutely right. Somehow your imagination has to wrap around whatever I have to offer you. That's the joy of a book as opposed to, say, a movie. In a movie, we watch what's presented to us. In a book, the decoding of the words on the pages, the images we have in our heads of the characters—we imagine ourselves in the story. When we're watching *The Godfather*, we're just seeing Al Pacino doing that—there's a slight identification with the character, but in a book there's so much more.

LW: That's a lack that I find in those bang-bang-you're-dead war books that leave nothing to the imagination. I can't connect with them at all.
TOB: I've been there and I can't connect either!

LW: Did you see the dramatization of "Sweetheart of the Song Tra Bong"? They changed the ending.
TOB: The ending was very confusing. I didn't understand it myself. I'm not sure what they were trying to do with it.

LW: I guess it was a cinematic ending, rather than a literary ending! They were trying to tie the two characters together, perhaps—Rat Kiley and Mary Anne—by implying that they stepped on a mine together.

TOB: I'm not sure—are they supposed to have died at the end?

LW: It was ambiguous.

TOB: I'll say! And the coincidence of her showing up, beyond belief! Very clumsily done—up till then it was reasonably well done. It was a little tedious in places, they could have cut it back, but by and large it was reasonably well done. But the ending—I didn't get it.

LW: I read somewhere that you said that story actually happened.

TOB: Well, I didn't see it. But it's one of the few things that has its root in any kind of reality. It's a story that was told as soon as I arrived in Vietnam, and I heard it maybe ten times, fifteen times, from various people, but I always discounted it as just another story that had gotten around. But after I got back to the States I kept hearing—especially after the publication of my story—"Yes, I was actually there." When one thinks about it, it's not any more strange than anything else I saw. There were civilians all over the place in Vietnam—secretaries, contractors, journalists, hippies—and logistically it may have been possible to do it. It'd take a lot of nerve, but it would have been possible. But finally, what matters is that it's rooted in reality, it's a story I heard and ended up believing, more or less. There's so much other stuff, much more bizarre, other things I'd seen all around me. But so many people told the same story, some had actually seen this woman. She was somewhat older, she was a college graduate, not a high school graduate, and she spent time up in the Song Tra Bong. Of course, finally, it's irrelevant—whether it was rooted in reality or not, I don't care, but it was a story I heard.

LW: How did you begin writing? Did you feel that you just had to write out your Vietnam experience?

TOB: No. I began as a kid, as a little boy. I can't remember what I wrote— short stories, whatever. I can't remember the content of the stories but I do remember the physical act of writing. I grew up loving books. I remember losing myself in books, escaping the world with them. I remember buying pads, paper, writing stories. Finally I found out how hard they were to do— incredible. You know, I'm eight years old and thinking, "This isn't any good!" So it began well before Vietnam. Vietnam was the catalyst where I think I had to write. I had no choice about that, I had to do it. Not for psychological reasons, so much as for reasons of just transmitting experience: "You've got to hear about this, you've got to know what happened—you've got to hear it." It wasn't therapeutic so much as it was this urgent desire to tell the world about the horror and the purposelessness of what I'd gone through, the absolute—all this death and no gain. So Vietnam was a catalyst but the literary impulse was there from when I was a little boy. Hence, the very first question you asked—why I prefer to talk about literary things rather than Vietnam, because it's a literary impulse.

LW: So you have no regrets about having chosen writing as your lifetime's occupation?
TOB: No, I can't imagine doing anything else. I can't think I'd be happy doing anything else.

LW: You don't regret, then, giving up your doctoral thesis?
TOB: Oh no. I have no regrets at all. I consider myself a writer who was really born in the United States. I'm widely read there, I'm quite a popular writer—I'm not John Irving, but I'm popular. But here [in the United Kingdom] I can be one of those writers who, like in the old days, can be popular but still serious. Here it's possible, whereas in the States it's very rare now. You're either one or the other. If you're literary you're unread, or you're read but, you know—for what purpose? The days of—the 1930s, '40s, '50s, even the '60s—you know, when popular writing could also be good writing—are almost gone. I'm one of the few people left who can do it, so I value what I do—what a waste it would have been if I'd been a teacher or a journalist or a scholar. A lot of this stuff for me goes back to childhood and this is like a dream come true, in a lot of ways. There are times when I wake up and wonder—what am I doing? This is one of them, coming here. Here I am, on a UK book tour, and I'm partly terrified and partly thinking of the little boy dreaming in the basement in southern Minnesota, reading his books and trying his little stories—hey! These things have happened, of course, over a lifetime for me.

LW: What would you like to be remembered for? If six of your books fell into a pit, which one would you want to survive?
TOB: Oh, I don't know. It's like choosing between your children! I know which ones for sure I would cast out—the son I wouldn't welcome home is *Northern Lights*. Unless I could rewrite it. It could be forgotten, but unfortunately you can't erase history. There it is. It's in the libraries, and now it's being reissued despite my desires that it should not. But the rest of my work,

to a greater or lesser degree, I'm proud of. I have a fondness for *The Nuclear Age*, which very few people have. Most people hate it. But I kind of like it. And I have a fondness for—I think probably my best book, technically, is *In the Lake of the Woods*. As a writer, you know where all the dials and switches are in a book and there, I'm delighted, it works really tightly. Other books, for example *The Things They Carried*, I look on, in a sense, as needing re-writing before publishing. Even small changes—for example, the little things like dialogue. There's a bit of dialogue followed by a lower-case "he smiled". Well, you can't smile words. So—"he said, smiling"? That's something I think I tried as a gimmick or a trick—will it work? I don't know, maybe nobody'll notice it—but it strikes me it was just not right, and so I'll change it. *Tomcat*, for me, is a book that I'm gratified with. I like the book, I find myself laughing and that's good for me! It's a book that I fear history will be unkind to, because I think people will think I'm endorsing this guy's behavior! Whereas I'm not. I'm of course criticizing it—that's why we're laughing at him, that's why it's a comedy, this guy is simply not doing the right things. But I think the fond part of my heart—the unruly child—is *Tomcat*. The children that succeeded most would be *The Things They Carried* and *Cacciato*. They're my success children. *If I Die* is the child who died—but it's probably my best-selling book in England. But it's a book that's really old, a lifetime ago, a long time ago. It barely seems mine any more—I read it, stunned, thinking, "I wrote this?" I now don't recognize much. I find myself reading along and liking it, but it doesn't seem like mine in the way the others do. Because it's old, you know. It's a nice way of talking about my books, as though they're children—I've never done that before!

LW: With *In the Lake of the Woods* were you consciously striving for a new form, or did it just happen? I've never seen another book with that kind of form, mixing speculation with evidence, fact, and fiction.

TOB: Every book is consciously striving for another form. Form is a crucial literary thing for me. Every book—say, *The Things They Carried*, for example, which is a novel in the form of a memoir, was following the conventions of its form: dedicating the book to the characters as though it's a memoir. The form of *In the Lake of the Woods* is also an invented new form: evidence, hypothesis. The form is there, at least for me, for a reason. In the case of *In the Lake of the Woods*, the reason for the form was that I've always been fascinated by the unknown and matters of magic, God, and so on, and things we'll never know. What happened to Lizzie Borden? Did Oswald act alone? Things we can never know. What is death? Is there a God? Do people love me? We can't know. It goes beyond the physical into the spiritual. We can't know. It's all fascinating. What was John Wilkes Booth like, the man who shot Lincoln? We'll never know. And so the form of *In the Lake of the Woods* was evidence-hypothesis-story, a way of eternally circling the characters John Wade and Kathy Wade. What happened during those hours at the lake? But because they're gone, we can't know. The best we can do is what we do when we talk about God. We can speculate, then we offer alternative possibilities. One religion will offer this, another this, an atheist this, an agnostic this, and all the gradations in between. But they're all circling the ineffable. The form of that book is circling. That's true of all my books, except maybe *If I Die*. There, I was consciously telling a story.

LW: Do you think you'll ever revisit Vietnam, either in literature or in reality?

TOB: I have been back. I went back in 1994. I don't know if I'll go back again in real life, but I know that in my writing I will. I'm doing it right now, in writing two separate short stories. The revisitive one is about a man who goes to Winnipeg, in Canada; it's about what his life is like.[2] But the other is a very simple story without any dialogue in it—it's a very hard story to write—about a man who's wounded, and the whole story will be making him crawling, more or less, with a leg hanging.[3] My thought, a page or two into it, well, so what? But that happens with every story—something's got to happen, obviously, beyond this man trying to survive. But that's the fun of it! I want to try, in this case, what's a very simple form—a man who's terribly, terribly injured, almost to the point of death, and trying to survive—a kind of survival story, but it's got to go beyond death for me. But what that will be, I don't know, because I haven't yet written it! Something strange will happen, out of the ordinary—but if it doesn't happen I'll never publish it. For me, I don't set out making the form, the form comes through the composition. That goes through all the books, including *Cacciato*. The dream idea came over me, when I was well into the book, about eighty pages—the observation post would be the focus, then it'd teeter back and forth, through flashbacks to the war, then the imaginary journey going to Paris. I was well into the book when it came to me. The same is true of every book, the form comes out of the content of what I'm writing. Then I'll go back and rewrite. I have to do a lot of rewriting.

2. "Winnipeg," first published in the *New Yorker*, 14 August 2000 (revised and later published as Chapter 9 of *July, July*).

3. "July '69", first published in *Esquire*, July 2000 (revised and later published as Chapter 2 of *July, July*).

Tim O'Brien: An Interview

Anthony Tambakis/1999

From *Five Points: A Journal of Literature and Arts* 4.1 (Fall 1999): 94–114. Reprinted with permission of *Five Points*.

Tim O'Brien is widely considered one of the best writers of his generation. He served as a foot soldier in Vietnam from 1969–1970, after which he pursued graduate studies in government at Harvard University. O'Brien later worked as a national affairs reporter for the *Washington Post* before publishing his first book, *If I Die in a Combat Zone*, in 1973. In 1979, his novel *Going After Cacciato* won the National Book Award in fiction. In 1990, his collection of linked stories *The Things They Carried* was nominated for a Pulitzer Prize and was chosen by the editors of the *New York Times Book Review* as one of the best books of the year. The title story won a National Magazine Award and was recently included in the *Best American Short Stories of the Twentieth Century*, edited by John Updike. O'Brien's most recent novel *Tomcat in Love* was an immediate best seller upon its publication in September of 1998. His previous novel *In the Lake of the Woods* was also selected by the *New York Times Book Review* as one of the best books of 1994, and by *Time* as the best work of fiction in 1994.

A native of Worthington, Minnesota, O'Brien lived in Cambridge, Massachusetts, for thirty years following his return from Vietnam. He recently moved to Austin, Texas, where he will be teaching at Southwest Texas State.

Five Points Assistant Editor Anthony Tambakis interviewed O'Brien at the Temple Bar in Cambridge on May 19, 1999.

Tambakis: You just got back from Hollywood, from a reading of the new screenplay for *Going After Cacciato*. Leonardo DiCaprio is involved, right?
O'Brien: Yeah, they flew me out for the reading in order to lend a little

literary cache to it. Nick Cassavetes has a nice script for it, and Leonardo is thinking of playing the lead. It was a lot of fun. They rented a big room in some fancy hotel and there were about twenty-five actors sitting around this huge table, not to mention all of these Hollywood types. Cassavetes assigned roles to everybody. Leonardo played the hero, of course, Paul Berlin, and Tobey Maguire played Cacciato. He was supposed to play Paul Berlin originally, but when Leonardo said yes they gave Tobey Maguire Cacciato. I think he was a little surprised at the reading because Cacciato hardly has any lines at all, as you would expect. His face will be on screen a lot, in the distance, but he doesn't have very many lines. Jon Voight was there, playing the old lieutenant. He was fabulous. There were also some other people I've never heard of—the star of *Felicity*—Carrie Russell I think. She played the little girl in the VW van. Leonardo brought along a lot of his buddies, so they all had roles, this whole pack of kids. They were good together, all laughing and having a good time. Cassavetes gave me the role of the promotions major to play, which is a great little role. I got to interrogate Leonardo. We were laughing and having a good time.

Tambakis: This isn't the first time you've had a book made into a movie. I know someone bought the rights to *The Things They Carried*. *In the Lake of the Woods* was a TV movie. Cinemax just did something based on "Sweetheart of the Song Tra Bong." Have you ever thought of writing a screenplay yourself?

O'Brien: No, I'm content to let someone else screw things up. The way movies are made, you basically have to take all the dreamlike elements out of your stories and tell a more straightforward, realistic story, which to me violates what the work is really about. The interweaving of memory and imagination, how one mingles with the other, doesn't come across in movies. If I were to write a screenplay for one of my books I'd probably screw it up as bad as anyone else. The guy who wrote the script for *Cacciato* did a good job. He used a lot of my dialogue, and it's nice to hear your words being spoken. If the movie gets made it would be great. Leonardo's father was there, and he's kind of the main guy decision-wise, so I was chatting him up. He doesn't look anything like you think he would. Nothing like Leonardo.

He's a flower child of the '60s kind of guy. Hawaiian shirt, long flowing hair. Pot belly. He's a great guy. Cassavetes is, too. He doesn't give a shit about money and all that other bottom-line movie stuff. It's probably because he grew up in Hollywood with his father and isn't impressed by all the bullshit. If he makes a good movie, I'll be happy. I've never had anything to do with the process before. Usually I just cash the check.

Tambakis: Thirty years ago you're trying to avoid land mines outside of My Lai and now you're hanging out with Leonardo DiCaprio.
O'Brien: What a journey, right? I don't know what I can even say about it. Writing was a dream I had ever since I was a little boy, but I never took the dream seriously. I just thought that it would be a cool thing to do when I grew up. I never studied writing. I took a lot of English courses when I was in college, but not for any writerly purpose. It's hard to look at the last thirty years and know what to make of it. It's like wanting to be a fireman when you're a kid, and then you grow up and suddenly, by chance, you become one. That's how I feel about writing a little bit. That by chance life intervened, and Vietnam happened, and that made me write.

Tambakis: Why do you think there's been so much important writing to come out of that particular war? Your work, *Dispatches*, *Paco's Story*—the list is long.
O'Brien: There are probably a few reasons for it, but one thing I think is that it had something to do with the clear-cut purposelessness of that particular war. All wars, finally, are stupid and ridiculous and horrid, but in the case of Vietnam it was crystal clear, even on the simplest terms, because it was a war that ultimately couldn't be won. Just taking it on that level—whether or not it was possible to triumph—it was plain to see that the whole thing was a mess. You didn't know who to kill, for one thing. You certainly can't win a war if you don't know who to shoot. There were no battle lines there. Instead of having a front and a rear there was nothing. The enemy was under you and above you. It was pointless. You'd hump all day, search a village, leave it, and as soon as you left it was the enemy's again. You didn't win ground and hold it. Everything you did was without purpose. Even the most uneducated ground soldier could see that we weren't gaining any ground, and we weren't winning hearts and minds. We were killing and dying for no purpose. Because that was so clear cut, the issues of violence and horror became more apparent. I think a veteran of World War II, like my father, might have felt some of the same things I felt in Vietnam—the insanity and horror of it all—and yet at least back then they had myths to rely on. That we were saving the world for democracy and all that. In Vietnam it was harder to rely on myth than it was in earlier wars. In Vietnam, myths were being crippled all around us, and we couldn't swallow them anymore.

I think that has something to do with it. The absence of moral rectitude and virtue. I'm not sure, though. What I do know is that they'll probably be reading those books you mentioned two hundred years from now. And rightfully so.

Tambakis: The Vietnam-writer label has got to irritate you.

O'Brien: Definitely. Definitely. It's like calling Toni Morrison a black writer, or Melville a whale writer, or Shakespeare a king writer. Or saying John Updike is a writer for the suburbs, which he isn't in the slightest. I understand that all writers get typecast. It's bound to happen, because all writers, all people, really, gravitate toward a center of concerns that are particular to their experiences. But it does irritate me, because no writer wants to be grouped in any kind of ready-made category. Writing is all about being an individual, an individual with your own vision, a vision unrelated to anything or anyone else. I don't write about bombs and bullets, after all. I write about the human heart. That's my subject matter more than anything else.

Tambakis: When you got back from the war you worked for the *Washington Post* for a while. As a reporter.

O'Brien: It started as a summer intern program at the *Post*. I did it just to make some money, basically. Then a guy went on leave and they hired me full time. It was good for me. I was interested in politics, and it was a hot paper at the time. I learned a lot about writing in the short time I was there. About how to tell a story concisely, and how to make revisions, and how to make every word count. I learned to crunch things down to ten inches or twenty inches or whatever they gave me. It was good training. You could probably go through a whole MFA program—unless you had really good instructors who were hardasses and really wanted to teach you—and you're not going to get the kind of training I got working at the newspaper. It was a serious business, and you had to do things right, no fucking around. I discarded some of what I learned later, because writing news is not like writing fiction, but at least I learned the bare bones of what storytelling is about.

Tambakis: You're not a reporter at heart, though. Not a facts-are-facts type.

O'Brien: You're right. I've believed all my life that truth is elusive. It's elusive in war, in love, in everything we do. The way we use the language has more to do with the truth of a story than any facts that may or may not go into it. A person can say the truest thing on earth and make it sound so trite and stereotypical and dumb as to make it feel untrue. On the other hand, a person can also tell a very convincing lie. Take that famous story of a man fall-ing on a grenade to save his buddies. It's a story we've all heard. A platoon is humping down a trail and a grenade comes flying out of nowhere and lands in the middle of a group of guys. In a few seconds it's going to explode. One of the guys jumps on the grenade and saves his buddies at the expense of his own life. Did that ever happen? I don't know. It may have, it could have happened somewhere, but the point is that it doesn't matter if it did or not, because it feels like something artificial, something phony and out of the movies. Whether it happened or not, it seems untrue and trite. But if you tell the story differently you can make it ring true, even if the story is made up. In a different version of that story, the platoon is humping and the gre-nade comes flying and one of the guys jumps on it to save his buddies, but before he dies, before the grenade goes off, one of the guys he's saving says, "What the fuck are you doing that for?" And the dead guy, the soon-to-be dead guy, says, "The story of my life, man," and grins. Now that never hap-pened, but there's something about the absurdity of the story, and the hor-ror that goes with it, also, which seems truer than the other version we've heard so many times. "What the fuck are you doing that for?" seems truer, right? So what I'm saying, what I'm always trying to say, is that the truth of stories isn't measured by genuine happening, or the truth of facts, but by the truth of fiction, which, done well, is greater than the truth of fact.

Tambakis: You wrote about that in "How to Tell a True War Story." It's a good example of the difference between reporting and inventing. Fact ver-sus fiction.

O'Brien: I'm not an absolutist and never have been. I'm a person who sees ambiguity everywhere; moral ambiguity, psychological ambiguity, ambi-guity even of memory. That's why I write fiction instead of scholarship or news reporting, where one has to have a kind of belief in the firmness of the world. To me, the world doesn't seem firm. It's malleable and very fluid and changeable. In fiction you can find truths that you can't find anywhere else.

Tambakis: Like you said in "Good Form," that story-truth is truer some-times than happening-truth? Can you explain that?

O'Brien: Yes. You can take any experience you might have had, and run it through your imagination and memory, and your imagination and memory will render what happened to you in an ordered, meaningful way. You forget some details and remember others, then you reorder the more conspicuous elements, and what you often have left is a power that the total experience did not have. All the random details, the minutiae of daily life, is forgotten, and in the new kind of experience your imagination gives you patterns and meaning you might not have had before. It's like when someone is dying, someone who may be important to you. In those real-life moments, the happening truth is that it's mostly monotony. Standing around or sitting down or performing small tasks. It's waiting, mostly, like in war, which is also mostly waiting. The imagination pushes those monotonous, unimportant things aside.

Tambakis: You can trace that kind of idea through your books. *If I Die in a Combat Zone*, your first book, is pretty much a straightforward account of your experiences in Vietnam, but there are points where you can see what will later become the ideas around which *The Things They Carried* and *In the Lake of the Woods* are centered. The fluidity of truth and reordering of memory.

O'Brien: Even from the beginning, even with *Combat Zone*, I restructured a lot of things unknowingly. I was writing about my experiences, so it seemed like a straight nonfiction piece, but I found myself doing other things, things I would become drawn to more down the road. I made up dialogue, for one thing. How often do you really remember what was said, or in what way? I restructured events, the chronology of things. The book starts out at the war and goes back to Minnesota before the war, so even then, unconsciously, I was working with some of the ideas we've been talking about. The world has never come at me in straight, linear ways, so even with that first effort, having absolutely no theoretical knowledge about philosophy or literature, it seemed the proper way to tell the story. As my career went on, what began as an intuitive thing crystalized into a general approach to the kind of art I like to do.

Tambakis: Art that's less concerned with what happened and more with what *might* have happened.

O'Brien: It's what we do as fiction writers. We're all doing fiction for a reason, which has to do somehow with our decision to make things up, to not put all of our faith in the literal world we all live in, but to instead commit ourselves to fiction. Otherwise, why not just tell the truth about everything? Those of us who do this have come to understand that faithfulness to the literal world, to the conventional ways of representing the world, may not be a faithfulness to the way we feel the world happen and unfold around us. The best writing is always explorative. Why do we do the things we do? What is love? What is courage?

Tambakis: You've written a great deal about courage, and you've said many times that you considered yourself a coward for going to Vietnam.

O'Brien: I felt that way, that I was a coward. I felt that the right thing to do would have been to go to jail or to Canada, considering what I believed, and still believe, about the wrongness of the war. I didn't have the guts to do it—going to war seemed to be the easy way out. Going to jail or to Canada seemed more difficult for psychological reasons, because I was afraid people would think I was a coward. I bowed to convention. To tradition. To small towns. To the mythology of service to my country, right or wrong. You do things because you want people to love you. I'm fascinated by that, the things we'll do to get love, to be loved. To stay loved. I'll always feel that I did a terrible thing when I was young. It'll be there forever, until the day I die, and I'll always carry a guilt with me, and yet you have to do something about that, so what I do is write stories. In a way, it relieves a little pressure on my soul, transfers some of Vietnam back to the country that sent me there. It doesn't end it, but I feel like it does two things: one, it relieves some of that pressure on my spirit, to acknowledge evil, like a confession, and two it might serve as a kind of warning to others. I hope that some kid in Sioux City reads *The Things They Carried*, and if he gets drafted to fight in a suspect war then maybe he might think about it just for a moment longer. I wonder if I had a book like *The Things They Carried* to read prior to my getting drafted if I might have thought, God, that guy thinks that. . . . Maybe it would have been one more little piece of weight towards Canada or jail. Away from Vietnam.

That kind of courage, the courage of conviction set up against the desire to be accepted and loved, is something that I've always been obsessed by. I never was one of those guys who felt he had something to prove to himself. I never looked at courage in that old Hemingway grace-under-pressure sense. I hated the war and didn't want to go to it. I had absolutely no desire to test myself by charging a hill or bunker. Some guys did, but I wasn't one of them. From the first moments of basic training, that was something I never understood. Why would anyone want to die? To take a chance like that? That was never a concern of mine, and so there's not a lot of that kind of thing in my writing. I'm more interested in things like guilt and memory. How people live with things.

Tambakis: You've said that stories can save us.

O'Brien: Stories can save us, but of course I don't mean that in just one sense. I don't mean it in a physical sense, that is to say they won't save our bodies, but stories can save us in the sense that whenever anyone opens up *Huckleberry Finn* it's alive again. Mark Twain is alive again. His ideas are alive. Stories can raise ghosts, in the way that someone may be gone, maybe a father, but then you remember him, and there he is in your imagination, throwing a baseball or whatever he used to do, and he's alive again. Writing stories is a way of doing that, of saving people like we save them in our memories. In fiction we can shuffle things around, like I said, and they can live again. We can live again. I also mean that in a spiritual sense, that stories can save us morally, save us from committing sin in our lives. Stories have a way of representing models of proper and improper human comportment. Stories can contain warnings to us. In my fiction about Vietnam I certainly have done what I can to hold up warning signs about war. About being careful about getting into wars. That they're not this glorious, patriotic enterprise that Hollywood has so often given us. Some guys will say "I served my country and I'm damn proud of that and I challenge anyone to say otherwise." There are a lot of guys like that. *Most* of them are like that. They're not my kind of guys. I'm kind of striking back at the proud-to-be-a-veteran notion.

Tambakis: How do you feel about Kosovo?

O'Brien: I'm reminded a little of Vietnam by it all. Obviously the parallels aren't exact by any means, but if you were to give a multiple choice test to two hundred random citizens on the street about the history of that area no one would get anything right. Nobody would pass it. Just like Vietnam. No one even knew the French were ever there. So there's that—that universal ignorance about the culture and history of the place, about nationalism and religion and other differences no one knows anything about. That kind of national ignorance is the same type of syndrome that got us into Vietnam. You have to remember that there was a great reluctance to use ground troops then, too. We tried to just drop bombs. Johnson was afraid of calling up reserves. It was all done in an incremental, step-by-step way, so as to not bring any waves on. There was a reluctance then, just like with Kosovo, and other recent conflicts.

Tambakis: I remember when Bush declared back during the Gulf War, "We've kicked the Vietnam Syndrome once and for all." Not quite true.

O'Brien: Yeah, that was about winning. Let's do it right this time. Let's win one. The thing about that is that we left the place with Saddam still in power, and what did we do, really, but save this oligarchy of Kuwait, which isn't exactly the greatest democracy on the planet. The Kurds are still getting hell, and Iraq hasn't changed a bit. Neither has the danger it represented. So yeah, we did it right in that a lot of Americans didn't die, but on the other hand, Americans have a way of wiping out the fact that a lot of other people died. We don't worry much about that. We live in a funny society. We have short term memories. If you went out into the square and asked ten people what the plot of *Hamlet* is, only one of them would know. And this is a very smart area. Then ask them who the star of *Frazier* is, and nine will know. It's just the way it is.

Tambakis: Bob McNamara was on TV again yesterday, peddling his new book. They only showed him from the waist up, so you couldn't see the blood on his hands.

O'Brien: I met the guy who ghost-wrote that book a couple of weeks ago at Brown University. Like on just about everything in life, I don't have any absolute things to say about it all. On one hand, I hold Bob McNamara and Dean Rusk and Walt Rostow and George Bundy responsible for what happened. You have to, because they're the people who brought us the war, and all the mea culpas in the world won't change that. There's just no getting around it. They were the decision makers. On the other hand, McNamara was the only one of that crew to even partially acknowledge the errors they made. He's taken a lot of shit, deservedly so, but at least he was able to say, all those years later, that he made a big mistake.

Tambakis: You returned to Vietnam in 1994 as the first soldier to go back to the My Lai area. What did that mean to you?

O'Brien: It's hard to sum up for me. It really is. I guess the central nugget, five years later, is that I'm very glad I went. Vietnam now, having gone back, isn't just a war anymore. It isn't just terror and death and horror and loss. Those memories will always be there, don't get me wrong, but now, at least, living alongside those memories is the picture of a country at peace, and a people I came to know a little bit in the brief two weeks I was there. I got to know more about the country and the people in two weeks than I did in the year I was there during the war. Actually meeting people, and having drinks with them, having fun together, was something I'll never forget. When I was there I didn't feel the things I do now about the country itself, or the people. When I was there I hated the place. I was scared. While I hated the war, I can't say that I sympathized with the Vietnamese, because I hated every bit of it—the paddies, the tunnels, the soil. I hated the fact that people I knew were dying. I hated the fact that I was terrified all the time. Until going back Vietnam was just a war to me, but now it's more, and I'm glad for that. I'm glad I made the journey. It's phenomenal how much the Vietnamese have forgiven us, or seem to have forgiven us. You see people crippled by the mines we left, and you wonder how it can be that they can forgive us like they have.

Tambakis: You served as a foot soldier around My Lai in 1969, a year after American troops massacred 504 Vietnamese villagers, and worked with what happened there in *In the Lake of the Woods*.

O'Brien: I went through exactly what those members of Charlie Company went through. I was a foot soldier, like you said, a year after the massacre occurred, and we helped pull security for the village when they started investigating what happened on that Saturday in March. Most of the casualties we took were from land mines, and it was frustrating because you couldn't strike back, and the land itself seemed to be the enemy. There's a sense of rage that develops when the ground itself seems to be killing you, and I understand what it is to have your blood sizzle with that rage. So I experienced the same frustrations they did, but I never crossed that line between rage and murder. I didn't cross the line, and neither did anybody in my unit. That said, the question becomes "Why?" Why did they cross the line and we didn't, even though our experiences were nearly the same? That's the mystery of it all. Evil is a mysterious thing. The question that I ask, the things that I'm curious about, lead me to try and discover other things, uncover mysteries, though most of the time I don't come to any neat conclusions. There usually aren't any. In *In the Lake of the Woods*, the mystery of Kathy Wade's disappearance remains a mystery. We don't find out what happened to her, whether she ran away or was killed or had an accident. I originally was going to end the book differently, but leaving it open seemed to be the right thing to do. Once a mystery is solved it's not a mystery anymore. What we seem to remember in life, what seems to capture our imaginations, is what we don't know. That's what keeps things like the Kennedy assassination alive. If we knew who did it, it wouldn't be a mystery anymore, and we wouldn't think about it anymore. It would be over.

Tambakis: You said once that writers should be scab pickers, because we lived in a society that was more concerned with healing than remembering.

O'Brien: I feel that we live in a mass psychology, from TV and movies on down the line, that tells everyone that you've got to heal your life. Part of that is true, and useful, but if one does it to the extent of forgetting the past, to where you're burying your head and saying that certain bad things never happened, then that's nothing more than denial. There's this kind of healing out there which involves denying the past, and when you do that you run the risk of repetition, of making the same mistakes again and again. You also run the risk of self-deception. Self-delusion. I don't think what happened at My Lai should be healed, necessarily. It was mass murder. They were killing babies. Old people. We know who they were—many of them have confessed. Yet nothing ever happened to them. Calley served four and a half months. That was it. Our country has an incredible facility for complacency and for forgetting our errors and blunders and evil deeds. My Lai is an example of that. Slavery and the genocide of the Indians are also good examples.

Tambakis: You've written that "Evil has no place in our national mythology."
O'Brien: Exactly. We've built a national story for ourselves which has to do with the rescue of the beleaguered and oppressed. Part of that is true, but along with the white knight we've also worn the black hat many, many times. People tell themselves stories to get through life, and our country does as well. For me, My Lai is part of the story we have to tell, because it staggers me when I go to universities and see the dumbfounded looks on the faces of the kids when I mention My Lai. They've never heard of it. Then I remember my own education, where I didn't learn a fucking thing about what was done to the Indians and damn little about slavery, too. There are certain things you can't put behind you—that you shouldn't put behind you. It's like putting the Holocaust behind you. You don't just forget about a thing like that. You've got to keep it alive. I feel the same way about Vietnam as Elie Wiesel does about the Holocaust. People call him a party pooper and want him to forget it, but you've got to bear witness in this life. You've got to bear witness. Someone should say something about the 504 Vietnamese who were slaughtered at My Lai that Saturday morning in March. I think that it's one thing to understand a thing and another to do it. It's like with Hitler—you can explain it, and understand it, read books, but to explain something is not to justify it. I can't conceive of what they did. I went through what they went through, like I said, losing friends, frustrated at having nothing to shoot back, not being able to find an enemy that was over us and under us and everywhere and nowhere at the same time. There was a frustration and rage that built up. But it makes you wonder what they think, even now.

Do they still try and justify it to themselves and to the world? Do they have trouble falling asleep at night? Do they try and reassure themselves that what they did was right? What kind of stories do they tell themselves?

Tambakis: That question seemed to sit at the center of John Wade's character in *In the Lake of the Woods*. He was a guy who hid what he did at My Lai.
O'Brien: The book was about the consequences of sin. Trying to hide it from yourself, the world, your own wife. My metaphorical expansion is the country itself—hiding our sins from ourselves, and the consequences of denying history in both a personal and a national way. It's about the consequences of telling lies to and about ourselves. We are compulsive liars as a nation, to ourselves and to the world, and the consequences of that are devastating. We lie in a repetitive, obsessive way. We're always trying to patch the truth, whether it's about slavery or Vietnam, because I think we're afraid of drowning in it. In a psychological and personal way, every veteran who went through the war in Vietnam does something like that on a more modest scale. John Wade was certainly one of those people.

Tambakis: You played a lot with form in that book. In all your books, it seems. *The Things They Carried* was heralded for inventing a new form entirely, one that seemed to mix fiction, nonfiction, and essay-like commentary. You dedicated the book to the characters in it, and even had a character named Tim O'Brien who was a writer your age. Many people think the book is nonfiction, but that's not true, is it? There was no Jimmy Cross, or Norman Bowker. "Speaking of Courage" was invented. All of it was, right?
O'Brien: "Speaking of Courage" came out of an idea I had about being home from the war, and getting a letter in the mail from a guy named Norman Bowker, who served in my unit in Vietnam. The idea was that I got the letter after having published *If I Die in a Combat Zone*, and in it he told me how he enjoyed the book, and how difficult it was for him to adjust to being home. He said he couldn't do much except for drive around the lake in his hometown in Iowa. He asked me to write a story about it, so I did. I sent him the story and he said he liked it, and I didn't hear from him until years later when I received a letter from his mother telling me that Norman Bowker had committed suicide. He hung himself at the YMCA. So I told that story, and commented on the telling of it, and the feelings I had, and that gave it an essay-like feel, like you said. But the truth of the matter is that it's all made up. The commentary is made up. There is no Norman Bowker. There never was. The idea that I was working with, especially using a character named

Tim O'Brien, is that in the world of fiction not only can we invent our own reality, but we can also invent our own autobiographies. Our own histories. *The Things They Carried* is a work of fiction, but it seems like something else. To me, that's the essence of a true story.

Tambakis: I see what you're saying, though one of my students was devastated to find out you didn't have a daughter. The O'Brien character in *Things* does, and she couldn't believe you made it up.

O'Brien: Well, in a way she is real. The child I do not have. Storytelling can even do that for you. Because I do not have a daughter, or because there's no Norman Bowker, doesn't make the stories any less true. Because these things didn't literally happen doesn't make them less true than if they did. It feels like they did, so in a sense they're more true. A story's truth should never be measured by actual happening. Fiction relies on a different standard, because good fiction is consumed with emotional truths, and those feelings, those truths, are what matters. "Does it ring true?" is a far more important question than "Is it true?" To try and classify different elements of a story like "Speaking of Courage," or "Good Form," or any of the stories in *The Things They Carried*, seems artificial to me. It's literature, and, as I said, it has to be looked at not for its literal truths but its emotional truths. In one hundred years it won't matter if Tim was really Tim the writer, or how much of it was made up. In a hundred years no one will care about that anymore. When it comes off the shelf the ideas will be alive again, and the truths in those ideas and stories will be alive again, and that's what matters. Nobody cares whether Mark Twain based Huck Finn on a real person or not anymore. It's irrelevant now. What matters in the fiction I read and the fiction I write is whether I'm moved by a story or not. Whether it rings true to me. Everything else is superfluous.

Tambakis: *The Things They Carried* seems to be the book most critics think is built to last the longest. Do you feel it's your strongest work?

O'Brien: You never know. There is no telling what will last and what won't. The best thing a writer can do is to get the work out, and not get too excited about good reviews or bad reviews, or what the critics are saying or not saying. Over time, things straighten themselves out. I don't get in the habit of defending my work, and if I get a bad review I feel it, but it only hurts for a short time, because I'm not writing stories for contemporary critics but for the ages. Every good writer will say the same thing—that their intent is to write for history, to create art that lasts, art that might be read and enjoyed a hundred or two hundred years from now. All you can control is the work. Getting it done. You can't worry about the rest of it. *Moby-Dick* was killed in its time. Trashed. The critics said it was the most hideous piece of garbage ever written. That didn't help Melville when he was alive and suffering, I know, but his intent was to write a book for the ages and he accomplished that. It's easy to say this now, because it feels true, and as I get older I think more about these kinds of things, but I'll tell you what: if I was lying on my death bed and you said, "Tim, I'll give you another two weeks of life if you give up all your stories and all your books," I'd probably say, "O.K., give me the two weeks." Take the books, give me the time. Isn't that something?

Tambakis: You'd probably use the two weeks to write one last story.
O'Brien: You're probably right. There's a story for you right there.

Tambakis: Your books and stories, from *Combat Zone* on to *Tomcat in Love*, seemed to be concerned with three things mainly: love, courage, and evil, and what those things are, and how we live with them.
O'Brien: That's right, those are the things I'm concerned with, and have always been concerned with and curious about. What bad things will people do to get love? To be loved? To keep love? We all have seeds of evil in us. Why do they grow in some people and not in others? To those things I would add the fluidity of truth is something I've always been obsessed by, the whole constellation of issues that go into that, that all have to do with fiction and storytelling in general. It's about expanding the world we live in, which is what I see largely as absolutism, and the consequences of absolutism, versus a more humble sense of the human spirit facing a veil of uncertainty and a veil of ambiguity. I think the human psyche is often overwhelmed by things like our own mortality, and the elusiveness of love, and all the things we're never going to get answers to. I try and explore all of those things in my work.

Tambakis: The things we'll do for love is a theme running through your most recent work, the short "Nogales," which was in the *New Yorker*, and of course *Tomcat in Love*, which was comedic and something of a departure for you.
O'Brien: I wanted to take some of the difficult things that had happened, some of the feelings of heartache and loss, and filter them through a comic lens. Love has at its center a kind of pitiful humor. I'm proud of Tom Chip-

pering as a character. It was tough to sustain that voice, that insensitive, self-justifying, politically incorrect voice. Though the tone is comic, the themes aren't. I'm still hung up on the idea we were talking about earlier, the idea of what we as people will do to win love and to keep it. *Tomcat* has its genesis in that idea, but I think it really goes all the way back to my first book. I've always been concerned with it. The most explicit representation of that idea was probably the *New York Times* article. That was really explicit.

Tambakis: Well, I wasn't going to bring it up, but since you did, that article, "The Vietnam in Me," was very raw and very moving. In it you frankly described your thoughts of suicide after your return from Vietnam in 1994 when your long-time girlfriend left you.
O'Brien: I really opened up in that article—everything I thought at the time is in there. It's hard to know what to say about it now, because everything I thought and went through is right there on the surface of the article. I've toyed with doing another piece like that, down the road maybe ten years later, but I don't know. The last I heard she's in California. I haven't seen her since that period. Since '94. The only real difficulty I had with that article is that it caused a lot of pain to the people I love. And to me, also. It's a perceptive piece, I think, about the inner penetration of love and war, and the similarities between the two, but I wish that maybe I held on to it and had it published posthumously. I don't know. The other side of it is that writing the article helped me through a tough time. There's nothing that can be done about it now anyway—at the time it was all I had, and you can't redo history.

Tambakis: You wrote about depression in that article. Seems like a lot of writers I know are depressives.
O'Brien: It's not surprising. You have to be kind of crazy to do this, and something of a depressive I'd have to imagine. If you weren't one when you started out you probably are now, because this is a field that is so subjective. There's always someone who's not satisfied, who wants things different. They don't like this ending, or this character. And then there's the doubt that all writers have to deal with. There are times when I don't think I can do this, times when I don't think I'll ever be able to write another story. The odds in blackjack are 48-52 at least—what are they in writing? A million to one? But I stick to it. I try to work constantly, and I'm stubborn about it, and I like doing it. If you're a writer you've got to like those times when you're digging and scratching your way out of things, when you're grinding through.

Tambakis: You're going to Texas this summer, where you're going to teach for the first time. Why Southwest Texas, and why now, after all these years?
O'Brien: It gets me the hell out of Cambridge for one thing. I've been here almost thirty years—since 1970. That's pretty much reason number one. I need a change of venue. There's too many bad memories associated with this neighborhood—even with this place we're at now. I'm sick of it. Sick of the cold. I like golf, and will be glad to play every now and then. That's it, essentially. I need some warm weather, and a new environment, and some new faces. I came here to go to grad school after the war and I'm still here. It's never felt like home to me. I never thought I'd go to Texas, though. Never thought of myself as a Texan, that's for sure.

I think the situation in Texas will be good though. It's a good set up. They're giving me a ton of money, and the workload isn't crippling. It's one class, once a week, for one semester, so it's not like I'm jumping into a full schedule. It'll only be about ten students, for four or five months. The second semester I have to give something like three public talks, which I can do easily. I'll be working with MFA students, and since I won't be loaded down I think I'll actually be able to help somebody. I think if you went in as a university professor with a full work load that it would be tough to help somebody through a thesis or a group of stories or a novel because you couldn't give enough time to it. You'd be overwhelmed by all the other crap you have to do, other classes and papers and committees, whereas I'll be able to work more closely with my small group, and do some of the things that a good editor can do, which is to make comments and very detailed suggestions. The first thing I think you have to do is put yourself in their heads and ask what it is they're trying to accomplish. So first you go drinking with them, talk, get to know them, and then you can get a notion for what kind of stories they're trying to tell and why. Sometimes that's one of the most fundamental questions that people never ask—why are you writing this? The answers can be incredibly surprising, everything from "I want to make a million dollars" to "It came right out of my life and I've been pained by it forever and I've got to get it out." The answer is very rarely "To make good art," and that's the answer that I'm most interested in. Even if they did go through it, that's not really what I give a shit about. It may mean something to the person but it doesn't make it fiction and it doesn't make it art. What I'm concerned with is a good, well-made piece of art, and the work that's necessary to progress towards that goal. That's what I'll try and get across to my students.

Tambakis: Where do you come out on the old question "Can writing be taught?"

O'Brien: I think it can be taught incrementally. On a day-by-day, sentence-by-sentence basis. Line by line. I'll try and teach them by what I know to be true about writing—you've got to work hard. I'll try and get them to understand what you need to give a story a chance at succeeding. What I want to know, what I want to feel, is extraordinariness and specificity. Why *this* love affair? Why *this* divorce? Why *this* cancer? They might say "Well, it happened to me" and think that it makes it true and interesting, but that's not the case. My job is to show them what can make it so, which is language. That's what we have to make it true and interesting—language. You have to know that, and also know that you've got to be at that typewriter all the time for something good to happen. You've got to stay after it. Stay after it all the time.

Tambakis: Raymond Carver said "Routine is no ugly word to a writer."
O'Brien: That's right. I think one of my best qualities as a writer is that I'm always at the typewriter. I'm tenacious. You've got be a mule, you know? Slowly climbing all the time, slowly moving forward all the time. Writing is like a dream to me. When I'm writing it's like a mixture of the directed and the subconscious. That's how my stories are written. It's like I'm sitting at the typewriter with one foot in the rational world and one foot in a dream world. I have no idea where a story is going to go. It's important for young writers to know that it's O.K. to sit down and see where a story takes you. Too much talking about writing theories can kill you, just like too much planning can kill a story. I'll try and tell the students that all you can try to do is write one good sentence. One sentence that's graceful and alive. And then you try and write another one. Then another. Anyone who writes knows how difficult it is. You have to love it. Me, I've always loved it. I've always been curious. As a boy, I had a curiosity about the world. You know, they say that Jeffrey Dahmer used to dissect road kill when he was a kid. Sometimes we become what we were. For good or for bad, we become what we were. The problem I'm having these days is that I always seem to be traveling somewhere for something that doesn't really have anything to do with writing, or with me getting my work done. I'm trying to put a curtain around my work. My time to work.

Tambakis: Well get back at it then.
O'Brien: I will. You get back at it, too.

Tim O'Brien: Author of *July, July* Talks with Robert Birnbaum

Robert Birnbaum/2002

From *Identity Theory*, 5 November 2002. Web. http://www.identitytheory.com/people/birn-baum72.html. Reprinted with permission of Robert Birnbaum.

Tim O'Brien was born in Minnesota and graduated from Macalester College in that state. He served in Vietnam and did graduate work in government at Harvard University. He was briefly a reporter for the *Washington Post*. Tim O'Brien has published the 1979 National Book Award–winning novel *Going After Cacciato*, in addition to *The Things They Carried, In the Lake of the Woods, If I Die in a Combat Zone, Northern Lights, The Nuclear Age, Tomcat in Love*, and now *July, July*. His writing has also appeared in the *New Yorker, Ploughshares, Harper's,* and the *Atlantic* and has been included in several editions of *Best American Short Stories* and *O. Henry Prize Stories*. Tim O'Brien has received numerous literary awards and fellowships. He is currently teaching at Southwest Texas State in San Marcos, Texas.

Robert Birnbaum: What was your starting point for *July, July*?
Tim O'Brien: Well, it's the story of a group of people who get together, a reunion, thirty years after graduating. And that seemed to me to be an interesting hilltop from which you could survey the past and see the person you were and who you are now and the person you may become. From there it goes into an investigation of each of my ten major characters and the turning point in that character's life. To me it's more a book about middle age and disappointment and joys that people have had that aren't commonly associated with what people call the '60s. It was more a look at life and what life had delivered to these people.

RB: I should have been more specific. I wanted to know what your starting point was in writing this novel.

TOB: I see what you mean. Just as a historical matter I was called by the fiction editor Rust Hills, at *Esquire* back then. There was a new feature that the magazine was running. A one-page story. He asked if I would do one. I agreed. I did a story about two people talking at a reunion. One had breast cancer and they knew each other all these years ago and she was just trying to get her old boyfriend to dance with her at a reunion. He keeps on saying no. Something about it intrigued me. I kept on picturing these nametags bobbing in the background—who are these people? I've never been to a reunion—what would it be like? It brought back a lot of ghosts from my own past as I was writing this story. And then one thing leads to another and I wanted to see who the name tag people were. So I did another chapter. And then another. And another. I found most of the chapters of the book were taking place not then but now. The things these people have gone through I had recently gone through. And then the troubles they brought to the reunion—they seemed to leave it a little bit lighter, marginally, so that tomorrow might be a little bit better than yesterday and that felt like my own life. All these things feed in, just story lines. The individual chapters intrigued me—writing about the death of Karen Burns intrigued me. Or about the dirty pictures and Jan Huebner or Marv's big lie or Dorothy's breast cancer. I became intrigued by each life and they became real people to me so the more I wrote about them the more I wanted to know about them.

RB: Is this a book you could have written any time before you wrote it?
TOB: No. No book has been that way.

RB: (laughs) No book was written before its time.
TOB: I couldn't have written *The Things They Carried* now . . . it's true of every book. What your interests are and what your psychology is as a human being have a lot to do with what your content or subject matter is going to be. Here I am at middle age and I'm interested in middle age.

RB: On looking back . . .
TOB: And forwards. Both. It's a time where you survey. You have some time left and it's not as much as it used to be and where have you been and where do you go from here? Of course, it varies radically by person and so I wanted a lot of people in the book to be able to look at different angles of this period of life.

RB: Did *July, July* require you to pay more or a lot of attention to structure and pacing? Or did it just come out?

TOB: I've always paid attention to structure and pacing. Because it's an ensemble novel I knew I couldn't do a whole life for each character. It would have been a 50,000-page book. So I had to find a structure—it seemed to me to be the natural thing to do. People in their lives more or less recall points of crisis, points of decision. Most everything else is erased. We're left with certain bundles and clusters of memory and images that have stuck and everything else is gone. So for each character I thought if I could find one of those clusters of moral choice, a period in life where something was done and there was no going back, where life would always be different afterwards. So when Dorothy walks out without her shirt on, that's something she would remember. It says a lot about the person she is. Not just the breast cancer. She needs to be loved and touched and she is desperate for contentment that she doesn't have. So it's a gallant move on her part.

RB: And unexpected, given her behavior so far in the story.

TOB: Yeah, it is unexpected. Almost inevitable too. Someone who has lived that kind of straight-laced life, sooner or later they all lose it (both laugh). Eventually, in modest ways.

RB: How much does what you have written before enter into your approach to a new story?

TOB: It enters in ways that are not related to plot or story. It enters in terms of style—the sentences in *July, July* are the equal of the sentences in *Things They Carried, In the Lake of the Woods,* or *Going After Cacciato*—they're good sentences and that enters in. One doesn't want to repeat oneself as a writer. I don't want to write a book I have already written. It enters in the sense that I had never done female characters and I had always wanted to. Lead characters and that kind of technical challenge and the fun of it came out of past work . . . I hadn't done it before in the past and I wanted to do it now.

RB: Is it a technical challenge?

TOB: Kind of. Technical may be too vague a term. It's a question of trying to enter the skin of another human being with whom I share little. Not just in terms of gender but in terms of experience. I never posed for dirty pictures and I've never won a lot of money playing blackjack. I've never done anything that these people did. After a while it felt like I was living in the skin of ten other human beings. I don't know if technical is the word. You write differently, not relying on the movie camera inside your head that has recorded your own experience. You are trying to imagine the movie camera inside the head of Dorothy or Jan or Amy—their lives. Even David Todd, I never went through anything like what he went through. I wasn't ever in danger of dying. But I watched it all around me. I know what morphine is. I took it once. I know the hallucinogenic properties and that kind of disembodied—it brings you into the center of your brain with this little bead in there and it seemed in that [David's] case a good place to go with the story.

RB: What's the value you place on accuracy? In the drug scenes, for example?
TOB: You want something interesting. There are a lot of uninteresting things that come out of drugs. I wanted something interesting to come out which is a voice of conscience or history.

RB: Or as in this novel, a deejay.
TOB: He also appears as a TV evangelist, a cop, and a blackjack dealer. To me, it's not meant to be supernatural. It's meant to be what all of us go through at some point just talking to ourselves those hours before sleep sometimes when we got fired or your girlfriend left you or something. You just talk to yourself saying, "How did I get in this fix? How do I get out of it? Why did I do what I did?" Sometimes in an alarmist voice and sometimes in a reassuring voice, "This was a tough divorce but not as bad as Anne Boleyn's." It comes out of us but it doesn't feel like our own voices—a mixture of us and our ideal selves. Then as a dramatist you try to give it a personality. Like with the deejay, I try to rev it up a little bit and it becomes an emblem of what all of us at some point or another do.

RB: In the past you have been identified as a Vietnam story writer and Vietnam has a presence in this novel. Has that been an issue in the critical reception of *July, July*?
TOB: Some reviewers really hated the book. Some loved it. That's been pretty much the case with all my books. Vietnam does figure in the book but obliquely. There is one chapter set there but aside from that, it's a backdrop for the '60s and the Baby Boomer generation. I'm flattered to be known as a Vietnam writer. I can't and I don't want to write the same books over and over. And haven't. *The Things They Carried*—I'd written *Cacciato* and *The Things They Carried* was another angle on it and way of looking at the ex-

perience. More about storytelling, about what stories do in our lives. About writing, about memory, reality. So Vietnam even in *The Things They Carried* wasn't the dominant topic—it's set there but it's not a rehashing of what happened in combat. I'm sure I'll return to it if some similar angle appears to me where something new can come of it.

RB: Were there many Korean War novels?
TOB: No, I've only read one. I'm not a historian or political scientist. I'm interested in human lives. All my books are—in some way or another—about the impact of big global things on individual human beings, what it does to people. Not the demography of it all or the sociology, that's for another province of writing. Mine is storytelling and I try to find stories that I care about. The things I care about have to do with people making choices and decisions in the context of what's right and wrong in the world, the political environment around the characters. But ultimately, especially in this book I almost write against that grain and say what mattered to these people were not just Vietnam and the '60s. What mattered to these people finally is what mattered to everybody—love. The trials of marriage and divorce and all these characters seeking love in one way or another and having a tough time finding it in every case.

RB: Is Vietnam in your books taken too literally?
TOB: Depends on the reader. My books are taught in schools—high schools and colleges—and there's a tendency to do what you just said, over-politicize the books and use them almost as history lessons. It's a bit like using *The Sun Also Rises* as a history lesson about the Lost Generation. It would be true in a way but it would undermine the artistry of the book. It's about Jake and Brett and their need for love.

RB: It's a story.
TOB: Yeah, it's a story. And you can talk about it in those terms. That's only one way of talking about it. If I close my eyes, I see Jake and Brett at the end of the book sitting in a cab. The Lost Generation is a backdrop for it and it's all related—but it's about Jake and Brett. (both laugh)

RB: Did I hear you correctly—you said most of the characters at the end of *July, July* are looking at their lives hopefully?
TOB: Oh yeah. Billy and Paulette might get married. Spook and Marv on a plane together. They are fantasizing together. Sure they go down but they

are together. Jan and Amy walk out, looking for a man. They haven't given up, despite all the bitterness, and through the whole book, in fact, looking around the corner for some possibility of happiness. Think of Marla and David—sure they've been divorced but for the first time in their lives they say, "Tell me about the river. Let's talk and sit on these chapel steps." And . . . there's not a character in the book that doesn't leave it—there's no glorious sunset happy ending that you're going to find in a Danielle Steele but by God, they make progress. Even Ellie when she goes into the shower and she's told her husband about the affair and the drowning and a hopeful breeze go through her thoughts and maybe it'll all be forgiven and the weight of confession or that secrecy, rather, is gone. "Maybe he'll forgive me and come back." That's why I said marginally. I mean there's . . . nothing huge in terms of Happy Birthday and Merry Christmas and the world's a bright place but there's a marginal improvement in these lives.

RB: That reminds me of the opening scene of the film *Milagro Beanfield War* where the aged Mexican peasant gets up and thanks God for one more day. (laughs)
TOB: Yeah! That's kind of how it is for these people. Tomorrow might be just a little better. And I think their characters are plucky. You know, they don't quit. And that seems to me how the world more or less is. Otherwise, we'd all be in Jonestown, drinking Kool-Aid, I mean we do have to have some . . . idea of a fantasy about a better tomorrow—even if it's a little better.

RB: One does have a sense of how many people do get to a certain point in their life and don't recognize the deep disappointment that they have.
TOB: Sure. I think you're right. Basically it's a bunch of love stories of various sorts. It's a book of love stories. I've never talked about it that way before but it's really what it is. It's hard. It's not romance but about things people will do for love.

RB: In Gail Caldwell's review in the *Boston Globe*, she took you to task for this dialogue about Karen's death. Early in the book they're talking about her death and someone says, "That's such a Karen thing to do." And Caldwell seems to think that's not the way women would talk.
TOB: I didn't read it.

RB: What's a womanly way to talk? Does a woman get to say that's not a womanly way to talk?

TOB: Everyone's entitled to their opinion. Lots of great reviews have come from women and they think the characters are great. Not all women talk the same nor do all men. How did she say women are supposed to talk?

RB: She didn't. Do you read reviews?
TOB: No. I don't read them. I mean I hear about them. I know my own book and I know it's a beautiful, beautiful book and so I really don't—I mean I hope people like it but I'm not going to change anything. I don't know many writers who really read them. . . . You can't really learn anything positive. You just get a general impression if people like it or they don't. It's a beautiful book. You have to reflect back—*Cacciato, Things They Carried, In the Lake of the Woods*, they're never unanimous. And in five years, the book will make it or not and succeed or not and it's not up to the contemporary reception—it just never is for any book. There will be five or ten years and then history will take charge after that and . . . books will surface or die over time. It depends more on the passage of time, history, and word of mouth.

RB: I recently watched *One Flew over the Cuckoo's Nest* and I started thinking about Ken Kesey and the books I was reading in 1969 and 1970 and 1971 and there's not a book that I'm really interested in rereading or that changed my life in the way I expect some books to do.
TOB: Yeah. Certain books do it for certain people. People for whom *Cuckoo's Nest* didn't change their lives . . . they read it in that facile, surfacy kind of way. For others, you know, it's a crucial book. It goes for *Catcher in the Rye* or lots of books. Some books, people are totally dead to it—they don't have the temperament. I remember reading *Catch-22* and at the time, it meant nothing to me. A couple of years back I read it again and it meant the world. I mean, time of life and . . . I think I read it first before Vietnam but I know it was just a funny book at the time and then later it meant a lot more. That's the part where the reader brings stuff to the book and the book has to deliver the goods in return.

RB: I have a sense—reconfirmed recently—that you're one of those writers' writers (whatever that means) and it was reconfirmed because I have a young friend who's out at a writing program in Montana and in his classes he says, "My god, whenever we mention Alice Munro or Tim O'Brien, the room gets hushed as if it's a religious ceremony or something like that." Do you have a sense of yourself as being revered by your peers?
TOB: I know my books are read, but I'm the guy who sits in his underwear

in front of the computer all day. People forget that. That's how I spend my days for four years in a row. I'm just sitting here in my underwear trying to write a book. So you're not aware of those things. You're kind of aware of them when you're on a book tour and many people come out but otherwise you just live your life.

RB: You're in contact with a lot of other writers, aren't you?
TOB: No.

RB: Were you teaching before you went to Southwest Texas?
TOB: No.

RB: This is your first real solid teaching job?
TOB: Well years ago I did it very briefly at Emerson—thirty years ago whenever *Cacciato* came out. Aside from that, this is the first time I've ever done it and even now I'm not teaching much. I teach for a semester then I have a year and a half off and then I do it for another semester so it's not a lot. It's embarrassing.

RB: Good deal! This is a kind of a change for a guy who grew up in Minnesota and spent his time in Cambridge and now you're in San Marcos, Texas. You're living in Austin, but San Marcos is very close isn't it?
TOB: Oh yeah it's like ten minutes away from where I live. It's a change but I arrived here in Boston and I realized why I had left . . . It's so cold! I got off the plane and it was snowing.

RB: Wait a minute, you grew up in Minnesota!
TOB: I know! That's what I mean. I'm getting old, can't take it anymore. Couldn't take it then either . . . I didn't like it then . . .

RB: One of my favorite lines in a recent movie [*Spy Game*]. Robert Redford gives some advice to his protégé, he says, "The point is to save up enough money so you can go die somewhere warm."
TOB: (laugh) That's a good line! There's a lot of truth in that. That's what 401k's are for.

RB: Judging from what you said it doesn't matter whether you're in Texas or Minnesota, you'd still be in front of your computer in your underwear writing . . .

TOB: Yeah . . . but it's just nice after you're done writing to be able to go outside and not freeze in October. There's something about the light that's mood enhancing. You feel better when it's not gray and dismal all the time. I'm not urging everybody to move to Texas, it does have its drawbacks. Politics of the state stink. The polyester crew is out in force but there's a lot of bad stuff here too. Austin is a kind of oasis—great music and a lot of great writers live there. I don't know 'em but they live there. Movies get made there. There's plenty to do. Dagoberto Gilb teaches at the school I'm at. He's a pretty good writer and he's a great guy, so I can hang with him when I get bored. So, it's a good place to live.

RB: Do you do a lot of reading?
TOB: Oh yeah.

RB: And how do you decide what you are going to read?
TOB: There are two main things. One route is blurbs. I am sent a lot of books. I'll read until I don't like it or finish if I do. Then I have a lot of debts to pay back. People helped me and I want to try to help others especially if I like the work. I know how hard it is especially for first novelists and novels in general are hard. Fiction's hard. If it's serious fiction, it's just hard to publish it, hard to sell it, hard to place it. Just always hard. So whatever I can do to help it feels like I am paying back. So I do a lot of that. I have authors that I have learned over the years I know I'm going to—if not love the book—at least I am going to really appreciate it. There's a list of writers that I really like. I always read those people when they have new books come out. I read all the time. I don't just read fiction I read other stuff too.

RB: Do you watch television?
TOB: Not much. I watch baseball. Not much to watch. I look now and then. There are 390,000 channels and I look and there is nothing to watch. Dismal. So I really end up watching baseball.

RB: Movies?
TOB: A little. Not much. I should do it more. I just don't like going out. I rent them now and then. My wife teaches acting so I go to the theater with her sometimes. Live theater. Now and then if there's a movie she says I'll love then we'll rent it.

RB: I'm dancing around asking the pretentious question of what informs your work?

TOB: There's no real answer to that question. Everything. It's not just stuff you've read. It's life in all its perverse variety. Dialogue comes at me and I just copy it and steal it from the world. Writers are noticers. Maybe not taking notes but I hear a bit of dialogue—I heard some people in a bar the other night in New York, sitting behind me. A guy and a girl and I guess they had gone out at some point. The guy says to her, "Why didn't we ever make it together?" (TOB snickers) She said, "You were suicidal and I was doing porno. That's why." (RB & TOB both laugh). I thought, "I'm going to use that line." What a weird line and you notice that stuff. I laughed but also in my writer's mind obviously I remember it and two days later I don't know where it will come in but little images will stick. Influences are not all literary. It's just the struggles of life itself where things that matter to you make good stories.

RB: Do you pay attention to the ebbs and flows in the book publishing world? Do you note the awards?

TOB: I know nothing about it. I never have. Even when I lived in Cambridge. I didn't subscribe to the *NY Times*. I read the sport section of the *Globe* and the front page. It doesn't interest me much. I don't know why it should. It's got little to do with what's inside books, with the story.

RB: Well, it's another setting where people act out their stories.

TOB: But when you do it for a living it doesn't interest many of us. It has to do with commerce. I'm not down on it. I'm not trying to say I'm above it. I'm just not interested in it. I never have been.

RB: When you read the sports page do you read about the managerial job competitions and such things?

TOB: Yeah, I follow all the little human ins and outs. That's what interests me about it. I'm interested in the psychology of competition. Always have been.

RB: Has there been a great baseball book?

TOB: I don't know if I know. I've read some. I wouldn't call them great. I read *The Natural*.

RB: Hey Rosie! [Rosie enters the room and tangles herself up in the microphone cord.] Do you like dogs?

TOB: Yeah. I've had three in my life. Mugs was a three-legged dog, eight years old and got caught in some hunter's trap and came back with his left hind leg dangling. Had it amputated. That dog would chase anything that moved. It was fast even with three legs. A great dog. He didn't slow down a step. Maybe a little faster, he didn't have the extra weight.

RB: Anyway, we were talking about baseball books and *The Natural*. I don't remember that it was much about baseball.
TOB: That's kind of what made it good. It wasn't all baseball.

RB: I liked the Mark Harris book, *Bang the Drum Slowly*.
TOB: I did too. I didn't like the movie much. I don't know what it was about the movie I didn't like. I don't even remember now.

RB: You spent four years writing *July, July*?
TOB: They are all the same. Four to five years.

RB: How do you know when it's finished?
TOB: It's like music. You hear the end and it sounds right to me. Like the end of a song sounds right to me. You hear the harmony and the closure and it sounds like it is finished, the way a song does. There's no real answer to it.

RB: Intuitive?
TOB: Not intuitive. It's like you are doing a painting and you see that it is finished and there is nothing more that you can add. You don't want to take away. So it looks and feels finished.

RB: When you get to that point is there much more to do?
TOB: I'm an endless tweaker. Every book I've ever written I've tweaked all the way through the paperback edition. If you can improve a book, even a little bit, there is no reason not to.

RB: Many writers tell me they don't reread their published work.
TOB: I don't really either. But I have to give readings. So when I notice something, I go, "Oh gosh, I can make that a little better, I think." And I'll do it. I find things over the course of having to go out and give talks. I notice a word here and phrase there, a paragraph there and I just adjust things and no one ever seems much to notice. Well, sometimes they have.

RB: Is there a book that you have been dying to write that you haven't written?
TOB: Yeah, I'm not sure how to approach it though. So it's hard to talk about it. It will probably be my next book. But I'm not sure how to get at it really. Something that happened in my own life.

RB: Some kind of looming presence on the periphery?
TOB: Yeah, a scary thing happened to me and I don't want to address it directly but I am still kind of frightened by it. So I have to find a back door where nobody will recognize themselves. The actual event is so compelling that it's going to be hard to leave behind the reality because it's so compelling. It's a real story and the details are so compelling. So you find yourself trying to find analogues for something but they are not sufficient to the real thing, the potency of what happened, that's the story. So I'm fishing around trying to find a way to get into the material. I haven't found a way to do it yet. I have been thinking a lot about it. Daydreaming about the story I could find to get at that story. I wish I could tell the real story but I can't.

RB: How long have you been thinking about it?
TOB: Ever since it happened. A long time.

RB: How do you try to "get at it?" You sit and try to write it down or does it only take place in your head?
TOB: Both. You have to think of a general story line that is compelling. Something like Huck on a raft. Something that will flow. If you chase a whale then you're going to chase a whale. It's got to be a simple way of entering a book. Simple for me, and yet compelling and that way has to approximate, more or less, what I went through in this experience. So it's doubly hard. You have to think of something interesting and simple and you want that thing to get at what happened. Ordinarily, I'll begin a book just from the story angle or from the real angle. This one is more difficult because it's so terrifying. So I have to find a story that will carry that freight for me, somehow. I will. I already have some ideas that in theory seem okay. They don't quite seem good enough yet.

RB: Are you able to start something and if it's not working put it down and come back to it?
TOB: Oh yeah. Absolutely. In *July, July*, the first chapter I wrote was not the reunion chapter but the drowning. It was written years ago and I knew

I wanted to make it part of something bigger because it was insufficient. I wanted consequences. And I put it aside until I saw her appear in this book. Yeah, I've done that a lot of times in my life. Some of them I never pick up again.

RB: Well good. Any predictions on the World Series?
TOB: I think Anaheim is going to win it. I felt that way before. They are a tough team. I didn't realize how tough they are. I didn't watch them much because they aren't shown in Texas except an occasional Game of the Week.

RB: What happened to your Red Sox hat?
TOB: I lost it on the tour so I bought this as a backstop hat.

RB: What do you make of the fact that *Sporting News* (this is a vote of the player's peers) voted Barry Zito AL pitcher of the year over Pedro Martinez?
TOB: There are a lot of good pitchers in the AL. And he (Pedro) may not be liked, personally. He's a tough customer. I don't know how much of it is personality but he is one tough customer.

RB: Well, who knows? Thanks very much.
TOB: A pleasure.

"Every question leads to the next": An Interview with Tim O'Brien

Jonathan D'Amore/2007

From *The Carolina Quarterly* 58.2 (Spring 2007): 31–40. Reprinted with permission of Jonathan D'Amore.

Tim O'Brien, author of *The Things They Carried, Going After Cacciato*, and *In the Lake of the Woods*, among other critically lauded works of fiction and memoir, visited the University of North Carolina as the Morgan Family Writer-in-Residence during the Spring 2007 semester. O'Brien spent part of an afternoon with me discussing his life in writing and how he writes about life. This author, who claims to feel most compelled to pursue in his books the questions that don't have definitive answers, graciously provided thoughtful and provocative—and occasionally definitive—answers to my many questions. We talked in Chapel Hill on February 27, 2007.

D'Amore: Vietnam, unsurprisingly, had a major impact on your life, and it's not too much of a stretch to say that the war is at the center of your writing life. I know I don't do more than invite speculation with this question, but I'll ask anyway: If you hadn't been drafted into Vietnam, if you'd crossed your metaphorical Rainy River, or if you'd been born five or ten years later, would you have become a writer anyway? Are you a writer by nature or by necessity?

O'Brien: Well, the short answer is: I don't know. A somewhat longer answer is that I think I'd still be a writer, but most likely writer in exile. Someone writing about leaving one's country, and the horrors of that: the dislocations, the lingering sense of moral failure, or moral rectitude, which can also haunt you. But I do guess that I would be writing. I'd be writing about those things, which I think would haunt me as much as Vietnam does.

JD: Writing about your experience in Vietnam in *If I Die in a Combat Zone* made you fairly well known when you were relatively young, just twenty-seven, and you became a National Book Award winner in your early thirties. You're often held up as one of your generation's best writers and certainly thought to be the preeminent literary chronicler of the Vietnam War. Now *The Things They Carried* is a core text in many classrooms. How has this literary fame affected you, personally, professionally, artistically?

TO: Again, the answer is that I don't know, because I don't know the alternative. It may have been otherwise, or it may have turned out that had the books not succeeded, my life would have been, in most meaningful ways, identical. And that's because my objective as a writer was never fame or money or awards; it was that story to be told as I'm sitting alone and staring at that blank page, writing about material that didn't just interest me but really inflamed me, made my stomach burn at night and kept me awake. And not just the horrors of Vietnam: I'm speaking about lost love, about childhood, about aspiration. The same types of things kept me awake when no one knew my name that keep me awake now that some people do know my name.

Some things are easier when you're well known. Certainly financially: you don't have to rely on a single success; you know that your next book doesn't have to sell a billion copies because you're secure already, so you can kind of do and try what you want. But you feel expectations, also. At least it feels as though there are expectations placed upon me. An expectation to revisit certain ground, for example, but to revisit it in a different way, and there are times when to me that ground is finally barren and dusty; when I see no promise there, and I don't want to revisit it, in a new way or not. And I fight that psychologically. I have to tell myself, "Tim, you've got one life to lead; you're sixty years old, you can probably write one more good book, so write the book that you want to write." That's basically what I've told myself with every book.

JD: Well, from book to book, can you see how you've changed or matured? At this point, has writing gotten easier for you? More challenging?

TO: Writing is not easier. I can flatly say that. I'm glad it's not easy though. I doubt I would do it if I weren't struggling over the language and the flow of stories. Because deciding how to tell a story that you think is extraordinary, with language that's appropriate to it, is a challenging enterprise that I find fun. It's a frustrating sort of fun, I must add in a hurry, like doing a difficult jigsaw puzzle when you lose focus on the whole scope of the picture you're trying to put together, because you're locked in on these individual little pieces of cardboard; then it can be frustrating, when you're locked on one sentence or just a noun. That locking sensation can be difficult because you've lost sight of the whole puzzle, you ought to just drop that piece and move on to the next. So as a general statement: writing is hard for me and yet really, really fun, simultaneously.

JD: Are there other particular authors you think make the pieces fit well? Whose texts might show you a way to grapple with your own, or inspire you to try something different?

TO: Of course. I have a whole slew of them, that at different stages of my life have had different degrees of influence. I choose to follow the influence of life over the influence of literature, but you do carry with you as a writer all the books you've read—good and bad, and even the bad ones are of influence in the sense of "avoid this" or "I don't want to sound like that terrible book"; then books you've loved or liked or admired will beckon, will say, "be more like me." But I don't ever make a conscious effort to model prose after the heroes of my past, Conrad being chief among them in my personal pantheon, which includes Borges and Márquez, Hemingway and Faulkner and Dos Passos.

JD: What about writers working today? Can you think of any who fit your way of looking at the world? Do you read any of your contemporaries with an appreciation that they're doing something you feel in concert with?

TO: Oh, constantly. There are people whom I admire immensely who do things that not only I couldn't do, but that I wouldn't do. John Updike, for example: I could no more write like John Updike than I could fly up to Mars and back, and I admire the beauty of his similes, the agility and fluidity of his prose—a fluidity and agility that would not come naturally to me. I'm a Midwesterner and I don't have or necessarily want that kind of diction, yet I admire immensely the intricate beauty of Updike's sentences. And many other writers, such as Robert Stone, who is a writer I admire for wholly different reasons—though he's a beautiful stylist in all kinds of ways—he has a knack for going after literary and philosophical big game. He's not hunting pigeons and squirrels, he's a big game hunter. He's hunting God and the dark curtain of life with an edginess of prose that I find fully admirable but wouldn't try to duplicate in a million years, because I'd only fail dismally.

JD: You teach writing—

TO: I try to teach.

JD: Fair enough: you try to teach writing, so you provide guidance to students in that way, and you're almost certainly a model for many aspiring writers, most likely for men and women of my generation who have done military service in one of our recent wars. For them, though they've not had the same experience you did, theirs is related. How would you advise someone who wanted to write about their experience in Iraq or Afghanistan or one of the conflicts in the 1990s? How should they approach that task?

TO: I think how and what you write is largely dependent on the temperament and baggage you bring to a war with you. What you're going to bring home and write about; what you're going to notice in the war. For example, if your politics are conservative and you've been deeply influenced by recent events, you're for the war, you're going to be writing a different kind of book than someone that brings a different temperament to it. And by different I don't necessarily mean opposed to the war: one might be indifferent to it, or scared out of one's mind. Or some people bring to war an adventuristic, I-want-to-find-out-about-death-and-myself attitude. Others bring a piety to it, see a kind of godliness in the proximity to death. So the literature that will ultimately come from social phenomenon like the war in Iraq or Vietnam or the Civil Rights struggle will finally bear the indelible stamp of individual temperaments or personalities.

JD: Soldiers, you say, are storytellers. And you identify yourself as a storyteller. In *The Things They Carried*, you wrote, "The thing about a story is that you dream it as you tell it, hoping that others might then dream along with you, and in this way memory and imagination and language combine to make spirits in the head." I wonder, do you feel a distinction between telling a story—that is, speaking it—and writing one? Do you feel differently telling a story to an audience—to an individual or group of people—as opposed to writing it down?

TO: For me there's a difference between storytelling and writing a story, though if I were to try to articulate it exactly, I'd probably fail. I can try inexactly though, and say that it has much to do with practical things such as revision.

Oftentimes, when I'm orally telling a story or an anecdote, say, about what might have happened to me last night in a bar, because of the pressures that are on your tongue as a result of your speaking to someone and looking them in the face and trying to get it done briskly and quickly, you're not going to have the time to find that right adjective or the right noun, and you'll sacrifice it in the interest of moving the story along. As a writer you don't make that sacrifice. At least I don't: I pause, and I try alternative bits of dialogue, with the hope of getting it right, telling the story right. And even knowing I'll probably fail anyway it will be more right than the oral version.

There's a beauty to both, to telling that story orally about what happened last night to that human being sitting across from you and to meticulously going over and over and over. They both have virtues. One may have more energy, may have a sense of spontaneity as you're listening to the teller tell it, but the other has the somewhat greater virtue of precision and harmony and beauty that the first didn't. To combine the energy of a tale or anecdote with the craft of applying language to event, to blend those two seems to me what art tries to be—what it should be.

JD: And when a story, spoken aloud or written down, becomes more like the dreaming and less like the actual happening, you don't feel troubled by it. You've said often that what you call "story-truth" can be more "true" than the happening truth.

TO: I think a story may contain nothing from the actual world or events that happened but may be nonetheless faithful to the world we live in, to the fears we all fear, and the joys we experience. As far as I know, no one has actually gone to Tralfamadore or played croquet with a flamingo for a mallet, and yet when you read *Slaughterhouse-Five* or *Alice in Wonderland*, even knowing that the events could not have happened in the world we live in, they still occur in a world of truth that is the world of the story, in which you suspend disbelief and you're dreaming along with the dreamer of that story. The relevance of the actual world that we've lived in to the story is, in some cases, nonexistent and, in other cases, marginal. And in other cases, like naturalistic fiction, it's very important. But nonetheless, when listening to a story or reading a story, if your effort is to connect literally the story to the world beyond the book, you're really beyond the intent of the storyteller.

JD: So that's a good writer: someone who can make the story true, make the story relevant, whether or not it's a representation in factual terms of the world. Making the story relevant, both to the author and hopefully a larger audience—would you say that's the skill of the writer?

TO: It's part of the skill of the writer, to have the details of the story activate the soul of the reader to feel pain and to feel joy and to feel terror, to wince and to wonder, to feel awe at the unfolding of the extents within the story, to feel suspense and ask, "What next?" The writer has to activate those senses of the spirit, direct all those senses at the ongoing story as it unfolds. That's my primary mission as a writer: to have a reader join the dream of the story, and want to be part of it, and not to be distracted by bad sentences and mistakes and infelicities and melodrama, by all the blunders that can be made in writing I don't like. I aim not to detract from the dreaming of the dream, so that it feels whole and continuous, uninterrupted by error or misjudgment. It also has to do with the sound of the prose, with the music beneath of the story. In the case of John Updike it's one kind of music; with Toni Morrison, it's another; with Raymond Carver, another—and there are recognizable musics or melodies beneath these tales being told by these people. And to be faithful to the voice one chooses to tell a story, and not just be faithful to but to exploit the voice in as many ways as you can and make the voice part of the story, even if it's a purely narrative voice, if it has no origin in the story, if it's just the voice of the author himself or herself. All those elements go into a single purpose for me, which is, academically, suspending disbelief, but which to me is much more little-boyish. There's a little-boyish feel to it. I don't want anything getting in the way of the dream of the dream.

JD: Well, the dream of the dream in your books often strikes a very ambiguous note.
TO: Yeah, I'd say.

JD: I think a big part of what your writing conveys is a sense of ambiguity about the world in your books and in the world outside them.
TO: That is my dream. A dream of ambiguity, of eternal and lasting uncertainty, which is an idea a good many Americans find less than palatable. I think Americans search for certainty and for hard edges to things, and part of the reason I'll never sell like, say, Elmore Leonard or James Patterson is because I admit of ambiguity. I like it. I'm tantalized onward by it. I wallow in it. I actually enjoy it.

JD: Have you come to appreciate that more and more as life has gone on? Or have you always been someone who's seen ambiguity in the world?
TO: For my whole life, I remember being tantalized by the Alamo, because there's such an absence of much record of what occurred there in the final hours. Even from the Mexican side, there's very little testimony, some, but not a lot. I'm tantalized by what happened in those final hours of Custer's Last Stand or what happened to Amelia Earhart. I'm tantalized by the Kennedy assassination—not so much asking, "Did Oswald act alone?" but "What were Kennedy's last thoughts as he was cruising down that street in

Dallas? What was in his mind? Dinner that night? Nothing?" These things are unknown and probably unknowable, and for many of us they're frustrating. We build religions to explain the unknowable, sometimes very odd religions, as a way of firming up the boundaries and saying, "Ah, I do know. Even if it's known only through faith, it's known."

I don't go for that. Maybe it's a temperamental thing, I suppose, but I'd prefer to have the mystery expanded as opposed to firmed up. That is to say, I want the mystery to get bigger and deeper and deeper. Hence, in all of my books, the character's problem, whatever it may be early on is not resolved in the end, it's compounded. By the end of the book, the mystery is only deeper. *In the Lake of the Woods* is the best example, but it's true also of *Going After Cacciato* and it's true of *The Things They Carried*. It's probably true of all my books, because that's the human being I am: I'm not an explainer or a tidier-upper, I'm a messer-upper, and by temperament I look for complication maybe where others probably don't.

JD: For you, asking questions is not about finding definitive answers? Maybe just more questions?
TO: Every question leads to the next.

JD: So ambiguity is reassuring to you.
TO: I love it. I love the feel of it because it has a hopeful sense of discovery at the end. It hasn't been discovered, but it might come around tomorrow, or the next day. It gives me a reason to draw the next breath, and light the next cigarette, and take the next step through life. I like that things haven't been neatly tidied up two decades ago or two centuries ago, but still remain open to us. There is something about the unknown that—even though it's frustrating to all of us—that's incredibly fascinating. All you need to do is turn on the History Channel for evidence of my proposition, in the latest show on Lizzie Borden or Amelia Earhart. We're fascinated by what's just beyond our grasp. We're always going after it like we're chasing a butterfly with a net, and the butterfly is just a little too small and fits right through the little spaces in the net, and we can't quite catch it, but by God we love chasing it. What we're chasing—at least, what I'm chasing—is that mutating thing we call the human spirit.

An Interview with Tim O'Brien

Steven Pressfield/2010

From *Steven Pressfield Online*, 1 March 2010. Web. http://www.stevenpressfield.com
/2010/03/the-creative-process-2-an-interview-with-tim-0%E2%80%99brien/. Reprinted
with permission of Steven Pressfield.

I read Tim O'Brien's book *The Things They Carried* right after it was published, and it blew me away. It is powerful—capturing the emotions, internal conflicts, and bravery of not just the Vietnam generation, but today's
soldiers and Marines, too. I've recommended it to many people since its
release, and the responses I've received from those who have read it have
always been moved and moving. It is an honor and privilege to do a Q&A
with Tim on the twentieth anniversary of the publishing of *The Things They
Carried.*

    The Things They Carried received France's Prix du Meilleur Livre Étrang-
er and was a finalist for both the Pulitzer Prize and the National Book Critics Circle Award. In 1987, O'Brien received the National Magazine Award
for the short story "The Things They Carried." In 1999, the story was selected
for inclusion in *The Best American Short Stories of the Century* edited by
John Updike.

    Tim is also the author of *Going After Cacciato*, which received the Na-
tional Book Award in fiction; *In the Lake of the Woods*, which received the
James Fenimore Cooper Prize from the Society of American Historians and
was named best novel of 1994 by *Time* magazine; *If I Die in a Combat Zone*;
Northern Lights; *The Nuclear Age*; *Tomcat in Love*; and *July, July*. His short
fiction has appeared in the *New Yorker, Esquire, Harper's*, the *Atlantic, Playboy*, and *Ploughshares*, and in several editions of *The Best American Short
Stories* and *The O. Henry Prize Stories*. O'Brien is the recipient of literary
awards from the American Academy of Arts and Letters, the Guggenheim
Foundation, and the National Endowment for the Arts. He has been elected

to both the Society of American Historians and the American Academy of Arts and Sciences. O'Brien currently holds the University Endowed Chair in Creative Writing at Texas State University. He lives with his wife and children in Austin, Texas.

S.P.: When it comes to generating ideas, what's your process? Solitary? Collaborative? Is it fun, is it grueling? How, exactly, do you work?

T.O.: Ideas seem to come (and go) as if by their own volition. A tantalizing story possibility will sometimes pop to mind, either out of memory or imagination, and I'll begin writing as a means of exploring the idea—its mysteries, its meanings, its facets, its moral import. The process of exploring and extending an "idea" through storytelling is for me wholly solitary. The process is collaborative only in the sense that the idea and I seem to work together on some occasions and at utter cross purposes on other occasions. I'm mostly a poor and pitiful supplicant, begging the story to reveal itself more fully. This process is sometimes fun, more often grueling, since I'm at the mercy of a story with its own secret purposes, ambitions, and desires.

S.P.: Do you experience Resistance (meaning self-sabotage, procrastination, self-doubt, etc.?) In what form does Resistance present itself?

T.O.: I work every day on a very rigorous schedule. I do not procrastinate. Sometimes the work goes well, in which case I might end up with a paragraph or two of decent prose; other times the work goes badly, in which case I end up with a foul temper. But the habits of regularity and discipline are necessary, at least for me. The resistances I encounter come in many forms and sizes—a truculent phrase, a noun that will not disclose itself, a character who refuses to utter anything but clichés, a turn of event that is neither interesting nor surprising, a story that will not take a single faltering stride out of the starting gate. And so on. And so on. A completed novel, in my experience, can be viewed as an unbroken chain of resistances overcome or evaded.

S.P.: How do you overcome Resistance? Do you have a specific technique or metaphor that you employ to fortify, encourage, or inspire yourself?

T.O.: As Joseph Conrad wrote, or said, somewhere: ". . . the sitting down is all." I take that to mean—even if Conrad didn't—that creative resistance can only be overcome, or artfully evaded, by the repetitive act of making oneself present. A writer must be there—at work—and not at a bowling alley.

S.P.: Once you have an idea, what's your process for taking it to a finished form? How do you decide whether an idea is worth pursuing? Is there a series of steps that take you from "germ" to "finished product?"

T.O.: Sad to say, but I have no conscious process by which I advance an idea toward its finished form. From the instant I embark on a story or a novel, I'm in search of some approximation of a "finished form." It's a quest, not a process. I may find an aspect here, another aspect there, but there is no method to it beyond trusting in my own story. To trust in story is to trust in something beyond the intellect, beyond "process," and beyond the sort of planning that an architect or an engineer or a plumber might do. I go to work each day trusting that my characters will utter interesting bits of dialogue, or that they will behave in interesting ways, or that might come up with interesting physical or linguistic replies to the moral paradoxes of being human.

S.P.: What do you do when you hit plateaus? How do you keep advancing? Is there one example of plateauing that you can share—and how you grew through it?

T.O.: When I hit plateaus, I head for the mountains. By that, I mean (or think I mean) that I do all I can to point a story or a novel toward its central human drama, toward its essential human mystery. Often, I've found that "plateaus" are the product of ill focus—an individual tree is in sharp relief, but the forest is blurry.

S.P.: Tim, much of what you wrote in *The Things They Carried* was based pretty closely (I assume) on actual events. Yet, being a fiction writer myself, I know that too intense an attachment to things-as-they-actually-happened or people-as-they-actually-are-or-were can work against the success of a story. How you do you handle the fact/fiction conundrum? Do ethical issues enter the equation, e.g. fidelity to an actual friend, in the sense of being reluctant to fictionalize anything he did . . . or simple fidelity to the truth of actual events? In your writing philosophy, what is the proper relation of fact to fiction?

T.O.: Since my work is very conspicuously labeled "fiction," I don't fret about issues of factuality. I would feel quite free, for instance, to write a story in which Germany wins World War II, or in which Richard Cheney is an angel of the Lord. My fidelity is to the story. To the story alone. As a fiction writer,

I'm interested not only in what "is," or in what "was," but also in what might have been or what almost was or what might still be or what should have been.

S.P.: I've been recommending *The Things They Carried* for years. If you have time, go check out Tim when he visits one of the following locations. Read the book.

On War, Heroes, and the Power of Literature: A Conversation with Tim O'Brien

Patrick A. Smith/2011

This interview is previously unpublished. Reprinted with the permission of Patrick A. Smith.

Four decades after returning from Vietnam, Tim O'Brien is one of the most recognizable, respected, and quoted authors of his generation.

This interview is meant to be a capstone piece for *Conversations*, exploring such topics as fatherhood, heroes, portrayals of Vietnam in film, and late-season collapses in baseball, and updating the author's thoughts on writing, his native Midwest, and the futility of war.

O'Brien spoke from his home near Austin, Texas, on October 12, 2011, and through subsequent correspondence.

Patrick A. Smith: Are you teaching this term?

Tim O'Brien: Yes, I'm teaching this semester—once a week for fourteen weeks and then I have a year and a half off—so it's not a lot to ask. Some of the work is encouraging, some is discouraging. There are always those students who are well read and who know what a sentence is. And there are always those who don't, those who aren't well read and don't have an ear for the language. Still, by and large, I'm encouraged. A reasonable share of my students have found important, unique stories to tell and have told them with grace and eloquence.

PAS: What are you reading?

TO: An interesting book in galleys called *Steinbeck in Vietnam*, a compilation of John Steinbeck's reporting for *Newsday* from the mid-sixties, edited by Thomas Barden and published by the University of Virginia Press. I had no idea that Steinbeck was so hawkish about Vietnam. A few times I've thrown down the book in disgust. Then I've picked it up, read another page or two, and thrown it at the wall. Yesterday I nearly decapitated my wife.

PAS: Are you writing?

TO: I'm working on a book. The project is hard to describe. I'm not sure what it is *exactly*, though I know inexactly—a mix of fiction and nonfiction, like many of my books—with a focus on my being an older father. Partly that, and partly a kind of memoir, the stories I tell my kids about my own life as a writer and a soldier and a father. It's partly fiction, too, little tales I tell to my kids at bedtime.

Also, the book is meant to be a record for Timmy and Tad of their own youth, the things they said or did or experienced. Most of what we experience as children is almost instantly erased, gone forever, and I'm hoping the book might preserve for my sons a few glimpses of their own swiftly passing childhoods. I look at the book as a little gift I can leave behind for Timmy and Tad. Being an older father, especially, you begin to meditate pretty intensely on human mortality and the implacable squeeze of biology. There's a sadness to that. Where will I be in twenty years? Where will my sons be? I take my role as a dad more seriously, probably, than I would have if I were thirty-four or forty-four. I want to make good use of the time I have with my children.

PAS: An admirable goal. I've got two boys, seven and five. It's been a wonderful experience. They've really come into their own. As you know, it's just one of life's great pleasures to watch.

TO: We're in the same boat! My sons are now eight and six. And what a treat to watch them begin to read and begin to write and begin to navigate between the natural world and the world of imagination. It's really quite astonishing to behold this miraculous blossoming of consciousness. And it's especially astonishing when you so vividly recall cradling your kids when they were infants, little packets of protein fresh from the womb. Now the older boy is playing lacrosse, the younger one is playing soccer, a little dynamo.

PAS: Sports tend to become a large part of life for kids that age. In fact, I was watching the American League Championship Series—the Rangers and the

Tigers—last night with my boys. I'm still pissed off at the Pirates, who had the lead at the All-Star break and ended up twenty games back at the end. Too good to last, of course. Just another season for the Pirates, but what happened to your Red Sox?

TO: No idea (laughs). Fate, I guess, the end predetermined millennia ago. Being a Red Sox fan can guarantee you a broken heart. This year I resigned my fandom. I'll no longer endure the emotional torture of those incredible collapses.

PAS: But they gave you two World Series!

TO: Yes, they finally managed to do that, but I'm not sure it made up for all the anguish along the way.

PAS: You've talked openly about your disdain for some of the things that you saw in your native Midwest. Have you made peace with those experiences in the last decade or so, or do they still weigh on you?

TO: I wouldn't say it weighs on me. In fact, it doesn't. But I'm resigned to the knowledge that I'm not going to change the Midwest, and the Midwest is not going to change me. By the Midwest, I'm talking about Babbitt country, the small-town, insular, sanctimonious, gossiping, absolutist America that simplifies the world down to the point of turning it all into a cartoon. That attitude irritated me as a kid, it irritated me as a young adult, and now it irritates me as an old adult. I'm just resigned to the irritation. I know that nothing I say or do or write will change anything. I feel the same powerlessness, I might add, in regard to mankind's appetite for war. I look back on my years as a writer—all those books, all those scenes and sentences and paragraphs, all that struggling over bits of language—but what real fruit did it bear? The world is as full of self-righteous bellicosity as when I began.

PAS: I think you're underestimating the influence of your writing.

TO: I wish I were. But the butchery goes on and on. *Slaughterhouse-Five* didn't stop it. Nor did *The Things They Carried*, or *The Naked and the Dead*, or *The Iliad*, or *The Red Badge of Courage*. It's not that I'm cynical. It's that the efficacy of humanism, including the efficacy of literature, seems far more limited than I envisioned as a naïve young writer.

PAS: I've had this conversation with Jim Harrison, among other writers, who bemoans the fact that America has so few readers of literature. People would rather turn on cable news in the morning and absorb whatever pabulum the talking heads dish out on a given day. If religion is the opium of the masses, cable news can't be far behind.

TO: That's pretty much my take, too.

PAS: But I've got to think—to hope, at least—that we still have heroes. There are those great passages in Homer's *Iliad* where Achilles considers his fate and asks his mother, Thetis, for advice. He's at a crossroads. Should he head to Troy to fulfill his destiny as a hero, one of the immortals, even though he's bound to die there? Or should he stay in his father Peleus's kingdom and rule that small plot of land, beloved by his family for generations, even if his legacy will eventually be lost in the mists of time? Of course, fetishizing war in the way that he and his culture do, Achilles goes to war and sacrifices his life, assuring his immortality. I see a great deal of that, writ small, in the literature of World War II and Vietnam. But those aren't our heroes anymore. Who are they?

TO: Oh, goodness. I'm not even sure I know what "heroic" means anymore. I'm pretty sure it does not mean marching like a cow to the slaughter, without conscience or willpower or volition or thought. Genuine heroism has very little to do, as far as I can tell, with the pursuit of glory or immortality. So-called heroes, many of them, are just plain *dead*. Nameless. Forgotten to history. Dust. Illegible etchings on tombstones. Partly because they tried to act heroically in the pursuit of wispy, false dreams of immortality or glory. And even those who survive, even those who are perhaps celebrated for a time, even they will eventually pass into the void. To pursue immortality is to pursue a fantasy, an old and discredited lie.

History has a way of effacing all of our lives, including the Audie Murphy and John Wayne wannabes. In war, there are times when to be heroic simply means to keep walking, to endure, to march on with full knowledge of this effacement. In Vietnam—a place littered with landmines—I felt that the most heroic thing I could do was just to move my legs, not knowing if the next step would kill me, or the next, or the next. There was very little charging the enemy, very little of the standard stuff we think of when we imagine wartime glory or heroism. Once in a great while, something like that may have occurred, but so rarely I can recollect only a couple of such incidents. To keep walking—to keep *humping*, as we called it—was its own modest sort of heroism.

But back to Homer. I would not want that lady, Thetis, for my mom. She casts the two choices in such a way that the outcome is virtually predetermined. She makes peace seem dull and insignificant, while making war seem exhilarating and glorious and wholly honorable. Who but a false-hearted, lying, bitch-of-a-goddess would view "immortality" in such loaded terms?

Heroes, too, are lost to history. Heroes, too, are mortal.

PAS: Thetis had the advantage of being immortal herself. Achilles's father, Peleus, wasn't so fortunate. Given how capricious the gods could be, Achilles's fate could have turned on the flip of a coin.

TO: Another difficulty I have with Homer has to do with divine intervention. It's another lie, another childish fantasy. And a dangerous one, at that. Sure, it would've been terrific if the gods had come down for a little chat at my foxhole, if they'd offered me sage advice, if they'd whispered emboldening imperatives in my ear, if they'd issued reliable prophecies about what would transpire during the next firefight, the next patrol, the next ambush, the next terrifying hour or two. No dice. Didn't happen. Maybe I went to war in the wrong millennium. I didn't bump into any gods, or God, in that godforsaken war.

PAS: When Robert McNamara died earlier this year, I remembered watching *Fog of War* and thought about my own tenuous references to war. One was my father, who was five or six years too old to be in the wheelhouse for the draft. He didn't go to Vietnam, though he asked me as a small boy—and I remember this clearly, at the age of seven or so—if it mattered to me that he had never fought in the war. It was obviously something that he had given a great deal of thought to and that bothered him, to some extent. The second point of contact was my brother, who was in the Air Force during the Cold War, sitting in Marquette, Michigan, waiting for the Soviets to come over the top of North America. So when I watched McNamara in front of the camera, I thought, "Here's this man admitting to mistakes that should have been clear to him initially and that directly resulted in the deaths of fifty-two thousand American men and women in Vietnam. He unburdened himself, but he had paid no personal price, made no sacrifice. It's cathartic for him. So many hundreds of thousands of people didn't have that opportunity." Is that naïve on my part, a case of having no frame of reference regarding war?

TO: I certainly share your point of view as to the latter part of the question. But with respect to McNamara, I cut him a break, in the sense that, after the die had been cast, what alternatives did he have afterward? You either say, "I was wrong," or you don't. And most of them didn't. The Rusks and the Bundys, for instance, never seemed to recognize, much less acknowledge, any errors or hubris or misjudgments. McNamara could have gone on believing in the rectitude of the American war in Vietnam. Or he could've refused to acknowledge his mistakes. He could've fallen silent. To his credit, he didn't.

I felt some relief, actually, at hearing McNamara finally validate what I'd believed for so many years: that the Vietnam War was misbegotten in the most fundamental ways. I felt a sense of vindication, even if it came way too late. Without someone such as McNamara making that admission, I probably would have gone to my grave thinking, "God, maybe these guys were right. Maybe they were smarter than I am, maybe they were more knowledgeable, maybe they had access to some secret reservoir of wisdom." To hear at least one of them admit error and express remorse helps me sleep better.

As you say, McNamara should have recognized these things much earlier, especially since they were being thrust in his face every day by a massive antiwar movement. He had full access to all the doubts and misgivings about what we were doing in Vietnam, yet he still staunchly defended and savagely prosecuted the war. The result was not just the deaths of fifty-two thousand Americans. Three million Vietnamese also died, and those dead Vietnamese should be entered into the arithmetic.

Hitler never apologized. And I don't think George W. Bush will be wringing his hands much over the absence of weapons of mass destruction in Iraq. That's a pretty big deal, isn't it? The *reason* for a war doesn't exist? It's as if the Japanese had never attacked Pearl Harbor, or as if Paris had never run off with Helen, or as if Hitler had never sent his armies into Poland. But I hear very damned little in the way of remorse or contrition from Rice or Cheney or any of the other people who led us into that war, either by incompetence or outright deception. And until McNamara, I didn't hear it from war-makers of the Vietnam era, either.

PAS: Colin Powell made a bad decision. His getting behind the idea of WMD was the point at which people started to support the effort.
TO: For me, the larger issue has to do with acknowledging error and expressing remorse in the face of error, especially when that word—*error*—incorporates a lot of dead people. And not just the dead, but their moms and their dads and their kids and their lovers. In the case of Vietnam, the casualties went way beyond fifty-two thousand Americans and three million Vietnamese. In any war, the multiplier effect is huge.

All those lives . . .

PAS: Has the way we conceive war now—in particular, the way we've waged war in Afghanistan and Iraq—changed the way writers record war in fiction and memoir? I'm thinking of recent books on Vietnam, like Karl Marlantes's *Matterhorn* and Denis Johnson's *Tree of Smoke*, both novels that come straight out of the heart of the Vietnam experience. Much of the work I've seen that draws on the experience of the second Gulf War is post-9/11 memoir. Thomas Ricks, Doug Stanton, and others have written solid current-events books. But we haven't seen much fiction yet. Is this a war that's hard to write about in the same way that Vietnam was written about?

TO: Harder, to be sure, because the pool of doubters—or at least the number of people ambivalent about these current wars—is small, relative to what we saw during the Vietnam era. Many of the people now in uniform signed up to go to war. And *all* of them are volunteers. They weren't drafted, or yanked out of school, or hauled away from their families. They've enlisted and been deployed of their own volition, and they're of a certain type, clearly much different from the guys I served with in Vietnam. Many of my fellow soldiers in Vietnam were brought in kicking and screaming. Other guys were utterly indifferent to the goals of the war and ended up in Vietnam for the same reasons I did—fear of embarrassment, fear of ridicule, fear of censure and humiliation. Now, because of the absence of the draft, a radically different soldier is returning from Afghanistan and Iraq. As a consequence, I think the public will entertain fewer doubts about it all and will ask fewer questions. In the end, I fear, fewer Americans will address even the most fundamental issue when it comes to war: Is the killing and dying really worth it? All the gore, all the lost arms and legs, all the widows, all the orphans, all the Gold Star mothers—is it *worth* it?

PAS: That overarching message in the media is disingenuous and intellectually dishonest. Turn on the television and we never see, except in the abstract, what you describe. Anything disquieting is pushed into the background.

TO: What's almost never acknowledged in our Fourth of July rhetoric, almost never alluded to on Veterans Day, is the overwhelming nastiness of war, a nastiness that goes beyond the common idea of soldier killing soldier. There is a day-by-day, hour-by-hour, minute-by-minute sinfulness of it all. You are immersed in evil. Beating up on people, kicking them around, peeing in their wells, burning down their houses, torturing detainees, strip-searching old ladies, racism of the most extravagant sort. On and on. Rape.

Theft. Homicide. Assault and battery. Arson. All to get rid of weapons of mass destruction that don't exist.

The nastiness is a poison that infects every minute, every second, of combat, and it accelerates throughout a soldier's tour of duty. You start losing people—fellow soldiers, friends—and it all gets worse. A friend gets killed, the hatred multiplies, the fear multiplies, the frustration and anger begins to vent itself. "But where's the enemy?" you ask. And if you can't find the enemy, you take out your grief and terror and rage on that old man over there, or his house, or his family, or whatever. The common conception of war is that the enemy soldiers are there, we're here, and we're going to battle it out. If only war were that clean. It is not. It's grubby. It's savage. It's mean-spirited. It's flat-out, stone-age evil. But none of that gets mentioned on Veterans Day or down at the local VFW. What we get instead is self-congratulatory, black and white, self-sacrificial, fake-heroic bullshit.

PAS: The new Marlantes book, the follow-up to *Matterhorn*, is a series of essays analyzing the psychological impact of war on soldiers. Marlantes, also a kind of scholar-warrior, says basically what you're saying, that we need to pay more attention to the individuals and put aside the ideology and the cheerleading and start taking care of returning soldiers in a way that they weren't taken care of when you came back, when Marlantes came back, when Phil Caputo came back.

TO: I think Marlantes celebrates the American soldier more than I would.

I think it's important that we be realistic. Even American soldiers do really bad stuff as part of war, bad stuff that goes way beyond just killing the enemy. And that aspect of war—the unsavory aspect that people would rather not deal with—isn't much acknowledged. It goes back, I guess, to an issue we discussed earlier—a falsely heroic conception of the warrior. Even brave men do terrible things. I don't exempt myself.

PAS: In *Going After Cacciato*, you write, "Facts are one thing, interpretation is something else." Paul Berlin's experiences transcend the day-to-day brutality of war, but as much as it's a flight of fancy, we also have to work within recognizable contexts, within limits, and we need to pay attention to political boundaries and the physical realities of that world. The "Observation Post" chapters anchor the narrative, it seems to me, and everything else is a cinematic reverie.

TO: Sure, the daydream of walking away from war, the reverie you mention, is anchored in reality. When you're in a war, you yearn for war's opposite: peace. Getting the hell out of this untenable situation. Virtually every well-known, canonized book about war incorporates that yearning for escape. Homer's *Iliad*, with Hector's futile attempt at fleeing from Achilles outside the gates of Troy; Stephen Crane in *The Red Badge of Courage*, with Henry Fleming's flight from battle, then later trying to atone for his act of cowardice; Heller does it in *Catch-22*—the character of Orr heading for Sweden; Hemingway's Frederic Henry rowing across the lake to flee from World War I. Very common—even necessary—in any book about war.

When you're in the nastiness, when you're immersed in the shit, you want out, no matter what your political values may be. Your head may believe in what you're doing, but your body doesn't believe. Your belly and legs and heart are screaming at you: Run! Yet the impulse to flee is counterbalanced by the overlay of duty, sacrifice for country, fear of embarrassment, love for your fellow soldiers, all those Fourth of July values. To a greater or lesser degree, I believe, every combat soldier has experienced that terrible tension between the desire to flee and the desire to endure.

PAS: When you talked to Daniel Bourne and Debra Shostak in the early '90s, they asked you what your thoughts were on the war twenty years after the fact. Another twenty years on, has the distance between you and the war grown? Between you and the writing of *The Things They Carried*? Do you still recognize the Tim O'Brien who came back from Vietnam and became a writer?

TO: I do recognize that person, just as I recognized the person of twenty years ago when I talked to Bourne. I feel now, as I did then, that there's a sense of unreality about one's own history, even if you're not in a war. I look back at myself as an eight-year-old and wonder, "Who was that kid sitting in that sandbox in Minnesota," just as I look back at Vietnam and think, "Who was that kid marching through the paddies?" Or: "How did I do it? Why did I keep going?" I sometimes wonder why I didn't go mad. In a sense, it seems impossible that any of it truly happened.

My next-door neighbor tells me, "I can't imagine being in a war." My response is, "Having been in a war, I can't imagine it, either." There's a dreamy feel to one's own history, no matter what it is, but especially when that history is full of unspeakable horror. "How did I survive? Why did I do the things I did?" Endless self-interrogation. Endless second-guessing. But it's a sterile, futile exercise. In the end we can never fix on any one motive, or even a set of motives, for our own behaviors. "Aha! There's why I went to war!"

you decide one day, thinking you've finally pinned it down, finally solved the puzzle. But you *never* know. Even with issues of the purest fact, there's a palpable and abiding sense of unreality.

Someone will say to me, "Did you ever kill anyone?" And I'll say, truthfully, "I don't know." Because war is chaotic. Triggers get pulled. Sightlines are obstructed. You're blinded by terror. And you have no idea whether a bullet from your weapon struck—much less killed—anyone. Looking back, I find it hard to fix *anything* with absolute certainty. There's a dreamy, otherworldly haze to my entire time in combat. And the uncertainty is compounded by a war with no front, no rear, no firm moral ground, no sense of purpose or accomplishment or righteous imperative. In Vietnam, at least for me, there were very few absolutes. For the most part, my infantry unit just blundered along from spot to spot, village to village, paddy to paddy, rarely knowing where we were, or why we were there, or what we were supposed to accomplish. We didn't know the language. We didn't know the land. We didn't know the culture. We didn't know which villagers were friendly, and which were not, and which were utterly indifferent. The whole war—it was a mystery.

Everything I've been talking about for the last two or three minutes militates against a firm sense of reality. There's very little you can hold on to. Except story. Maybe, finally, that's why I write novels.

PAS: Do you revisit your enigmatic character John Wade and *In the Lake of the Woods* every now and then? In the wake of 9/11, I read Wade as a more sympathetic character, for many of the reasons you just discussed.

TO: I do, too. He's a man overwhelmed by his participation in an atrocity of war. He just wants to erase those memories completely. Who wouldn't? Or, if he can't erase it, he can try to keep it secret from his wife and friends and family. Based on the e-mails I receive from guys with whom I served in Vietnam, I suspect that if we got together, I would see a lot of such erasure of nasty memories. A certain nostalgia seems to set in. Mythology replaces reality.

The consequence of such erasures, of course, is that war gets sanitized. A big can of Ajax is sprinkled on our own misdeeds, our own racism, our own bullyism, our own arrogance, our own atrocities, our own acts of daily, petty evil. The things we celebrate, we seem to pluck out and rinse them off and get all the filth and the grime off them and hold them up on the Fourth of July and celebrate them. I find that false and dishonest and despicable.

It goes back to where we started with our discussion of Homer. Immortality. Heroism. The age-old lie. Nothing I say and nothing I write can change it. The glorious lie will be told and retold.

PAS: The book you're working on now will make a difference . . .
TO: I hope it will make a difference in my kids' lives, at least.

PAS: In *The Things They Carried*, the phrase "This is true" explores the gray area between truth and fiction. Has that notion gotten even more nebulous in the last decade? In war, the truth is the first casualty . . .
TO: Truth is the first casualty not just in war, but in the build-up to war. How can you expect some seventeen-year-old kid to go off and kill people and maybe die himself by telling him the truth of it all? He'd say, "Fuck you! I won't do that!" And we make up these grand, beautiful lies and half-truths: we're going to save the world for democracy, we're going to rid the world of weapons of mass destruction.

Within the lies, of course, little beads of truth are sprinkled in. But our perceptions are formed by the larger and grander deceit. The nastiness I keep coming back to, that's relentlessly avoided. It's relentlessly eradicated from the saber-rattling, gung-ho, self-righteous, black-and-white rhetoric that precedes any war. The recruiters talk about glory, about making you a man, about giving you skills for a later career. But they don't utter a syllable about the coffins, the lost legs, the deadened souls, the never-ending nightmares. Like Thetis, the recruiters and war hawks load up the dice with their half-truths and skewed rhetoric.

PAS: How much has cinema fed into the notion of honor?
TO: That mythology is propagated not just by cinema, but by Marine Corps posters and TV ads and our celebrations on July Fourth and Veterans' Day. As a nation we're swamped by a kind of everyday, common-man rhetoric about supporting our soldiers because they're the greatest people on earth and can do no wrong. Well, I was one of them. You don't just do wrong, you do *big* wrong. And you do it endlessly, if you're on a tour of combat. And then you dream about it afterward, for the rest of your life, trying as best you can to erase those memories but never wholly succeeding. Only a handful of films even *try* to portray any of this.

PAS: What do you think about the film of Vietnam? *Apocalypse Now, Deer Hunter, Coming Home*?
TO: Some of them I thought were good. Others were awful. *Apocalypse*

Now captured the absurdity of 'Nam. The way 'Nam felt to me, anyway. A little crazy, where the ordinary conventions we live by are turned upside-down, right spills over into wrong, the old commandments are no longer true. Vietnam had the feel of *Alice in Wonderland* with a *Heart of Darkness* spin to it. The whole spine of *Apocalypse Now* strikes me as genuine, as a descent into this pit of sin and evil and horror.

Deer Hunter appealed to me in a different way. A pretty good movie, too, though it's been criticized by a great many combat veterans, who often say, "Well that never happened, that never happened, that never happened. I never saw anyone playing Russian roulette." Of course they're right, on a literal level. I never saw that either. But the Russian roulette scenes are intended as metaphor, not as a literal representation of the war, and on a metaphorical level as metaphor those scenes seem to me very powerful and very telling. Russian roulette captures the feel and the essence of combat. *Click*, I'm alive. *Click*, I'm alive. Those scenes where the pistols are put to people's heads—John Savage, Christopher Walken, Robert DeNiro—that's what combat felt like. The operative word there is "like." True, I didn't witness anyone playing Russian roulette in Vietnam, but when those guns go *click*, that's what combat felt like. *I'm alive.* And you do it again, the next minute or the next day. And you hear that sound: *click*. And you're still alive. The tightening of the cords on their necks and their red faces as they screw up the courage to pull those triggers—that's what it felt like to be in a firefight.

PAS: I grew up in the Pittsburgh area, where *Deer Hunter* was set. In the mid-1980s, I took a job in a brick factory in my hometown, Summerville, and the guys I worked with—older brothers and uncles of classmates— would have been ten years out of Vietnam, not yet thirty years old. When you talk about Russian roulette as a metaphor for the war experience, I think back to their conversations. Although much of the talk didn't pertain *directly* to their experiences in Vietnam, their conversations spoke volumes about what they had been through.

TO: Sometimes people speak indirectly about things, if they speak about them at all. *Deer Hunter* tries to do that and, for the most part, succeeds. No film I've ever seen has come so close to capturing the physical sensations of combat. The failures of realism are myriad. Not just bad John Wayne movies, but also well-intended movies that eventually collapse into stereotype or melodrama or simple-minded "messages." A realistic war movie is almost an oxymoron, since war itself is so incredibly surreal. For me, the films and the books that succeed in portraying war are those that take into account, one way or another, the surreal, chaotic, hallucinatory, morally ambiguous qualities that will forever haunt me.

Key Resources

Interviews and Profiles

Blades, John. "Prisoners of War." *Chicago Tribune* 9 December 1994. Tempo: 1–2.

"Bold Type: Interview with Tim O'Brien." 13 January 2004. http://www.randomhouse.com/boldtype/0998/obrien/interview.html.

Boog, Jason. "Novelist Tim O'Brien Reflects on the 20th Anniversary of *The Things They Carried*." *Media Bistro* 22 March 2010. Web. http://www.mediabistro.com/galleycat/novelist-tim-obrien-reflects-on-the-20th-anniversary-of-the-things-they-carried_b11338.

Bruckner, D. J. R. "A Storyteller for the War That Won't End." *New York Times* 3 April 1990: C15+.

Capuzzo, Mike. "A Novelist's Inner War." *Philadelphia Inquirer* 27 October 1994. G1+.

Coffey, Michael. "Tim O'Brien: Inventing a New Form Helps the Author Talk about War, Memory, and Storytelling." *Publishers Weekly* 237 (16 February 1990): 60–61.

Cryer, Dan. "Talking with Tim O'Brien: Goodbye to All That." *Newsday* 16 October 1994: 32.

Edelman, David Louis. "Tim O'Brien Full Interview Transcript." 1 October 1994. http://www.davidlouisedelman.com/author-interviews/tim-obri-en-full/.

Grossman, Mary Ann. "Reality Doesn't Matter." *St. Paul Pioneer Press* 11 March 1990: 1D.

———. "Secret Life of Tim O'Brien." *St. Paul Pioneer Press* 17 October 1994: 1C.

Hicks, Patrick. "A Conversation with Tim O'Brien." *Indiana Review* 27.2 (2005): 85–95.

Kahn, Joseph P. "The Things He Carries: Vietnam's Sins Still Haunt Tim O'Brien." *Boston Globe* 19 October 1994: 69+.

Karp, Josh. "The 'What if?' Game." *Atlantic Monthly* 30 October 2002. http://www.theatlantic.com/unbound/interviews/int2002-10-30.htm.

Lannon, Linnea. "In War, Reality Becomes Surreal." *Detroit Free Press* 17 April 1991: 3E+.

Lowenthal, Michael. "Lying for Love: What Does It Mean When Tim O'Brien Gets Funny?" *Boston Phoenix* October 1998: 15–21.

McMurtrie, John. "Interview with Tim O'Brien." *SFGate*, 4 April 2010. Web. http://articles.sfgate.com/2010-04-04/books/20833716_1_tim-o-brien -book-things.

Marquiss, Twister. "Westward Ho! (Chi Minh): Tim O'Brien and the Wounding of the American Cowboy Mythos. *Southwestern American Literature* 29.2 (Spring 2004): 9–15.

Mehegan, David. "New Terrain." *Boston Globe* 8 October 2002: E1.

Muro, Mark. "Believer in the Grand Theme." *Boston Globe* 10 October 1985: 85–86.

Rosica, Karen. "Interview with Tim O'Brien—From Life to Fiction." 15 May 2004. http://www.lighthousewriters.com/newslet/timobrie.htm.

Sawyer, Scott. "In the Name of Love: An Interview with Tim O'Brien." *Mars Hill Review* 4 (Winter/Spring 1996): 117–26.

Schumacher, Michael. "Writing Stories from Life." *Writer's Digest* 71 (April 1991): 34–39.

Slater, Judith. "An Interview with Tim O'Brien." *The Short Story Review* Spring 1987: 1–5.

Streitfeld, David. "The Writer Wounded by Friendly Fire: Vietnam Vet Tim O'Brien, Still at War with Himself." *Washington Post* 25 November 1994: B1.

Weber, Bruce. "War and Peace." *Esquire* September 1985: 269.

———. "Wrestling with War and Love: Raw Pain, Relived Tim O'Brien's Way." *New York Times* 2 September 1998: E1, 4.

Articles, Essays, and Books

Barden, Thomas E. "Urban Legends in Tim O'Brien's *The Things They Carried*." *War, Literature, and the Arts: An International Journal of the Humanities* 22 (2010): 1–14.

Bates, Milton. "Tim O'Brien's Myth of Courage." *Modern Fiction Studies* 33.2 (Summer 1987): 263–79.

Bonn, Maria. "Can Stories Save Us? Tim O'Brien and the Efficacy of the Text." *Critique* 36.1 (Fall 1994): 2–15.

Calloway, Catherine. "How to Tell a True War Story: Metafiction in *The Things They Carried*." *Critique* 36.4 (Summer 1995): 249–57.

———. "Pluralities of Vision: *Going After Cacciato* and Tim O'Brien's Short Fiction." In *America Rediscovered*. Ed. Owen W. Gilman, Jr., and Lorrie Smith. 213–24.

Chen, Tina. "Unraveling the Deeper Meaning: Exile and the Embodied Poetics of Displacement in Tim O'Brien's *The Things They Carried*." *Contemporary Literature* 39.1 (Spring 1998): 77–99.

Couser, G. Thomas. "*Going After Cacciato*: The Romance and the Real War." *Journal of Narrative Technique* 13.1 (Winter 1983): 1–10.

Dayley, Glenn. "Familiar Ghosts, New Voices: Tim O'Brien's *July, July*." *War, Literature and the Arts: An International Journal of the Humanities* 15.1/2 (2003): 316–22.

Epstein, Renee. "Talking Dirty: Memories of War and the Vietnam War Novel." *Massachusetts Review* 34.3 (Autumn 1993): 457–70.

Farrell, Susan. "Tim O'Brien and Gender: A Defense of *The Things They Carried*." *CEA Critic: An Official Journal of the College English Association* 66.1 (2003): 1–21.

Franklin, H. Bruce. "Plausibility of Denial: Tim O'Brien, My Lai, and America." *Progressive* 58.12 (December 1994): 40–44.

Gilman, Owen W., Jr., and Lorrie Smith, eds. *America Rediscovered: Critical Essays on Literature and Film of the Vietnam War*. New York: Garland, 1990.

Goluboff, Benjamin. "Tim O'Brien's Quang Ngai." *ANQ: A Quarterly Journal of Short Articles, Notes, and Reviews* 17.2 (Spring 2004): 53–58.

Grossman, Mary Ann. "Fighting Words." *St. Paul Pioneer Press* April 30, 1995: 1E.

Heberle, Mark A. *A Trauma Artist: Tim O'Brien and the Fiction of Vietnam*. Iowa City: U of Iowa P, 2001.

Herzog, Tobey C. "*Going After Cacciato*: The Soldier-Author-Character Seeking Control." *Critique* 24.2 (Winter 1983): 88–96.

———. *Tim O'Brien*. New York: Twayne, 1997.

———. "Tim O'Brien's True Lies (?)." *Modern Fiction Studies* 46.4 (Winter 2000): 893–916.

———. "Writing about Vietnam: A Heavy Heart-of-Darkness Trip." *College English* 41 (February 1980): 680–95.

———. *Writing Vietnam, Writing Life: Caputo, Heinemann, O'Brien, Butler*. Iowa City, IA: U of Iowa P, 2008.

Horner, Carl S. "Challenging the Law of Courage and Heroic Identification in Tim O'Brien's *If I Die in a Combat Zone* and *The Things They Carried*." *War, Literature and the Arts: An International Journal of the Humanities* Spring/Summer 1999: 256–67.

Jarraway, David R. "Excremental Assault in Tim O'Brien: Trauma and Recovery in Vietnam War Literature." *Modern Fiction Studies* 44.3 (1998): 695–711.

Jones, Dale W. "The Vietnams of Michael Herr and Tim O'Brien: Tales of Disintegration and Integration." *Canadian Review of American Studies* 13.3 (Winter 1982): 309–20.

Kaplan, Steven. *Understanding Tim O'Brien*. Columbia: U of South Carolina P, 1995.

———. "The Undying Uncertainty of the Narrator in Tim O'Brien's *The Things They Carried*." *Critique* 35.1 (Fall 1993): 43–52.

Kearns, George. "Revolutionary Women and Others." *Hudson Review* 39 (Spring 1986): 121–34.

Kinney, Katherine. "American Exceptionalism and Empire in Tim O'Brien's *Going After Cacciato*." *American Literary History* 7.4 (Winter 1995): 633–53.

Liparulo, Steven P. "'Incense and Ashes': The Postmodern Work of Refutation in Three Vietnam War Novels." *War, Literature and the Arts: An International Journal of the Humanities* 15.1/2 (2003): 71–94.

McCay, Mary. "The Autobiography of Guilt: Tim O'Brien and Vietnam." *Writing Lives: American Biography and Autobiography* 39 (1998): 115–21.

Melley, Timothy. "Postmodern Amnesia: Trauma and Forgetting in Tim O'Brien's *In the Lake of the Woods*." *Contemporary Literature* 44.1 (Spring 2003): 106–31.

Nelson, Marie. "Two Consciences: A Reading of Tim O'Brien's Vietnam Trilogy: *If I Die in a Combat Zone, Going After Cacciato*, and *Northern Lights*." In *Third Force Psychology and the Study of Literature*. Ed. Bernard J. Paris. Rutherford, NJ: Fairleigh Dickinson UP, 1986. 262–79.

O'Gorman, Farrell. "*The Things They Carried* as Composite Novel." *War, Literature and the Arts: An International Journal of the Humanities* Fall/Winter 1998: 289–309.

O'Nan, Stewart. *The Vietnam Reader: The Definitive Collection of American Fiction and Nonfiction on the War*. New York: Anchor, 1998.

Oldham, Perry. "On Teaching Vietnam Literature." *The English Journal* 75.2 (February 1986): 55–56.

Palaima, Thomas G. "Courage and Prowess Afoot in Homer and the Vietnam of Tim O'Brien." *Classical and Modern Literature: A Quarterly* 20.3 (2000): 1–22.

Piwinski, David J. "My Lai, Flies, and Beelzebub in Tim O'Brien's *In the Lake of the Woods*." *War, Literature and the Arts: An International Journal of the Humanities* 12.2 (Fall/Winter 2000): 196–202.

Raymond, Michael W. "Imagined Responses to Vietnam: Tim O'Brien's *Going After Cacciato*." *Critique* 24.2 (Winter 1983): 97–104.

Ringnalda, Don. "Tim O'Brien's Understood Confusion." *Fighting and Writing the Vietnam War*. Jackson, MS: UP of Mississippi, 1994. 90–114.

Robinson, Daniel. "Getting It Right: The Short Fiction of Tim O'Brien." *Critique* 40.3 (Spring 1999): 257–64.

Schroeder, Eric James. "The Past and the Possible: Tim O'Brien's Dialectic of Meaning and Imagination." In *Search and Clear: Critical Response to Selected Literature and Films of the Vietnam War*. Ed. W. J. Searle. Bowling Green, OH: Bowling Green State U Popular P, 1988. 116–34.

Silbergleid, Robin. "Making Things Present: Tim O'Brien's Autobiographical Meta-fiction." *Contemporary Literature* 50.1 (2009): 129–55.

Slabey, Richard. *"Going After Cacciato*: Tim O'Brien's 'Separate Peace.'" In *America Rediscovered*. Ed. Owen W. Gilman, Jr., and Lorrie Smith. 205–12.

Smiley, Pamela. "The Role of the Ideal (Female) Reader in Tim O'Brien's *The Things They Carried*: Why Should Real Women Play?" *Massachusetts Review* 43.4 (Winter 2002/2003): 602–14.

Smith, Lorrie N. "The Things Men Do: The Gendered Subtext in Tim O'Brien's *Esquire* Stories." *Critique* 36.1 (Fall 1994): 16–40.

Smith, Patrick A. *Tim O'Brien: A Critical Companion*. Westport, CT: Greenwood, 2005.

Taylor, Mark. "Tim O'Brien's War." *Centennial Review* 34.2 (Spring 1995): 213–30.

Timmerman, John H. "Tim O'Brien and the Art of the True War Story: 'Night March' and 'Speaking of Courage.'" *Twentieth-Century Literature* 46.1 (Spring 2000): 100–114.

Vernon, Alex, and Catherine Calloway, eds. *Approaches to Teaching the Works of Tim O'Brien*. New York: The Modern Language Association of America, 2010.

Volkmer, John. "Telling the Truth about Vietnam: Episteme and Narrative Structure in *The Green Berets* and *The Things They Carried*." *War, Literature and the Arts: An International Journal of the Humanities* (Spring/Summer 1999): 240–55.

Wesley, Marilyn. "Truth and Fiction in Tim O'Brien's *If I Die in a Combat Zone* and *The Things They Carried*." *College Literature* 29.2 (Spring 2002): 1–18.

Wharton, Lynn. "Hand, Head, and Artifice: The Fictive World of Tim O'Brien." *Interdisciplinary Literary Studies: A Journal of Criticism and Theory* 3.1 (2001): 131–35.

Young, William. "Missing In Action: Vietnam and Sadism in Tim O'Brien's *In the Lake Of The Woods*." *Midwest Quarterly: A Journal of Contemporary Thought* 47.2 (2006): 131–43.

Zins, Daniel L. "Imagining the Real: The Fiction of Tim O'Brien." *Hollins Critic* 23.3 (June 1986): 1–12.

Index

Achilles (in Homer's *Iliad*), 187, 188, 192

Afghanistan, 38; war in, 176, 190

Alamo, the, 178

Alice in Wonderland (Lewis Carroll), 25, 50, 177, 195

Alzheimer's Disease, 132

American Colonial period writers, 107

Apocalypse Now (film), 9, 10, 35, 63–64, 194–95

Atlantic, 68, 160, 180

Autry, Gene, 102

Baby Boomer generation, 163

Bambi, 72

Bao Dai, 80

Barth, John, 12

Baumer, Paul, 109

Bible, 14, 27, 57

Birnbaum, Robert (interviewer), ix, xv, 160–72

Boer War, 112

Booth, John Wilkes, 142

Borden, Lizzie, 97, 141, 179

Borges, Jorge Luis, xv, 12, 15, 26, 65, 77, 81, 175

Boston Red Sox, 52, 172, 186

Bourne, Daniel (interviewer), xiii, 68–87, 192

Breadloaf Writers' Conference, 51

Brooke, Rupert, 9

Broyles, Bill, 49

Bundy, George, 151, 188

Bundy, Ted, 43, 44

Bush, George H. W., 80, 150

Bush, George W., 189

Cacciato, Richard, 91–92

Caldwell, Gail (*Boston Globe*), vii, xii, 52–57, 165

Calley, Lieutenant William, xiii, 153. *See also* My Lai

Caputo, Philip (*A Rumor of War*), xv, 109, 191

Carson, Johnny, 131

Carver, Raymond, 159, 178

Cassavetes, Nick, 144

Catherine the Great, 97

Charlie Company, 152

Cheever, John (*Stories*), ix, 117

Cheney, Richard, 182, 189

Chu Lai (Vietnam), 93

Civil Rights Movement, 176

Clinton, Bill, 122

Cold War, ix, 188

College of Wooster, 69

Coming Home (film), 10, 194

Conrad, Joseph, ix, xv, xix, 44, 59, 61, 62, 65, 71, 84, 98, 114, 119, 128, 175, 181; *Heart of Darkness*, 59–60, 65, 66, 71, 195; *Lord Jim*, 61, 65, 71,

114; *Nigger of the* Narcissus, 114; *Nostromo*, 71; *Typhoon*, 71; *Victory*, 114; *Youth*, 71
Coover, Robert (*The Public Burning*), 4
Crane, Stephen, 78, 192; *The Red Badge of Courage*, 9, 109, 186, 192
Crimea, 112
Crosby, Bing, 79
Custer, George Armstrong, 178

Dahmer, Jeffrey, 159
Damon, Matt, 122
D'Amore, Jonathan (interviewer), xv, 173–79
De Niro, Robert, 195
Deer Hunter, The (film), 10, 194–96
Del Vecchio, John (*The 13th Valley*), xv
Desert Storm, 98
DiCaprio, Leonardo, 143–45
Dickens, Charles, 82
Dos Passos, John, xv, 107, 175
Dostoyevsky, Fyodor, 65, 95; *The Brothers Karamazov*, 65; *Crime and Punishment*, 65, 95
Dr. Strangelove (film), 14

Earhart, Amelia, 178, 179
Eastlake, William (*The Bamboo Bed*), 8
Eliot, T. S. ("objective correlative"), 135
Emerson, Gloria, 23
Esquire, xxii, xxiii, 124, 142, 161, 180

Faulkner, William, ix, xv, 42, 82, 107, 119, 127–28, 175; *The Sound and the Fury*, 107
Fitzgerald, F. Scott, 61, 62, 107
Flaubert, Gustave (*Madame Bovary*), 96
Fort Lewis, Washington, 4, 7

Fourteenth Amendment (Constitution), 97
Fowles, John, 21, 65, 81; "Poor Cocoa," 65
Frazier (television show), 151
French colonialism, 80
Freud, Sigmund, 131
Fussell, Paul (*The Great War and Modern Memory*), 109

Gass, William, 11
Gilb, Dagoberto, 168
Gipson, Hoot, 102
Godfather, The (film), 138
Goldilocks, 72
Graves, Robert, 9
Green Berets, 56
Grimm's Fairy Tales, 101
Gulf of Tonkin, 108
Gulf War, 150, 176, 190

Hanks, Tom, 122
Hansen, Erik, 27, 39
Harris, Mark (*Bang the Drum Slowly*), 170
Harrison, Jim, 186
Harper's, 160, 180
Hasford, Gustav (*The Short-Timers*), 35
Hawthorne, Nathaniel, 107
Hector (in Homer's *Iliad*), 192
Heinemann, Larry (*Paco's Story*), 145
Heller, Joseph, 192; *Catch-22*, 9, 166
Hemingway, Ernest, viii, xv, 4, 13–14, 32, 42–43, 61–62, 107, 128, 149, 175, 192; *Farewell to Arms*, 43, 78; *The Sun Also Rises*, 14, 43, 62, 107, 164
Heroes (Vietnam film), 10
Herr, Michael (*Dispatches*), xv, 8, 10, 27, 31, 34, 36–37, 116, 119

Herzog, Tobey C. (interviewer), viii, xi, 100–14

Hills, Rust, 161

History Channel, 179

Hitler, Adolf, 112, 153, 189

Ho Chi Minh, 80

Hobbit, The (J. R. R. Tolkien), 50

Hoffman, Abbie, 107

Holocaust, 153

Homer, 187–88, 192–93; *The Iliad*, 27, 78, 186–87, 192; *The Odyssey*, 27, 78

Hope, Bob, 79

Houghton Mifflin (publisher). *See* Lawrence, Seymour

Hugo, Victor (*Les Misérables*), 65

Humphrey, Hubert H., 106

Hussein, Saddam, xv, 80–81, 151

Iraq, war in, xv, 151, 176, 189–90

Irving, John, ix, xxii, 21, 117, 140; *The Hotel New Hampshire*, 21; *The World According to Garp*, ix, xxii, 4, 21, 117

Iwo Jima, 116

James, Henry, 19

Johnson, Denis (*Tree of Smoke*), 190

Johnson, Lyndon B., 3, 102, 150

Jonestown (Guyana), 165

Joyce, James, 126–28, 130; *Ulysses*, 107, 126, 129

Judge Crater, 64

Kalevalan mythology, 13–14

Kaplan, Steven (interviewer), ix, x, xiii, 58–67

Kennedy, John F., 3, 102–3, 152, 178

Kesey, Ken (*One Flew Over the Cuckoo's Nest*), 166

Korean War, 105, 164

Kosovo, 150

Kovic, Ron (*Born on the Fourth of July*), xv, 37, 44–45, 109

Kuwait, 151

Larry of the Little League, 101, 102

LaRue, Lash, 30, 102

Lawrence, Seymour (Houghton Mifflin), xii, xxii, 52–53, 116, 119

Lee, Don (interviewer), vii, ix, 115–19

Lei Lu (Vietnamese writer), 83

Leonard, Elmore, 178

Lindbloom, James (interviewer), 120–24

Lone Ranger, xv, 102, 105

Lost Generation, 164

Lou Tannon's Magic Store (New York City), 104

Magical realism, xv, 4, 15, 26, 48

Magician's Handbook, 101

Maguire, Tobey, 144

Mailer, Norman, xv, 21; *The Armies of the Night*, xv; *The Naked and the Dead*, 9, 24, 32, 186

Malamud, Bernard (*The Natural*), 169

Marlantes, Karl (*Matterhorn*), 190–91

Marquette, Michigan, 188

Márquez, Gabriel García, xv, 4, 15, 26, 81, 175; *Autumn of the Patriarch*, 26; *One Hundred Years of Solitude*, 4, 26–27

McCaffery, Larry (interviewer), vii–ix, xvii, 3–21

McCarthy, Eugene, xxi, 3, 6, 107

McGuane, Tom, 21

McNamara, Robert, 151, 188–89; *Fog of War*, 188

McNerney, Brian (interviewer), xi, xiii, 88–99

Melville, Herman, ix, 44, 48, 146, 156; *Moby-Dick*, 46, 48, 85, 156

Milagro Beanfield War, The (film), 165

Minneapolis Star, xxi, 110

Minneapolis Tribune, 37

Mitau, Ted, 106

Mix, Tom, 102

Mondale, Walter, 106

Morrison, Toni, ix, xv, 4, 81–82, 114, 146, 178; *Song of Solomon*, 4, 82

Munro, Alice, 166

Murdoch, Iris, 132

Murphy, Audie, 74, 105, 109, 187; *To Hell and Back*, 105

My Lai, xiii–xv, 63, 110–11, 115, 118, 145, 151–54

Naparsteck, Martin (interviewer), xii, 41–51

National Archives (Washington, D.C.), 88, 90

National Geographic, 79–80

Native Americans (Indians), 153

New Journalism, xv, 22

New York Times, xiii, xxii, 26, 58, 68, 115, 116, 120, 123, 143, 157

New York Yankees, 102

New Yorker, 123, 124, 129, 142, 156, 160, 180

Objective correlative. *See* Eliot, T. S.

O'Brien, Tim (William Timothy):
  Life of: baseball, xv, 118, 138, 150, 168, 169–70, 172, 184, 185–86; desertion, thoughts of (Vietnam), 4, 6, 7–8, 10, 55, 62, 108, 116; fatherhood, xv, xvi, xxiii, 184, 185; films portraying Vietnam, attitude toward, 48, 63–64, 66, 143–45, 184, 194–95; golf, xviii, xxi, 51, 59, 104, 105, 108, 109, 118, 158; Harvard (graduate school), xi, xxi, 5, 55, 57, 100, 108, 112, 116, 118, 140, 143, 160; Macalester College (St. Paul, MN), x, xxi, 6, 55, 100, 106–7, 116, 160; magic, xi, xxi, 17, 101, 104, 106, 116, 131–32, 141; Midwest, influence of and attitude toward, vii, x–xi, xxi, 61–62, 80–81, 102, 119, 128, 131, 175, 184, 186; Minnesota, vii, x, xii, xxi, 4, 55, 80, 102, 103, 106, 116, 117, 128, 129, 143, 160, 167, 192; parents, x, xi, xviii, xxi, 6–7, 101–5, 116, 129–31; politics, influence of and attitude toward, xxi, 3, 5, 6, 46, 71, 80, 102–3, 105, 106–7, 108, 146, 176; Purple Heart and Bronze Star (Vietnam), viii, xxi, 52, 109–10, 116; religion and spirituality, influence of and attitude toward, 65, 102, 129, 134, 135–36, 141–42, 150, 179, 187, 188; teaching, xv, 51, 143, 158–59, 160, 167, 184; Texas State University, San Marcos, xv, 143, 158, 160, 184; travel, 5, 132–33; Vietnam draft, viii, xxi, 3, 4, 5, 55, 58, 97, 108, 116, 117, 127, 149, 173, 190; Vietnam experience and psychological impact, vii, viii, xii, xiii, xv, xvi, 4–5, 8–10, 12, 22, 24, 29, 33, 35, 37, 41, 44, 49, 52–53, 55, 63, 69, 71, 80, 88, 98, 108, 111–13, 115, 120, 122, 125–26, 138, 139–40, 148, 152, 171, 173–74, 176, 190, 195;

Washington Post, reporting for, xii, xxii, 5, 117, 143, 146, 160

Writing, aspects of: antiwar sentiment, 18, 106, 111–12, 189; *Best American Short Stories,* 41, 160, 180; *Best American Short Stories of the Century,* xxiii, 143, 180; death, x, 14, 16, 19, 21, 31, 42–43, 46, 50, 63, 65, 67, 70–74, 78–79, 89–90, 96, 97–98, 125–26, 134, 140, 141, 142, 151, 161, 165, 176, 188–89; courage and cowardice, x, 4, 10, 13, 33–34, 44–46, 55, 62–63, 71, 91, 97–98, 109–10, 117, 148–49, 156, 180, 192, 195; dialogue, 19–20, 22, 23, 37, 40, 45, 52, 53, 69–70, 74, 114, 123, 137, 141–42, 144, 148, 165–66, 169, 176–77, 182; drama and melodrama, 10–13, 15, 17, 20–23, 28–29, 34, 36, 51, 59, 68, 74, 78, 83–84, 86, 95, 96, 131, 163, 178, 195; dreams and daydreams, xv, xvi, 7, 12, 14, 15–16, 18, 24–25, 30–31, 34, 39, 48, 50–51, 53, 58, 59, 74, 77–79, 81, 111, 118, 142, 144, 159, 171, 176–78, 187, 191; escape and fantasy, ix, 7, 8–9, 12, 15–16, 19, 25, 27, 31, 36, 105, 106, 108, 114, 165, 192; Guggenheim Foundation, 68, 180; "happeningness" in the work of, 17, 23, 68; heroes and heroism, 13, 15, 45, 76, 102–3, 105, 108–9, 117, 144, 175, 184, 187–88, 191, 194; honor, notions of, xi, 109, 180, 188, 194; humor and comedy, xv, 13–14, 18, 20–21, 46, 120, 127, 135–36, 141, 156–57; imagination, vii, viii–ix, xvi, 4, 7, 9, 15–16, 24–26, 28, 31–32, 35–36, 38, 50, 54, 56, 57, 60, 64–65, 79–80, 89–90, 96, 105–6, 108, 114, 117, 126, 138, 147–48, 150, 152, 176, 181, 185; love and the human heart, vii, ix, xiii, 54, 55–56, 60–61, 63, 66, 68–69, 71, 72, 75, 76, 86, 96–98, 99, 103–5, 115, 118, 119–20, 122, 123, 126–27, 128, 130, 131, 133, 135, 141, 146, 148–49, 156–57, 159, 162, 164–65, 174, 192; Massachusetts Arts and Humanities Foundation, 68; memoir and pseudo-memoir (see also *If I Die* under O'Brien, Tim (William Timothy): Works), 75–77, 82; memory, vii, xiii–xiv, xvi, 20, 25, 27, 31–32, 35–36, 38, 48–50, 54–57, 88–89, 90, 114, 117–18, 121, 125–26, 132, 134, 135, 137–38, 144, 147–48, 149, 162, 163–64, 176, 181; metaphor, use of, 10, 14, 33, 71–72, 75, 86, 101, 117, 154, 173, 181, 195; morals and morality, ix–x, xvi, 8, 10, 12–13, 16, 18, 21, 26, 27, 30, 32–34, 36, 44–45, 59, 62, 66, 86, 105, 108, 109, 122, 145–46, 147, 150, 162, 173, 182, 193, 195–96; mystery and the unknown, xiii, 17–18, 40, 62–63, 64–65, 69, 82, 86, 100–101, 118, 152, 179, 182, 193; mythology, xiv, 13–14, 149, 153, 193, 194; myths and myth-making, 24, 27, 73–74, 82, 111, 145; narrative points of view, x, xvi, 20, 30, 50, 53–54, 58, 59–60, 64, 65, 74–75, 79–80, 82–85, 94, 118, 121; National Endowment for the Arts, xxiii, 68, 180; *O. Henry Prize Stories*, xxii, xxiii, 41, 160, 180; place and setting, ix, xi, xiv, xv, 9, 15, 17, 19, 42, 56, 58, 60, 62, 77, 79–80, 84, 88, 89–91, 95, 111, 114, 115, 128, 133–34, 150, 151, 169, 187; Prix du Meilleur Livre Étranger (*The Things They Carried*), xxii, 120, 180; stories and storytelling, xi, xvi, 21, 27, 56–57, 58–59, 60–62, 66, 68, 69–72, 77, 85–86, 116, 117, 129, 146, 156, 163–64, 176, 181; "truth" in the work of, vii, xii–xiii, xvi, 28–29, 49–50, 55–56, 59, 69–70, 73, 74–77, 83–84, 86–87, 110, 117–18, 121–22, 131, 138, 146–49, 154–56, 177, 182, 194; "Vietnam Writer," reputation as, vii, 5, 44, 68, 146, 119, 163; women, portrayals of, 60–62, 76–77, 83–86, 93–99, 162, 165–66; writing process and technique, vii, xi, xiii, xv, 4, 5, 10–11, 22–23, 33–34, 51, 67, 70, 74, 86–87, 107, 127, 130, 136–38, 159, 162–63, 166–67, 174–75, 177, 181

Works:

"Faith" (story), 123

Going After Cacciato (novel), vii–ix, xv, xvi, xxii, 4–8, 10–13, 15–19, 24, 26–34, 36–40, 41–43, 45–48, 50, 52, 54, 56–57, 58–59, 65–66, 68, 78, 79, 91–92, 94, 117–18, 120, 141–42, 143–44, 160, 162–63, 166, 167, 173, 179, 180, 191; National Book Award for, vii, ix, xxii, 4, 41, 52, 58, 68, 117, 120, 143, 160, 174, 180; "Observation Post" chapters, ix, 12, 31, 50, 54, 56, 142, 191

If I Die in a Combat Zone (memoir), vii, viii, x, xv, xxi, xxii, 4–7, 10, 21, 22–24, 27, 29–30, 34, 36–37, 39, 40, 41, 46–47, 52, 54, 58, 62, 68–70, 89, 92–93, 95, 106, 109–12, 116, 117, 127, 129, 141, 142, 143, 148, 154, 160, 174, 180

In the Lake of the Woods (novel), ix, x, xiii–xiv, xxii, 100, 101, 115, 117–18, 120, 121, 123, 126, 128, 133, 135, 141–42, 143, 144, 148, 152–54, 160, 162, 166, 173, 179, 180, 193

July, July (novel), ix, x, xv, xvi, xxi, xxiii, 137, 142, 160–66, 170–71, 180

"Loon Point" (story), 124

"Nogales" (story), 129–30, 156

Northern Lights (novel), viii, x, xi, xxii, 4–5, 10–11, 13–15, 19–20, 41, 42–43, 44, 58, 61–62, 68, 73, 117, 121, 127–29, 133, 140–41, 160, 180

Nuclear Age, The (novel), ix, xii, xv, xviii, xxii, 5, 14, 15, 20–21, 34, 41, 44–46, 48, 52, 58, 60–62, 65, 68, 117, 118, 141, 160, 180

"People We Marry, The" (story), 68

"Step Lively" (story), 70

Stories and essays appearing in: *Atlantic*, 68, 160, 180; *Esquire*, xxii, xxiii, 124, 142, 161, 180; *Harper's*, 160, 180; *New Yorker*, 123, 124, 129, 142, 156, 160, 180; *New York Times*, xiii, xxii, 115, 120, 123, 157; *Ploughshares*, 115, 160, 180

"Streak, The" (story), 124

Things They Carried, The (novel), ix, xii, xiii, xv, xxii, 41, 47–49, 52–57, 58, 59–63, 66, 68, 69, 72–77,

81–84, 88, 89, 94, 117, 118, 120, 121, 124, 125, 134, 141, 143, 144, 148, 149, 154–55, 160, 161, 162, 163–64, 166, 173, 174, 176, 179, 180–83, 186, 192, 194; "Field Trip," 89–90; "Good Form," 75, 77, 147, 155; "The Ghost Soldiers," xxii, 66–67; "How to Tell a True War Story," xii, 49–50, 56, 85, 95–97, 147; "The Lives of the Dead," 47, 126; "Notes," 77; "On the Rainy River," 58–59, 66, 108, 134, 173; "Speaking of Courage," xxii, 47, 134, 154, 155; "Sweetheart of the Song Tra Bong," 56, 74, 76, 84–85, 95, 138, 144; "The Things They Carried," x, xxii, xxiii, 180

Tomcat in Love (novel), ix, x, xv, xxiii, 120–21, 123, 126–27, 129–30, 135, 141, 143, 156–57, 160, 180

"Vietnam in Me, The" (essay), xiii, xxii, 115–16, 123, 157

Your Play (drama), 66

O'Connor, Flannery ("A Good Man Is Hard to Find"), 67, 129–30

Okinawa, 110, 116

Oswald, Lee Harvey, 141, 178

Pacino, Al, 138

Patterson, James, 178

Peace of Paris, 19, 33

Pearl Harbor, 189

Peleus (father of Achilles), 187–88

Percy, Walker, 21

Pinkville, 93, 110–11

Pinter, Harold, 66

Plato, 6, 45, 52, 121–22, 132

Playboy, xxii, 6, 37, 110, 180

Ploughshares, 115, 160, 180

Poe, Edgar Allan, 65

Popeye (cartoon character), 62

Pork Chop Hill (Korean War film), 105

Posttraumatic stress disorder (PTSD), 113

Powell, Colin, 189

Pressfield, Steven (interviewer), vii, 180–83

Quang Ngai (Vietnam), xxi, 115

Rabe, David, xv

Redford, Robert (*Spy Game*), 167

Remarque, Erich (*All Quiet on the Western Front*), 9

"Resistance" in writing, 181

Reynolds, Quentin, 32

Rice, Condoleezza, 189

Ricks, Thomas, 190

Road to Mandalay, The (film), 79

Rogers, Roy, 102

Rosica, Karen, xii

Rostow, Walt, 151

Roth, Philip, 82

Rubins, Jerry, 107

Rusk, Dean, 151, 188

Russell, Carrie (*Felicity*), 144

Salinger, J. D. (*Catcher in the Rye*), 166

Sassoon, Siegfried, 9

Savage, John, 195

Saving Private Ryan (film), 122

Sawyer, Scott, xvi

Schroeder, Eric James (interviewer), ix, xvi, 22–40

SDS (Students for a Democratic Society), 106

SEATO (Southeast Asia Treaty Organization), 80

Sevron, Bruce, 104

Shakespeare, William, ix, 44, 46, 62, 119, 146, 151; *Hamlet*, 151

Shostak, Debra (interviewer), xiii, 68–87, 192

Skowron, Bill "Moose," 102

Smith, Patrick A. (interviewer), 184–96

Socrates, 44

Spanish-American War, 112

Speer, Albert, 16

Stanton, Doug, 190

State Department, 116

Steele, Danielle, 165

Steinbeck in Vietnam (Ed. Thomas Barden), 184–85

Stone, Robert, 22, 36, 175; *Dog Soldiers*, 36; *A Flag for Sunrise*, 36

Talese, Gay, 22

Tambakis, Anthony (interviewer), ix, 143–59

Ted Mack Amateur Hour, 121

Television, 35, 102, 137, 168, 190

Thetis (mother of Achilles), 187–88, 194

Thompson, Hunter S., xvi

Timmy Is a Big Boy Now, 101, 102

Tolstoy, Leo, 78–79, 84; *Sevastopol Sketches*, 79; *War and Peace*, 78, 84

Trader Vic's (Statler Hilton, Boston), 117

Troy, city of (Homer's *Iliad*), 187, 192

Trudeau, Garry (*Doonesbury*), 62

Twain, Mark, 39, 74, 126, 150, 155; *Connecticut Yankee in King Arthur's Court*, 74; *Huckleberry Finn*, 39, 66, 75, 85, 101, 102, 126, 129, 150, 155, 171; *Tom Sawyer*, 101

Tyler, Anne, 81

Updike, John, ix, xxiii, 21, 44, 143, 146, 175, 178, 180

Veterans Day, 190, 191, 194

Viet Cong (VC), 73, 91–94

Vietnam Veterans Against the War (VVAW), 112

Vonnegut, Kurt (*Slaughterhouse-Five*), 9, 177, 186

Wabash College, 109

Walken, Christopher, 195

Wayne, John, 44, 74, 187, 195

Weapons of mass destruction, 189, 191, 194

Webb, Jim (*Fields of Fire*), 35

Weigl, Bruce, xv

Wharton, Lynn (interviewer), xi, 125–42

Wiesel, Elie, 153

Williams, Ted, 102

Wolfe, Tom, xv–xvi

Wonder Books, 101

World War I, 62, 109, 192

World War II, x, xi, xxi, 24, 35, 64, 116, 145, 182

Worthington Daily Globe, xxi, 110

Wouk, Herman (*The Winds of War*), 83, 84

Wright, Stephen, xv

Yippie movement, 107

CPSIA information can be obtained at www.ICGtesting.com
Printed in the USA
BVOW071141141012

302491BV00002B/5/P

PS
3565
B75
Z465
2012

Conversations with
Tim O'Brien.

$40.00

DATE		

Library & Media Ctr.
Carroll Community College
1601 Washington Rd.
Westminster, MD 21157

WITHDRAWN

DEC 13 2012

BAKER & TAYLOR